'I started to read then paused while I fetched my Bible; then a pen to underline wisdom. Then I prayed. Then I started to tell someone else all about it. It is like having an amazingly wise old uncle showing you how to live; to truly be alive. I wish it had been available years ago. It should be required reading.'
Roy Godwin, Executive Director, The Ffald-y-Brenin Trust, and author of The Grace Outpouring

'In the midst of the complexities of life today, it would be hard to find a more comprehensive guide. What is here given us is not so much a book to be read but rather a treasure house in which to linger and frequently revisit. On every page, to facilitate growth towards wholeness and holiness, there's insight and wisdom, encouragement and challenge. Although written from a Christian perspective, the author is nevertheless open to truth wherever it's to be found, and he speaks with the authority that can only come from personally lived experience. His style is such as to repay careful bite-sized reading and continual reflection. The reward for doing so will yield a rich harvest. Highly recommended!'
Brian M. Noble, Emeritus Bishop of Shrewsbury

'Reading this book is like being taken into a beautiful garden by a Renaissance man, who shows you how the different layers of reality revealed by music, art, poetry, psychology, nature and science can bring you into a place of awareness. I believe the aim of the book is enabling others to develop what the early Christian contemplatives called *diorasis*, a clear seeing into the reality of things – and above all their createdness.'
Shaun Lambert, Senior Minister, Stanmore Baptist Church; author of A Book of Sparks *and* Putting on the Wakeful One

'This wonderful book is a fount of wisdom. It is beautifully written, in inspirational language, and is obviously the fruit of lived experience. It contains a wealth of uplifting quotations, gleaned from the wisdom of the ages. It covers the whole

gamut of human existence, and our relationship to the divine. There is richness on every page – for this reason, the book needs to be taken slowly and reflectively. It is indeed a treasure.'
Fr Vincent O'Hara OCD, Director, Avila Centre, Dublin

'Good spiritual reading is sacramental. It takes us there. To where truth lies. It makes us present. It paves the way for and makes possible an encounter with the Lord. This book does just that. It is a goldmine. I have found nuggets for my own inner journey and for those whom I accompany on theirs. It will be a blessing for all into whose hands it happens to fall.'
Canon John Udris, Spiritual Director, St Mary's College, Oscott

'This work is to be relished, not rushed. Drawing on deep wells of experience and insight, Robin Daniels opens doors which enable us to see with artistic precision and radical freshness the wonder of God. With unique ability he speaks to the soul, bringing to consciousness the seemingly indescribable. It is less a book and more a journey which will not fail to transform your relationship with God, self and others.'
Teresa Onions, Director of Pastoral Care UK for the Association of Christian Counsellors

'Kierkegaard, the great Danish existentialist, claimed that God has a prophetic vision of what each of us could be with His grace. Daniels shows us how to escape from the foam and splash of our often ego-driven lives, to enter into that true self.

'*The Virgin Eye* is a remarkable blending of insights from poetry, Jungian psychology, Scripture and the words of spiritual writers. In fact, the style of *The Virgin Eye*, with its beautifully paced insights, invites the reader to enter into the peace that is its goal. Yet *The Virgin Eye* is not an ethereal treatise for momentary escape from the problems of life. Each chapter squarely faces the deformations of life in our times dealing with such topics as stress, workaholism, micro-managing others. To all these familiar albatrosses Daniels brings fresh spiritual remedies.

'I rate this one of the best contemporary books on spirituality.'
Ronda Chervin, PhD, Professor of Philosophy at Holy Apostles College and Seminary, USA; author of spirituality books

THE VIRGIN EYE

TOWARDS A CONTEMPLATIVE VIEW OF LIFE

ROBIN DANIELS

Edited by Katherine Daniels

instant
apostle

'To appreciate' is to perceive what is of value; to see everyone as precious; to see a friend, a familiar face, as if for the first time. To the virgin eye, nothing and no one is ordinary.

I dedicate this book to
KATHERINE
who does with grace what I just write about

First published in Great Britain by Instant Apostle, 2016.

Instant Apostle

The Barn
1 Watford House Lane
Watford
Herts
WD17 1BJ

British Library Cataloguing-in-Publication Data

A catalogue record for this book is available from the British Library

This book and all other Instant Apostle books are available from Instant Apostle:

Website: www.instantapostle.com

E-mail: info@instantapostle.com

ISBN 978 1 909728 52 3

Printed in Great Britain

Contents

Acknowledgements

Sister Rosemary Bayne HHS read, and helpfully commented on, the penultimate text. A very dear friend, she gave generously of her time, her wisdom, and her experience of life (inner and outer).

Lisa Vas-Diass, Barbara Macanas, Jan Dunsford and Teresa O'Neill have typed a succession of drafts with skill, patience and cheerful cooperation.

Lisa Vas-Diass worked with devotion on the final drafts, which were also the longest. Her support has been vital both to me and this book: the quality of her work was exemplary, over a sustained period.

Robin Daniels
Blackpool, 8th July 2007

Since Robin's death, others have helped to bring this book to the light of day. I would like to thank Fr Vincent O'Hara OCD for mentoring me through the editing process, and for believing in the value of the book. I would also like to thank Jeremy Boreham and Nigel Freeman for their tremendously thorough proofreading and comments. I thank Sr Anne Stewart for encouraging me to devote time to the book, to Sr Zela Proctor for reminding me that the book is my priority. Thank you Nicki Briggs for marketing ideas. I thank a kind person for her careful explanations and reflections, and Joyce

Simpson for generously checking the quotes. I thank Nicki Copeland, Manoj Raithatha and Sheila Jacobs for the copy editing, formatting, generous marketing, design expertise and help all along the way. Thank you Lisa Vas-Diass for all your careful typing for Robin, and for teaching me how to make formatting changes. I would like to thank Sr Wendy Beckett for her generous foreword.

Katherine Daniels
21st March 2016

Foreword

This book is a gladness to the heart that seeks God and a strengthener to the will. It both inspires and gives practical advice. It is, in fact, a treasure. But it is not a treasure that can be easily put into practice. Parts of this book are very simple and obvious though also very difficult to achieve. Other parts are pure inspiration and open the eye to what the hard work of practice will enable us to see. On almost every page there are profound insights, and if that were not enough, there is an extraordinary richness of quotation.

If I too may quote, I am reminded of Simone Weil's quotation: 'Attente au Dieu'. The author wants us to be able truly to see, and the wonders of the created world can only be seen in their truth if we are attentive to God. It is His light that shines within all that is, drawing us upwards and inwards and outwards in love.

For me, the heart of the book is the small paragraph about halfway through in which Robin Daniels describes St Thérèse, sick, lonely and suffering, scratching on her cell wall, 'Jesus is my only love'. I say this is the heart of the book for me, but it is a hidden heart. The presence of Christ is all-pervasive but hardly ever explicit.

Clearly the author wants his book to be of service to all men and women of whatever religion or no religion, who long to be complete human beings, and in that fullness glorify the God who made them. The Christian will read it in a Christian context, but it is one of those wonderful books that does not need this context to be full of life and meaning. Whether we are at the very beginning of a serious search of God, still embroiled and clogged with the complexities of life, or whether time and grace have purified us over the years and washed our eyes so that we see with innocence and brightness, we can learn from this book.

Daniels quotes F. H. Bradley's wonderful remark in his 'Aphorisms': 'One cannot remain in love unless perpetually one falls in love anew.' This book helps us to do that.

Sister Wendy Beckett

Notes about the author and book

The author: life and work

Robin Daniels was born in Blackpool in the middle of an air
raid during the Second World War. His mother was American,
and father English. He spent happy years of early childhood in
San Francisco while his father fought in Burma. The family
returned to England – to post-war rationing – when his father
took on the family leather business. For a sensitive boy –
initially with an American accent – the British public school
system was a culture shock.

Robin studied music for four years with Alan Rowlands. His
lifelong loves of music (especially Handel, Mozart and
Beethoven) and sport (cricket, tennis and football) are evident
in the imagery and examples he uses throughout the book.

Robin worked in the wool trade, as a music critic for *The
Croydon Times*, and in the work-study department of W. H.
Smith, before taking on a publicity manager role at the charity
we now know as Scope. This contact with people in need drew
him into training as a counsellor at the Westminster Pastoral
Foundation, then led by Methodist minister and founder, Bill
Kyle. There Robin was taught and supervised by the great
Jungian analyst, David Holt. He undertook further training as a
social worker and then as a psychoanalyst at the Lincoln Clinic,
where the key components of his training were Jungian.

Robin was on Westminster Central Hall's Social
Responsibility (visiting) Group. He ran marriage enrichment
and bereavement groups in church settings and, latterly, a

reflecting group for hospital chaplains. He was a supervisor at the St Marylebone Centre for Healing and Counselling.

Robin's previously published books are: *Blackpool Football* (Robert Hale, 1972); *Conversations with Cardus* (Gollancz, 1976); *Conversations with Menuhin* (Time-Warner, 1979); *Conversations with Coggan* (Hodder, 1982); and *Cardus: Celebrant of Beauty* (Palatine, 2009).

Robin looked out for, and appreciated, the good and beautiful things of life – in people, art, music, poetry and the park. His social encounters were well spaced, but those he had were deep, and he gave time and encouragement to people in his day-to-day interactions – on buses, in shops.

He was an extraordinarily single-pointed person. Prioritising prayer, writing and the counselling work involved a pruning of other things, and often saying 'no' to good things. He lived a rhythmical life, at an *adagio* pace. He was a very pure man; rather quiet, spacious and simple; always grateful; and experiencing sporadic ill health all through life (yet remaining joyful). The insights of this book were won from hard experience, and many knocks.

Though generally he followed a rather consistent and stable pattern, Robin could make major and surprising changes. He married late in life. And he entered the Catholic Church in 2011, a year and half before he died, and after most of this book was written.

The book

The book was originally conceived in the 1990s when Fr Laurence Freeman OSB invited Robin to lead a retreat at Camden Hill Road on the interface between psychology and spirituality. Robin expanded his notes from that weekend, and honed his reflections over a further decade or two. This book is the long-awaited result.

Part 1 sets out the main challenges facing us today: the extent of change we have collectively experienced since the Second World War, and the stresses caused by modern life, particularly our misuse of technology and our chronically rushed pace. Robin makes a case for slowing down, guarding peace, silence and solitude, and prioritising the inner life.

A theme of the book – and one which supplies its title – is seeing things from a wider perspective, as if for the first time, with a virginal innocence. This is the subject of Part 2. The book might equally have been titled *The Poet's Eye*, or *The Child's Eye*, as it calls us to infuse a spirit of play into all our everyday activities and to see these – and other people – as so many windows into the life of God.

The concept of 'the Triad' supplies the structure of Parts 3 to 5. The Triad refers to the threefold attention we need to give to our relationship with *God*, to growing in *self-awareness* and to *loving others*. As we encounter God's redeeming love through prayer, and courageously facing our darker side (or 'shadow'), He restores our original innocence, and this makes truer and deeper our personal encounters. A further theme is learning to perceive and embrace the God-givenness of all events and relationships, including difficult ones, as being for our ultimate growth.

Particular chapters set out Robin's take on decision-making; mindfulness (as it relates to eating, walking, taming the tongue and speaking on the phone); grace and non-striving; combating the wiles of often subtle pride with humility; radical purity (for the celibate and the married); and features of a lasting relationship. Prayer is woven through all the Parts. For the most part, Robin refers to God rather than members of the Trinity by name, so that the book can be readily assimilated by readers from a variety of backgrounds.

It is poignant that this book is being published after Robin's death (to bronchopneumonia) in December 2012. The editing process has involved making a few final insertions from notes Robin had left, reducing duplications, removing and adding to footnotes, reordering some material by subject, pruning, subdividing longer chapters, and adding the subheadings. The broad structure is that conceived by Robin. Only the equivalent of three pages has actually been written in the editing process. Readers will need to regard the dedication as expressing the idealism of a man who has just fallen in love, but will understand why I have not wanted to delete it. Editing this book has been – in a certain sense – a way of continuing a relationship beyond death, and of bringing forth, for Robin, progeny.

The man

The qualities that most stand out to me about the man I fell in love with – and am still in love with – are the quality and depth of his listening. He never imposed his own opinions, only sharing if asked. He seemed to be listening simultaneously to God, to his own depths and to the other person. This gave him a rare gift of encouraging and drawing out the eloquence and wisdom of others. He helped people to tap into their own intuitive side.

He was very much his own person – never one to follow the crowd. He would not want his own routine or discipline set out here; he would want you to find your own approach through creative experimentation and careful listening to the body and to God's promptings.

Robin was a very appreciative person – always finding things to thank God for. He kept upbeat, even when suffering ill health or pain. A friend of ours once asked Robin what he thought the spiritual life was about and Robin said, 'Attention and Praise.'

He was tremendously disciplined, not curious about the business of other people, abstemious in food, vegetarian, and teetotal (or, it would be more accurate to say, 'hot-chocolate-total'). He had a high pain threshold – not taking painkillers even when he suffered ten wedge fractures in the spine through osteoporosis. He was very aware of the power (for good or ill) of words. In six and a half years of marriage, I never heard him utter an irritable word towards me, nor an indiscreet or unkind word towards someone else. He was vigilant about the guarding of his peace and his senses, and avoiding shadow (except where work called for it to be faced and transformed).

He did little things for me – and for others – with a lot of love. For instance, he would turn the outside light on if I was returning in the dark, and often phoned back to thank a person's boss for good service received (with specific examples). If something good happened to someone, he would say, 'Maybe you deserve it!' When asked what he'd like prayer for, for himself, he would say, 'Just to be more grateful.' His usual farewell was, 'Blessings.' A man's last words express his priorities. Like a little boy calling for his mother, Robin called out, 'All I have is God; I want God. Bye-bye, Katherine.'

As Sr Rosemary Bayne HHS said after her reading, 'This is a book to be prayed through.' As Robin's widow, I pray that your reading and praying through this book – and the impact it has on your life, and the lives of those you connect with – will be his way of 'leaving footprints on the sands of time' (Longfellow, 'A Psalm of Life').

Katherine Daniels
Solemnity of St Joseph, 2016

For self-help and other resources, or to book a talk, please visit: www.mindfulnessforchristians.com

But often, in the world's most crowded streets,
But often, in the din of strife,
There rises an unspeakable desire
After the knowledge of our buried life;
A thirst to spend our fire and restless force
In tracking out our true, original course;

A longing to inquire
Into the mystery of this heart which beats
So wild, so deep in us – to know
Whence our lives come and where they go.
And many a man in his own breast then delves,
But deep enough, alas! none ever mines.
And we have been on many thousand lines,
And we have shown, on each, spirit and power;
But hardly have we, for one little hour,
Been on our own line, have we been ourselves –
Hardly had skill to utter one of all
The nameless feelings that course through our breast,
But they course on for ever unexpress'd.
And long we try in vain to speak and act
Our hidden self, and what we say and do
Is eloquent, is well – but 'tis not true!
And then we will no more be rack'd
With inward striving, and demand
Of all the thousand nothings of the hour
Their stupefying power;
Ah yes, and they benumb us at our call!
Yet still, from time to time, vague and forlorn,
From the soul's subterranean depth upborne
As from an infinitely distant land,
Come airs, and floating echoes, and convey
A melancholy into all our day.

Matthew Arnold, 'The Buried Life'

Preface: Quest

And the end of all our exploring
Will be to arrive where we started
And to know the place for the first time.

T. S. Eliot, 'Little Gidding'[1]

When the ocean of life is experienced mainly on the surface, our focus will be on foam and splash. If we live at depth, we are centred in our undercurrent, or soul. This current is strong enough to keep flowing in its chosen direction – sometimes against the prevailing tide. Thus whenever I write about wholehearted living, I always imply a rich inner life as the basis for all that we say and do.

In this book we often use journey as a metaphor for the adventure of becoming one's self, fulfilled as God intends and for His greater glory. Each generation has applauded Cook and Columbus, the first daring expeditions to the North and South Pole, the first solo flight across the Atlantic, the historic final conquering of Everest in coronation year, and the first moon landing. Yes, but have I found my place under the sun? We can each make a special contribution to His kingdom:

> I believe, if we cannot discover a terrestrial America, there are new continents of the soul for us to land upon. Virgin soil.[2]

---

[1] T. S. Eliot, *Four Quartets* (London: Faber & Faber, 1943).

frozen up within

When ancient myths tell of a journey to a far-distant priceless goal, they point the way not only to material treasure, but to an inner journey to an inner kingdom where I can better enjoy being my self, and where those closest to me, and also colleagues, will treasure me more because I am my own person. This inspires others to continue their own journey, an often rough route that leads to joy, but which needs reserves of courage and stamina, physical and emotional.

This book begins with three main chapters – Change, Stress and Time – which explore the many ways in which our current lifestyle hinders – and subversively conspires against – this quest. In attitude and in behaviour, people in contemporary Western society tend to be one-sidedly extrovert: mind and body and senses intoxicated by 'the busy dance of things that pass away' (Wordsworth, *The Prelude*, Book XIII). We have externalised our endeavours, skewing our vision, yet never slaking our thirst for more and more stimulus. Have we, in Arnold's phrase, become 'frozen up within' ('Growing Up')?

Comparative neglect of the inner life leads to imbalance and even harm – from depression to self-destructive tendencies in the form of drink, drugs, promiscuity and violence. By creative contrast, the more fully we inhabit our own inner space (what Hopkins called our 'inscape'), the more richly we value our experience of the visible world.[3]

The next step is to outline where people could be; and how they could evolve, thanks to a constant review of personal priorities (Romans 12:2), an increase in self-understanding, and a prayerful life, leading to service of others. The threefold attention to God, self-work and others is the 'Triad' which forms the basic structure of this book.

---

[2] D. H. Lawrence, Letter to Catherine Carswell, 25th February 1916, in George Zytaruk and James T. Boulton, eds., *Letters of D. H. Lawrence, Volume II (1913–1916)* (Cambridge: Cambridge University Press, 1981).

[3] Gerard Manley Hopkins, ed. Humphrey House, *The Journals and Papers of Gerard Manley Hopkins* (Oxford: Oxford University Press, 1959) pp.221, 218.

It is wise to embark on spiritual pilgrimage not (or not just) with a stack of 'how to do it' nostrums, but in a spirit of openness and wide-angled seeing. God is best approached allusively – not as an engineer but as an artist. The French Impressionists, who teach us to observe ever-shifting halftones of light, can show us the way to eternal Light: by suggestion, reflection and intimations of the Immortal.

We each of us have our moments – or, if blessed, our periods – of clarity: rich experiences of life and love, new perceptions of meaning and best purpose. These moments are precious and lucid. They are memorable precisely because they are suffused with mystery. Worthy and complete in themselves, they point beyond. The more we see, the more we realise has yet to be seen. The more we love, the readier we are to call ourselves 'beginners' – first-graders, if even that!

Our humility, our not-abject smallness, is our salvation: it prompts us to be ever on the alert for the divine presence, the prime source of our affirmation – in my soul, in my home, in my beloved, in my neighbour. God's affirmation heals me, helps me to become more self accepting, and hence more accommodating of other people – all parts and aspects of them. If I fully accept and acknowledge – even as I write – that God is designing me for His kingdom, can I any longer feel estranged from any aspect of my self? By extension, if I honour our Father, can I regard anyone as a stranger? The parable of the Good Samaritan does not define or limit who our neighbour is. 'Veiled in flesh the Godhead see!' (Charles Wesley, 'Hark the Herald Angels Sing').

'The truth shall be thy warrant' (Sir Walter Raleigh, 'The Lie', i). The truth is our password for entry, but much more is required of us. We have to ask ourselves how consistent we are to the faithful living of the Word: 'Am I loyal, night and day?'

'Art is a jealous mistress', Emerson says: so is the spiritual journey.[4]

No palace, no retinue, is worth the sacrifice – or even the temporary destabilising – of your integrity. The integrity is all. Your morale and your reputation and the 'the immortal part of yourself' depend on it.

Shakespeare's Proteus warns us that we are on a slippery slope from our very first detour or deviation from absolute truth and rectitude:

> That one error
> Fills him with faults; makes him run through all th'
> sins.

> *The Two Gentlemen of Verona*, V iv

Nowhere on the gate of the Citadel of Truth, nor on the walls inside, will we find the word 'compromise' (Matthew 10; Luke 9:62).[5] We can be true, or we can be false, to every moment, every encounter. Each word I utter (and its tone), every activity, every stirring of my heart, is an entry test. This very moment is alive with its own special offering or invitation, and a deeply relational petition for each of us to love and to serve our God and our neighbour. How will I respond to this moment? Will I be true to it, true to my self, serving the gracious Giver of time?

Is the voice of this moment soft or demanding, or both? The standard is love. Rilke writes: 'Fondness between human beings: that is ... the ultimate, the final test, the aim for which

---

[4] Ralph Waldo Emerson, *The Conduct of Life* (Boston, MA: Houghton, Mifflin and Co., 1860), 'Wealth', p.114.

[5] *Cf* Hubert van Zeller: 'There is all the difference in the world between legitimate adaptation and convenient compromise' in *Considerations* (London: Sheed & Ward, 1973) p.81.

mysting hermit
elusive yet palpable!

all other activity is only preparation.'[6] The essence of love is kindness. I need to start by being kind to myself, embracing all that I am, past and present. The poet sees truth as synonymous with beauty. The aesthetic and consoling sides of life with God may ameliorate the tone of our enterprise, but they do not lower the bar or the criteria for our spiritual quest by a single centimetre.

The Way is hard and humorous, relentless and peaceful, high-toned and gentle. This very morning, He who is all-mercy is beckoning to each one of us, saying, 'I give you a new day. You can start again.' When did you last see the sun rise?

At every fork and turn in this noblest of ventures, we rejoice, stumble, wait; get up, recover, and set forth again – renewed in our strength and stature by the Almighty, He who is elusive yet palpable.

We want answers to the puzzles, the mysteries, of life, both personal and collective. A pilgrim looks for solutions – even if they are only ever partially revealed – during his walking of the Way. Each footfall could precipitate a fall, but thanks to God's companionship he learns to tread without undue dread. Our goal (personal and collective) opens out and is revealed stage by stage. It is the bliss of converse with the Creator, day and night, in the depths of my soul. Could any outer pleasure equal this excitement? A feeling of surprise is a sign that we are in or near the presence of treasure.

The journey is a metaphor for this unfolding of our inherent destiny to abide in Him. Then let us begin. Because we must anticipate a sore back and blistered feet, this setting out is itself a cause for celebration. Much courage is needed at the start as well as along the way, because we do not yet have the impetus of outer momentum. We can only progress if we are prepared to take calculated risks. We must listen to – even respect – doubts but not be confused or corralled by them:

---

[6] Rainer Maria Rilke, trans. M. D. Herter Norton, Letter to Franz Kappus dated 14th May 1904 in *Letters to a Young Poet* (London: W.W. Norton, 1934) pp.40–45.

> Present fears
> Are less than horrible imaginings;
> My thought ...
> Shakes so my single state of man that function
> Is smother'd in surmise, and nothing is
> But what is not.

Macbeth, I iii

We shall be guided and accompanied along the way by saints of the past and present, who each long for us to manifest His presence in our lives (Galatians 2:20). Our predecessors tell of their dark nights, their valleys and peaks. But their description is of their own experience: one peak, many routes (as many as there are people). The stages and the topography are generic, not cartographical. Our spiritual guides – we can choose our own favourites for our expedition – have written their journals and memoirs to encourage us and to reassure.

Our mentors say, 'The journey has been made. "The gate is narrow and the way is hard, that leads to life" (Matthew 7:14), but we have travelled it. You can too. We are counting on you to join us now. You must.'

> Square your shoulders, lift your pack ...
> and go.

Housman, *A Shropshire Lad*, LX

Why do they insist? First, in order to fulfil God's design: this is what our soul longs for above all else. And because this quest is really their bequest to me and to you.

> What light of unremembered skies
> Hast Thou relumed within our eyes,
> Thou whom we seek, whom we shall find? ...
> A certain odour on the wind,

Thy hidden face beyond the west,
These things have called us; on a quest
Older than any road we trod,
More endless than desire ...

Rupert Brooke, 'The Song of the Pilgrims'

Prayers

May I live ever-constant in the search for unblemished truth.

May I live according to the following values and virtues – the tenets of justice and moral behaviour, simplicity and sincerity, unity and goodness, integrity and loving-kindness.

May I make this and every day a kind of summary of my whole life, the life in miniature, including all outer duties and all aspects of interior work and spiritual life. And may I never allow outer to submerge inner.

In Your mercy, in Your infinite goodness, I am on my journey home to life eternal. Please then take me to Yourself, to be at one with You for ever.

CONTEMPORARY CHALLENGES

I
Change

Jack Kennedy said that 'Change is the law of life'. Change is endemic in all aspects of life today, with frequent changes of where we live, who we live with and who we work for. In his third play, *Death of a Salesman* – which began its first run in February 1949 – Arthur Miller foreshadows the personal and family angst of the era of hire and fire. Willy Loman is a washed-up salesman who has spent 34 years on the road, trying to earn both money and recognition. He and his employer,

---

[7] T. S. Eliot, *The Complete Poems and Plays of T. S. Eliot* (London: Faber & Faber, 1969).

Howard Wagner, measure worth by the volume of sales. At the start of act 2, Willy Loman is being sacked by Howard Wagner:

> Howard [*starting to go off*]: I've got to see some people, kid.
> Willy [*stopping him*]: I'm talking about your father! There were promises made across this desk! You mustn't tell me you got people to see – I put thirty-four years into this firm, Howard, and now I can't pay my insurance! You can't eat the orange and throw the peel away – a man is not a piece of fruit![8]

A repair culture has been superseded by a throwaway culture. In only a couple of decades, the prospect of 'a job for life' has been replaced by six-month contracts and natural wastage of the workforce. In spite – or partly because – of feeling insecure or unstable, our expectations of life continue to rise. Many of us will have a longer, healthier and more active retirement than our parents did. We live in an age of novelty, diversity and transience.

Shifting values

Artists express the collective. They give early warning signals of dangers in our values, our behaviour, our lifestyle, our level of respect. Artists are a mirror to what we are or will be. They give voice to our imminent mood, about to erupt.

Nietzsche, Kierkegaard, Huxley (*Brave New World, Eyeless in Gaza*), Orwell, Eliot (*The Hollow Men*), Sartre, Camus (*L'Etranger*) and Kafka (*The Trial, The Castle,* and his parable *The Metamorphosis*) each foresaw the shaking of values that would

---

[8] Arthur Miller, *Death of a Salesman* (New York: Viking Press, 1949) Act 2, scene 1.

soon occur; and the underlying anxiety, the loneliness and the emptiness:

> Whence this secret dread, and inward horror,
> Of falling into naught? Why shrinks the soul
> Back on herself, and startles at destruction?

Addison, *Cato*, V i

In an age of the brief and transitory we are losing the long-term view which helps us read context and interpret events, and enables us to feel that we are a vital and treasured part of a fast-moving collective story.

The signs of change that we see everywhere around us engender new forms (and spans) of relationship, and new dilemmas. Ethicists now have to wade through a quagmire of moral dilemmas, safety and quality-of-life issues, and medical-scientific controversy, such as: Should joint consent continue to be required from a couple who have split up, for the continued storage and possible future use of frozen eggs, sperm or embryos?

Paradox in society adds to our confusion about values. Government blindly increases access to abortion, yet (rightly) tightens measures to safeguard children and babies. Taste and humour, reflecting social attitudes, have their own double standards (but perhaps they always have). Jokes about race, disability or sexual orientation are now, and rightly, suspect or taboo, but jokes about drugs, genitals or the slurred speech of binge drinkers cause hilarity. Francis Gilbert, in his book *Yob Nation*, highlights the widespread use and acceptance of profanity, and 'the normalisation of pornography in everyday imagery'.[9]

---

[9] Francis Gilbert, *Yob Nation* (London: Portrait, 2007).

One of the benefits of living in what W. H. Auden called 'an age of anxiety'[10] is the prompt it gives us to become much more aware of our self. A former psychotherapy client once said, 'I am just a gallery of mirrors, reflecting what people expect of me.' The biggest problem is not being connected to one's self. In his provocative late-1920s essay 'The State of Funk', D. H. Lawrence wrote:

> What really torments civilized people is that they are full of feelings they know nothing about; they can't realize them, they can't fulfil them, they can't *live* them. ... It is like having energy you can't use – it destroys you.[11]

Too much change in too short a time is destabilising – causing shock and even disorientation. Sociologists have compared the impact of change to the bewilderment of a peripatetic asylum-seeker who, with his family, is forced to adapt to a series of countries and cultures, all within a brief span of time. At a time of such rapid and potentially destabilising change, many people retreat into a state of denial – refusing to face reality, trying to hide from the inevitable.

Because our society does not give us a firm enough anchor, we need to find more of our security within. Personal stability is shored up by health in six main areas: acknowledging and befriending your emotional life; having a set of coherent values and personal standards; a commitment to personal growth; a supportive spouse and/or family; fulfilment in one's vocation; and identification with a place – including home, friends and community, country, culture. I belong, therefore I have meaning. Investing one's energy in a wider entity (such as family, church or charity, or community service), and aligning

[10] W. H. Auden, *The Age of Anxiety* (New York: Random House, 1947).
[11] D. H. Lawrence, *Late Essays and Articles, Volume 2* (Cambridge: Cambridge University Press, 2004) p.221.

one's interests with God Himself (the Kingdom of Love), is the ultimate commitment and the ultimate finding.

The impact of information techology

In 1943, Thomas Watson, then Chair of IBM, is reputed to have said, 'I think there is a world market for maybe five computers.' The first computers were made in the Second World War for decoding, to develop bombs and launch rockets. The biggest computer, known as Colossus, weighed a tonne but had less power than a laptop.

Now the internet offers round the clock research facilities, news, entertainment and games, advertising, banking and commerce, shopping, auctions, holiday booking, flat or house purchase, job search facilities, voting, gambling, dating and healthcare advice. The internet is by far the most powerful free-market system ever created. It gives unprecedented power to the individual, and a global reach to even small enterprises. It forces people, groups and nations to be much more competitive.

But the demands of ever-faster technology, and the expectations of civilisation in the twenty-first century, far outstrip the ability of body and mind to adapt. In former times, people got up at sunrise and returned home when it began to get dark. The 24/7 society divorces us from our natural rhythms, and from Sabbath rest. We suffer when we neglect, or overrule, them. Jet lag and shift work impose swift penalties.

The Cartesian aphorism, 'I think, therefore I am', has now been usurped by, 'I log on, therefore I can know'. The result is the mind in constant fast-forward, under siege from a glut of information. Every day we are subjected to an estimated 3,000–5,000 marketing messages. Dr Martin Hilbert and his team at the University of Southern California estimate that we receive the equivalent of 174 newspapers of information per day. That is five times as much as in 1986.[12]

The new technology is intended to liberate. But our use, or abuse and overuse, of it makes us surfeited and exhausted.

Goethe illustrated one of humankind's fundamental dilemmas – in any period of history, but especially today. In his 'bargain' with Mephistopheles, Doctor Faustus gains knowledge and power, but at the cost of disharmony in his mind and soul. He has – to quote D. H. Lawrence – 'a state of mind made up of apparently irrelevant thoughts that scurry in different directions... each with its own small head and tail, trotting its own little way'.[13] We cram our mind, and then complain of information overload. We fire up our senses, and then bemoan our emotional burnout.

Many of us overrate our knowledge and our cleverness. Communion with God and compassion for our neighbour: these constitute true intelligence. Alexander Pope well describes the person of real culture and learning:

> The learned...
> Careless of censure, nor too fond of fame,
> Still pleas'd to praise, nor yet afraid to blame,
> Averse alike to flatter, or offend,
> Not free from faults, nor yet too vain to mend.

An Essay on Criticism

Moreover, such a person, says Pope, is reluctant to give advice without being invited. I should like to be a creative partner on my neighbour's Way, without getting in the way. Some of us perhaps focus too much on the genuine good we do. However, the greatest good is not to display our own gifts

---

12 Richard Alleyne, *The Daily Telegraph*, 11th February 2011.
13 D. H. Lawrence, *Complete Poems* (Harmondsworth: Penguin, 1993) Introduction to *Pansies*.

but to help other people reveal their own. What better epitaph could anyone have than 'He/she was an encourager'?

We are entertained, but burdened, by a surfeit of stimulus. We hear muzak, but do we ever listen to it? Alistair Cooke said, 'Canned music is like audible wallpaper.' In the mid-1990s, the World Health Organization warned that noise is a major threat to health and well-being. It affects digestion, blood pressure, foetal development, mental and emotional health, and our quality and length of sleep. Many families have their television on in the background all day. Like the mobile phone, a noisy environment gives a pseudo-sense of continuity, but at what a cost! It makes us restless, increases the already driven pace of city life, and cramps listening and breadth in conversation. Noise also curbs concentration and creativity. In a letter, Rilke laments:

> My beautiful silence! Where are the days when I wrote that the lovely fountain set the measure for all the noises here? This [recent] disturbance of one's pure hearing is so frightful to me, because for any thought to become real, I must first be able to state it in sound equivalents, projecting it onto the purest possible surface. To find my hearing crammed with such an alien din is just like having to write on paper that has been blotted and scribbled-on all over.[14]

As with the use of recreational drugs, so also with overstimulation of the senses – by eye, ear and loins – there is a tolerance effect: the desensitised self now has a need or craving for more noise (at the cost of stupor) – more that is coarse and novel, even depraved – in order to achieve the previous level of satisfaction.

---

[14] Rainer Maria Rilke, *Letters to Merline, 1919–1922* (London: Methuen, 1951) p.119.

space / peace / Silence

The new technology increasingly impinges on home life, even our sick days or holidays. The outcome is less face-to-face time with friends and family, clients and colleagues. Cable, internet and handset can prevent us from ever being alone: indeed, many of us avoid solitude. Banquo spoke for many of us when he wailed:

> Merciful powers,
> Restrain in me the cursed thoughts that nature
> Gives way to in repose!

Macbeth, II i

The more gifted you are, the more demands on your skills, and thus the more processing time you need. Our health and our emotional state depend on maintaining a daily balance between inner and outer. He only can relate fully who can *face his solitude*.

Boredom is the much-feared nadir of our times. We could end up like the restaurant owner in Sartre's *Nausea*: his mind emptied when his café closed and all his customers went home. Sartre's solution was threefold – space, peace and silence. Creative people always relish the chance to let their mind and imagination roam. For them, Sartre's trio form the atmosphere they most need and prize. I predict that the new chic could be more time offline.

Constantly receiving messages and being always on the lookout for more information makes workers tired and anxious. Their concentration suffers. They doubt their own often hasty replies and decisions. And their attention span shortens – thus reducing their stamina for longer-term projects. Paranoia in the office is evident. When seated at the computer, normally polite people shed their inhibitions and spice emails to colleagues with invective and intimidation, full of capitalised words and exclamation marks. Some people – afraid of confrontation or intimacy, at work and in their social life – use email to avoid personal contact.

We have a love/hate relationship with the new technology. We are addicted to the buzz of new data, and we are afraid of missing a vital phone call. Getting many emails makes us feel that people need us and want us. Being asked for advice or information flatters our sense of worth, and that self-importance makes us want to know everything that is going on.

The frontal lobes of the brain can get overloaded. When we are faced with making the fifth decision after the fourth interruption, in the middle of searching for the tenth missing piece of data, we panic. The deeper, more primitive parts of the brain shift into survivor mode, dimming clarity and creativity. Workers then tend to forget the big picture. They may avoid taking decisions, or they may react impulsively to ward off the perceived danger.

Much of the time that labour-saving devices bring us is wasted. It brings little increase in output because so much of the sending and receiving of messages is defensive in nature. Executives increasingly extend their working day, and erode holiday time, by staying connected outside the office. They are afraid of what may happen to them and their department if they were to lose touch, even briefly, with work issues, office gossip and company politics. We are only just beginning to see and assess the downsides of this blurring between work and home. A few years, in an era of rapid change, is not enough time for healthy social norms to be established.

Those whom social scientists now call 'robo-communicators' live in fear of losing their all-covering security blanket, even for a short time: 'telecocooned' is the new word for this obsession. Instant messaging and a long list of Facebook 'friends' give a sense of relatedness. Some undergraduates recently admitted that they feel unloved if they find no messages waiting for reply when they wake up. Maintaining social bonds, almost non-stop, is seen as more important than having something vital to convey or discuss – think of the choreographed ritual of short messages that precede a rendezvous.

Yet, handsets can also reduce one's sense of being in control: they give the person one is about to meet the ability to cancel or delay a meeting – and to convey that message at the last moment. And many young people use text messaging as a way of avoiding face-to-face contact – especially for embarrassing situations, such as the ending of a relationship.

Almost a century ago, members of the adult education committee of the Knights of Columbus – part of a Catholic fraternity in the USA dedicated to self-help – posed warnings and questions about the telephone: 'Unless people individually master these things, the things will weaken them.'[15]

The world's first telephone exchange was set up in 1878 in New Haven, Connecticut. By the turn of the century, only 15 per cent of American homes had a telephone, and it was not until after the Second World War that more than half were connected. By contrast, the cellular phone – introduced in 1983 – became ubiquitous in less than 20 years. The technological infantry of our era has sped from novelty to familiarity, and at low cost, faster than any other socio-economic expansion in history. We have scarcely begun to discuss or question and debate the social consequences.

Technology is changing the way we relate: work and family and social relationships are becoming more wired and virtual than real and tangible. We are seeing a convergence of the written and the spoken word, and there is a loss of precision in the way we think and express ourselves. Can swifter and often superficial communication ever add up to better and more meaningful dialogue? The next generation of communication products may have an even more pervasive impact on our life – and in ways we cannot yet foresee.

---

[15] Claude Fischer, *America Calling: A Social History of the Telephone to 1940* (Berkeley, CA: University of California Press, 1992) p.1.

Childhood: journey or race?

How much breathing space do children have in the cyber age, with so many seductive choices, and laden with 'the weight of too much liberty' (Wordsworth, 'Nuns Fret Not', *Miscellaneous Sonnets*, Part I, i)? They are sophisticated, streetwise, widely travelled and sexually active, years earlier than their parents or grandparents were. And, at a biological level, the turmoil and temptations of puberty come sooner and last longer. Thus the distinction between the adult world and the child world has become blurred.

Many parts of early life have a competitive edge already: being popular with peers, coursework and exams, sports and other extracurricular activities, preoccupation with dieting and body shape. Like their parents, children now have much less unstructured time. The motto, the imperative, for all ages is, 'I must make every minute count.' Children pressed by tests and timetables become adults stressed by targets and tailgating. Childhood is designed to be a journey, not a race, but for youngsters (as well as adults) life has become an unending succession of things to do – with little or no time in between.

Their bedrooms have become centres of information, entertainment and communication – equipped with smartphone, games console, television and laptop, with constant access to the internet. Studies at the Kaiser Family Foundation, based in California, have found that American children spend an average of seven and a half hours a day using electronic media. Too much time spent sitting in front of a screen can lead to antisocial tendencies. This is the combined result of both content and the daily average number of hours spent watching. For example, before finishing elementary school, most American children will have seen about 8,000 fictional murders on television.[16]

---

[16] Kaiser Foundation, *Generation M2: Media in the Lives of 8- to 18-Year-Olds*. http://kff.org/other/report (2nd March 2016).

According to a recent government-backed survey, the average British working parent spends twice as long dealing with email (at home) as playing with their children. Even bedtime rituals are no longer sacrosanct. In order to help parents cope with time-consuming youngsters, a group of authors have condensed classic fairy tales into one-minute, one-page stories. Is it any surprise that, in the absence of adult attention, millions of children throughout affluent nations have been diagnosed as suffering from attention-deficit hyperactivity disorder?

Romance: the wisdom of gradations

Adult culture too has lost the joy of anticipation, and the wisdom and beauty of gradations – such as in the early stages of a relationship. Dating agencies, internet chat rooms, singles nights at the supermarket, and ads on the lonely hearts page, all promise a partner after only a short overture. But shopping around for partners and accelerating the pace of intimacy can never guarantee lasting happiness and fulfilment. Erich Fromm points out in *The Art of Loving* that if physical closeness occurs without love (or outpaces it), when the mirage of unity is exposed for a sham the two feel alienated from one another and themselves.

Recent adaptations of *Pride and Prejudice* show that the slow rituals of courtship still appeal. Romance needs all the drama of challenge and mutual discovery. Every act of this drama has its own tempo and duration, its own delights and despairs. Saint-Exupéry writes with touching simplicity about the gradual unfolding of love, and the trust that allows us to yield to love's embrace.

> 'Each day we will sit a little closer to one another',
> says the fox to the Little Prince.

The Little Prince asks, 'What does it mean "to tame"?'

The Fox replies, 'It means "to create connections" ... If you tame me we shall need each other. ... You will be unique for me. ... if you tame me my life will be full of sunshine. Your footsteps will sound different to all the others ... Yours will call me out from my burrow like music ... You have hair the colour of gold ... When you have tamed me, the golden wheat will remind me of you ... You become responsible for ever for the creature you have tamed.'[17]

The age of impatience

We are living in an age of impatience. A poster on the window of a bank which urged people to come in and discuss a new credit card offer, reading, 'Don't wait!' is surely a sign of the times. People are constantly seeking – mainly unconsciously – people on to whom to discharge their negativity and unmediated tension (physical and emotional). This manifests in traffic or parking rage, office or mobile phone rage, gym rage, bar or restaurant rage, cigarette-smoke rage, check-in and in-flight rage, even checkout rage in supermarkets. We pound the steering wheel, we scowl, we snarl like Long John Silver, because we have to wait.

When we are in public, frustration (and worse) is lurking, just waiting to erupt at even the smallest provocation, real or presumed. Rage is a by-product of rush. Anyone who steps across our path, who slows us down – who delays (even slightly) our getting what we want when we want it – can provoke anger from normally mild-mannered people. Instead, heed Alexander Pope's advice:

---

[17] Editor's translation from Antoine St Exupéry, *Le Petit Prince* (Paris: Gallimard, 1945) pp.78–80.

At every trifle, scorn to take offence,
That always shows great pride, or little sense.

An Essay on Criticism, II

What we do not acknowledge in ourselves we project on to others.[18] Matthew 10:16 speaks of the need – the urgent need – to protect oneself and guard our loved ones: 'I send you out as sheep in the midst of wolves; so be wise as serpents and innocent as doves.'

The economics of happiness

For the first time, the main problem for many nations is shifting from scarcity and survival to surfeit. Too many cars clog the roads. Too much junk food (high in fat and sugar) causes obesity which, in many Western nations, rivals smoking as the main preventable cause of death. So vast a choice of products dazzles our ability to select. Do we have enough time to enjoy what we have bought? Affluence broadens choice; choice multiplies dilemmas. Discernment is the safeguard of the new freedoms posed by higher income and a more liberal society. In his essay *The Economic Possibilities for our Grandchildren* (1930), John Maynard Keynes forecast that – for much of the human race – the new challenge would be how to live wisely in a more affluent society.

In the 85 years since Keynes wrote his essay, the per capita income of Americans, inflation-adjusted, is six times larger. Yet since 1960 the divorce rate has doubled, and cases of alcoholism and clinical depression have tripled, as have the number of teenage suicides. The recorded level of violent crime has quadrupled, and the prison population has quintupled. With good reason, 'Rising GDP' is no longer seen as a panacea,

---

[18] Carl Jung in 'Two Essays on Analytical Psychology' (*Collected Works* 'CW':7).

proxy term for personal satisfaction, except in the poorest countries.

Studies of well-being – in Britain, the USA and Europe – show that, after a society reaches a certain level of economic improvement, further increases in earnings and material comfort make little difference to individuals.[19] Indeed, self-perceived personal satisfaction may even decline.[20] When we enjoy material prosperity and satisfactions, pleasure seems to emanate directly from these good things of life, rather than from their origin and essence.

Where, then, do we look for contentment? Indeed, would we ever, like St Paul, be 'content' 'in whatever state I am' (Philippians 4:11)? Happiness is seldom found in a cult of having: a bigger house, a higher bank balance, and a wardrobe packed with designer clothes.

> Happiness depends, as nature shows,
> Less on exterior things than most suppose.
>
> William Cowper, *Table Talk*

When he drafted the American constitution, Thomas Jefferson put the pursuit of happiness early on (paragraph 2), as a core aim for the people of the new republic. But even the most enterprising of us seldom succeed by *trying to be happy*. Edward Diener, Professor of Happiness Studies at the University of Illinois, says that the expectation that one should be happy most of the time is itself a frequent cause of discontent.[21] The pleasure derived from getting what the false

---

[19] John Talberth, Clifford Cobb and Noah Slattery, *The Genuine Progress Indication*, (Oakland, CA: Redefining Progress, 2006).
[20] See Oliver James, *Affluenza: How to be Successful and Stay Sane* (London: Vermillion, 2007).
[21] E. Diener, Rober-Biswas Diener, *Happiness: Unlocking the Mysteries of Psychological Wealth* (Blackwell: Oxford, 2008).

self wants does not last for long, and is frequently followed by guilt, disappointment or spiralling cravings.[22]

At one level, happiness is an occasional by-product of doing what you enjoy and deem worthwhile, and of being with life-enhancing people. More deeply, happiness is – like hope – a spiritual state. Joy arises from the soul, first and last because of God's constant presence in our life, within and all around us.

We can prepare for happiness – such as by guarding our integrity and all aspects of our health (physical, mental, emotional, spiritual), and by full-hearted devotion to a worthy aim – but happiness eludes full-on pursuit. It often comes as a gift – unbidden, unexpected. Our role is then threefold: to be thankful; to be opportunist in glad acceptance; and to show – by attitude and by action – that we want to be worthy of what (or whom) we have been given to cherish.

Many people live their life back to front: they accumulate more money and possessions and status in order to do more of what they enjoy, so as to be happier. But the reverse is the surest way. First, be who you really are, by using your talents in service of ultimate good. 'What I do is me: for that I came' (Gerard Manley Hopkins, 'As kingfishers catch fire').

In St Augustine's view, the peak of wisdom is contemplative entry into the will of God: the aligning (or realigning) of yourself with the outpouring of His goodness. This entails first a new befriending of yourself, your uniqueness, and a welcoming of all that happens. Not denying or avoiding, not rationalising, not fighting against pain; but facing and working through. Not restlessly seeking pleasures, nor trying to hold on to those that come. When you stop chasing after pleasures, you open up to the givenness of joy.

One sign of maturity is the acceptance – not just the tolerance – of ambiguity. A spirituality that understates – slurs

---

22 The false self refers to the narrow, egoistic self, as well as the mask or *persona* we present to the outside world. It is a negation of truth, an aspect of God which grows in us as we grow more and more into His likeness.

over – sorrow and emotional winters (which are part of all human life, and especially of all religious journeys) will produce too much leaf and too little fruit. Learning from both light and darkness develops and enriches our humanity – especially faith, compassion, and stamina:

> Oh Life! without thy chequered scene
> Of right and wrong, of weal and woe,
> Success and failure, could a ground
> For magnanimity be found;
> For faith, 'mid ruined hopes, serene?
> Or whence could virtue flow?
>
> William Wordsworth, 'After-Thought'

Anticipating and managing change

The rate of change is far more rapid and more widespread than in any previous era of human history. The present is fast; the future will be even faster. Most insidiously of all, the pace and diversity of change outrun humankind's ability to cope and adapt (let alone anticipate). So much change in a relatively short time causes what William Ogburn has termed 'cultural lag'.

At times of major change (and/or disruption), some of us hunker down in a state of denial. The less one thinks about the future and plans ahead, the more intimidating that period may feel when it eventually arrives. This Latin proverb is still pertinent: *Praemonitus, praemunitus* – Forewarned, forearmed. We need to spend more time, alone and in groups, mobilising curiosity and intuition, imagination and long-range thinking. The only safe way to relate to the future, according to C. P. Snow, is to have 'the future in our bones'.[23]

---

[23] C. P. Snow, 'The Two Cultures', Rede Lecture (Cambridge: Cambridge University Press, 1959).

We must not stand Canute-like before the advancing tide. When a situation or an inner state is not made fully conscious, it hits us as fate. The way down is the way up. The way in is the way out.

We need to invest in preparing people of all ages not only for the possible, but also for the unexpected. We all need to look to the future – our own and society's – with elasticity of mind. In an age gushing with choice – so many attractive possibilities beckoning, giving us their 'come hither' look – we need to be ever more astute, shrewd in the investing of our energy, time and talents. Where? With whom? To what extent – as to intensity and likely duration? And for what – or Whose – ultimate purpose?

There are six main ways of managing change. First, to nurture more (and more enduring) friendships, and widen one's contacts in the neighbourhood. Second, not to take on more than one or two of the major life changes at the same time: grief, separation, illness, house move, job change (as far as this is within our control). Third, plans need to be kept fluid, and adapted as circumstances change.

Fourth, remember that every situation (no matter how large, how complex or how painful) can be divided into its constituent parts. This brings two benefits: it promotes ease and economy of action and, by reducing the size of each task, it boosts momentum and morale.

> I never ran 1,000 miles: I could never have done that. I ran one mile 1,000 times.
>
> Stu Mittleman, long-distance runner

Fifth, in order to survive (let alone thrive) in an era of headlong speed and change, it is vital to maintain good health (so far as hereditary factors allow).

Last of all, it is so often proved that the more input, the greater the need for assimilation and reflection. Personal equilibrium depends on having enough breathing space: time to pause, absorb, reflect, read, discuss, learn and grow. The more breathless the society, the less responsive people are to the breath of the Spirit. There is a wisdom in modulating to the rhythms of, and respecting the distinctions between, day and night, workdays and Sabbath rest, and the seasons: times to mourn and rejoice, times to sow, and times to let the land lie fallow.

St John of the Cross, Spanish Carmelite friar (1542–1591), gives this advice for the world's sickness:

> That which we most require for our spiritual growth is the silence of the desire and of the tongue before God, Who is so high: the language He most listens to is that of silent love.[24]

The faster and more complex the rate of change, the greater our responsibility, and the more we need to peer into the future. We cannot prevent personal or collective change, but we can learn to move from the futility of denial to an attitude of watchful acceptance. Without loss of integrity, we need to become part of the change.

Prayers

May I detach myself from anxiety, from temptations, from superficial preoccupations, from anything that might confine or impoverish my soul, so that my whole being may live this earthly stage of its existence in its richest and most noble expression.

---

[24] St John of the Cross, trans. David Lewis, *Spiritual Sentences and Maxims* (London: Longman Green, 1864).

I thank You for Your companionship – ever-present, ever-available, ever-new and yet changeless.

I listen for the sound of the music of peace. May my life be one continuous act of praise, worship, and self-offering.

II
Stress

*If people but provided for eternity with the same
solicitude and real care as they do for this life, they
could not fail to reach heaven.*

*Archbishop John Tillotson, 'On Covetousness',
Sermon XXXIX*

The word 'stress' was first used about tests to destruction – in the fields of physics, engineering and manufacturing. Robert Hooke, the seventeenth-century inventor, used this concept in experiments to test the tolerance of load-bearing materials. The human counterpart is to be overburdened for a long period: taking on too much, our balance (sometimes also our reason) is disturbed.

Physiological and behavioural effects of stress

In the 1930s, an Austrian-born Canadian endocrinologist, Hans Selye, formulated the modern medical concept of stress, which he defined as the rate of wear and tear on the body, such as in response to injury, disease or trauma.

Our ancestors evolved the fight-or-flight response in order to cope with sudden physical threats (such as predators) or environmental threats (such as bad weather). Energy is mobilised for muscular exertion by diverting resources from the body's housekeeping functions – tissue maintenance and repair, digestion, growth and care of the immune system – which are not essential for a rapid, and relatively short-lived, reaction to danger.

Blood supply is also diverted to the brain, to boost its power through a supply of oxygen and glucose. Stress happens when the adrenaline and cortisol levels continue to be high, putting the body on emergency alert over a prolonged period. The symptoms – such as anxiety, insomnia and reduced functioning – often persist long after the source of stress has ended. The consequent changes in body chemistry and balance (homeostasis) can affect metabolic function and weaken the immune system, making the stressed person more prone to infection or disease.

Stress is a constant adjunct to major conditions – from strokes to cancer. Stress can precipitate a latent condition, such as heart disease, because it increases blood pressure, and can cause behaviours destructive of health – such as seeking refuge in alcohol, cigarettes and/or drugs; unhealthy eating patterns; and reduced physical activity. Coffee, alcohol and junk foods all increase stress: stimulants and processed, chemical-laden foods deplete adrenal function.

Stress thus contributes to obesity. Stress hormones release sugar into the blood to fuel rapid thought and movement. When stress is a constant part of everyday life, the body's blood sugar levels are on an all-day roller coaster ride of highs and lows, thus overstimulating the appetite.

A feverish state of mind can cause psychosomatic illness. Stress and/or anger raise acid production, leading to heartburn, and colonic disorders such as irritable bowel syndrome. With almost as many nerve endings as the brain, the digestive system is one of the first areas of the body to suffer from chronic stress.

A healthy level of stress (optimum stimulus) is needed for peak performance in any field of human endeavour. The hormones released aid speed of decision and movement. Jonny

Wilkinson spoke for many top sportsmen when he said, 'The greater the pressure, the better I play.' The Lorme school of doctors contends that short bursts of purposeful activity are beneficial to body and morale. But when the limits of strength are breached, the result is nervous breakdown: the human equivalent of blowing a fuse.

Among the time loss and behavioural costs of stress are accidents and forgetting: leaving keys or wallet at home, the mobile in the bus, the shopping list in the car, or school books at Dad's. Prolonged stress, or severe short-term strain, can inflame a latent mental disorder, or cause regression to any stage(s) of life during which conflicts were least adequately resolved. The earlier the developmental stage, the more severe the new emotional disturbance is likely to be.

Stress is linked to at least two in every five GP consultations. At any one time, one in five of the adult population is suffering from stress. In the USA, the stress-management industry is huge and expanding, comprising a range of services from stress audits to dreamweaver goggles, noise cancelling headphones, relaxation drinks and luxury massage chairs.[25]

Personal causes of stress

We are influenced not only by circumstances, but also by our perception of, and reaction to, circumstances. One person's threat is another person's challenge. Shakespeare exaggerates to make his point: 'There is nothing either good or bad, but thinking makes it so' (*Hamlet*, II ii). People vary in their coping strategies for dealing with hassle or threat (real or imagined).

In the 1960s, two American psychologists/medical researchers, Richard Rahe and Thomas Holmes, compiled a list

---

[25] Bruce Horowitz, 'All stressed out? Businesses will sell you some peace', in *USA Today*, 5th August 2013.

of major life events (some positive, some negative), which tend to cause stress.[26] The higher the number of simultaneous life changes, and the more radical or substantial they are, the greater the cost to body and mind. Such events include:

- setting up a home with one's partner;
- pregnancy, childbirth and the integration of a new (and needy) member of the family;
- trouble with in-laws;
- financial worries, such as being responsible for more than one family;
- mounting debts; large mortgage;
- move of home;
- tense relationship with boss;
- promotion or demotion at work – up or down the management ladder – increases job insecurity;
- change of employer;
- change of type of job; retraining;
- redundancy, prolonged unemployment;
- child leaving home;
- relationship problems;
- sexual difficulties;
- own separation, divorce;
- retirement;
- parents' separation or divorce;
- death of parent or other close family member;

---

[26] T. H. Holmes and R. H. Rahe (1967), 'The social readjustment rating scale', *Journal of Psychosomatic Research*, 11, p.213.

- death of partner, child or friend;

- injury, illness, some form of trauma;

- recovery period: after injury, illness or any form of loss;

- caring for someone who is ill and/or aged; and

- coping with one's own disease or disability, or that of a significant other person.

Collective causes of stress

A number of collective fears contribute to personal insecurity. The world's population is expected to reach 9 billion by 2050, an increase of 2 billion from current levels: that's equivalent to two Indias. The need to provide food, fuel and other resources will be acute.

Poverty will increasingly be the biggest challenge in history, coupled with balancing the needs of human beings and nature. One-third of deaths (18 million people a year) are caused by poverty. Approximately one-third of the world's population live in a slum or shanty town, frequently without running water, mains sewerage or proper roads; and where criminal gangs are rampant.[27] More than 1 billion people lack access to safe drinking water. And, according to the United Nations, half of the world's hospital beds are occupied by patients with waterborne diseases. The debt burden of many of the poorest nations far exceeds their entire annual exports.

UNICEF has reported that half of all the world's children are directly exposed to war, extreme poverty, disease, famine or some other major deprivation or danger. In a world that is ever-more socially integrated – through commerce, information technology and immigration – it will be increasingly destabilising to have a billion who live on less than one dollar a

---

[27] Mike Davis, *Planet of Slums* (London: Verso, 2006) pp.136–144.

day, 70 per cent of them in Africa. When adjusted for purchasing-power parity, the richest countries are more than 70 times richer than the poorest, in per capita GDP. Here are conditions for disease, civil war and terrorism.[28]

Sixty per cent of the systems that support life on Earth – such as climate, fresh water and clear air – are being degraded or used unsustainably. The main threats from climate change are rapidly rising sea levels, massive biological extinction, intensifying storm systems, widespread drought and desertification, famine and water shortage, and the personal/social/political disruption (such as forced migration) caused by these major pressures. With each sunrise, God reminds us that the world is ours on lease. For the sake of life tomorrow, may our love for the Earth increase.

By 2050, world oil output is forecast to be only ten per cent of its 2010 levels.[29] We consume three barrels for every new one discovered. When oil production begins an irreversible decline – in the 2020s or possibly sooner – geopolitical tension and conflict will sharpen.[30] Each of us (especially the Western societies) will be forced to radically simplify our lifestyle.

The world is a more dangerous place than it has ever been, because of the rise in fundamentalism, the miniaturisation of weapons, and because the global community is now so 'small', porous and interconnected. Everyone's home is on the front line of all the dangers – and all the benefits – that our closely linked world threatens or offers.

Digital technology has closed the former gap in time between atrocity and worldwide awareness. By contrast,

---

[28] Ronald Wright, *A Short History of Progress* (Toronto: House of Anansi Press, 2004).
[29] Elizabeth Kolbert, *Field Notes from a Catastrophe*; John Lanchester, 'Warmer, Warmer' in *London Review of Books*, 22nd March 2007; *Summary for Policymakers*, 2007, Intergovernmental Panel on Climate Change; UN's *The Millennium Ecosystem Assessment Synthesis Report* (March 2005).
[30] David Strahan, *The Last Oil Shock: A Survival Guide to the Imminent Extinction of Petroleum Man* (London: John Murray, 2008).

Picasso's most famous work, *Guernica* – produced for the Spanish Pavilion at the Paris Exposition Universelle of 1937 – expresses his horror at the bombing of the Basque capital during the civil war of 1936–39. It was market day. This mural is an artist's immediate but considered response to mass brutality and bloodlust. The mural – with its bullfight imagery, disembowelled horses and screaming mothers – is a twentieth-century icon of fear and guilt. Postcard reproductions of the mural were banned in Spain during Franco's rule. The mythic monsters and tormented statues recast the event as classical tragedy. Today we would see live video footage of the bloodshed. Terror thrives on spectacle.

A related and equally tormenting trend is the West's voyeuristic obsession with reality television, especially when – as so often nowadays – it shows the breaking, even the sundering, of taboos: bullying, humiliation, confession, physical and emotional exposure. It is beyond the scope of this book to explore the many and complex reasons for this disturbing and increasing trend. The factors include short attention span, the craving for ever-more stark stimulus, vicarious thrill, the wish to compare self with others, projection of our own shadow, and the loss of our moral compass.

This compass is a who, not a what: it is you and me. In his wise book, *Man's Search for Himself,* Rollo May shows how the weakened sense of self erodes our ethical base. Prior to values is the valuer – a person who can choose and affirm, and with the force of character to live what he believes, rather than be blown by every wind of trend or fashion, preoccupied, like the hapless Macbeth, with buying 'Golden opinions from all sorts of people' (I vii).

> To know what you prefer – instead of humbly saying 'Amen' to what the world says you ought to like, is to keep your soul alive.
>
> R. L. Stevenson, *An Inland Voyage*, chapter IV

Causes of stress in childhood and adolescence

Events that often cause stress in children include:

- moving house;
- starting at playgroup or school;
- a new baby in the family;
- emotional and/or physical abuse;
- parental conflict, and domestic violence;
- death of a relative, friend or favourite pet;
- parental mental health problems;
- bullying;
- separation from a parent, and family break-up.

To these events, children may show their distress through nightmares, bed-wetting, jealousy, aggressive behaviour, temper tantrums, regression, somatic illnesses, withdrawal or speech impediments. One in five British schoolchildren has an illness (physical and/or psychological) which is stress-related.

Many children may be in deficit emotionally if both parents invest excessive time and energy in their career. Building up financial capital should not sacrifice the nurturing of human capital. In Britain, eight out of ten working fathers and more than half of all working mothers often (or usually) have to work antisocial hours – i.e., outside 8am to 7pm, Monday to Friday. This means that millions of young children are likely to spend more time with a childminder, nanny or au pair, in a nursery or at school, than with their parents.

Returning home at the end of a tiring day at work, exhausted parents have less time and energy to attend to the needs of their children. Less family time weakens family bonds. If the evening's conversation between parent and child is reduced to an unvaried five-word litany – 'How was school today?' ... 'OK' – then the adult will not be able to foresee, empathise, support and guide.

American teenagers now spend an average of three and a half hours alone each day: more time alone than with friends and family combined. Not wanting to add to the burden of their parents, youngsters tend to hide their worries. The number of teenage suicides has more than doubled in the past 20 years, with dramatic rises also in truancy, binge drinking, drug addiction and eating disorders. In the USA, use of prescription drugs is rising faster among children than among the elderly.[31]

Family meals offer a regular routine, and enable parents to monitor their children's behaviour. But the family meal is in decline because parents work longer and children spend more time in front of televisions and computers. One in four British homes does not have a dining table that can accommodate all members of the immediate family.[32]

Children are becoming more bedroom-bound – partly because of their love affair with technology and entertainment, and lack of quality time with parents, and also because of health and safety fears: far fewer children, especially in cities, are now allowed to play outside or walk to school. When young children are outside, they are often seen on reins, or strapped into a buggy or a car seat. These factors combined contribute to obesity, impaired social skills and a delay in learning about appropriate risk-taking.

Personality and the capacity to learn, interact and regulate emotions are shaped by the amount and the depth of affection and attention given in the early years. The more conversation children have as toddlers, and the more they are encouraged to sing, the better they read, write, speak and relate later on. This

---

[31] Mary Eberstadt, *Home-Alone America: The Hidden Toll of Day Care, Wonder Drugs, and Other Parent Substitutes* (New York: Sentinel HC, 2004).
[32] 2005 study undertaken by Cranks, the restaurant and food brand.

quality attention on a daily basis affects both emotional and intellectual growth. Today's children are being raised more by interactive computer games than by care and cuddles. It is said that 'a family who pray together, stay together'. Perhaps this maxim is also valid if we substitute 'play' for 'pray'.

A long-lasting influence, which can trigger (or exacerbate) stress, is the childhood observation and subsequent memory (conscious and unconscious) of the way parents, teachers and other role models coped with difficulty or conflict. 'Were they tense? Were they mature? Did they use me as a confidant, or try to make me a pawn in their own battles?'

The recurring danger to the balance, adjustment and well-being of a child is when one or both parents use them as a confidant, and as a substitute for the love, security and emotional warmth that are missing in the parental relationship. Whenever parents relate to a child on any basis but that of the child's own needs and individuality – such as by casting him or her in an inappropriate role – they violate the child's freedom, and seriously delay them becoming themselves.

Jung (in *Collected Works:* 15) said that the strongest negative psychic effect on a child – especially if the overt parent–child relationship is overclose and overintense, and in some families, mutually dependent – is the unlived life (inner and outer) of one or both parents (and ancestors too). One of the best and most creative gifts to a child is for the parents to focus more on their own personal growth. This helps to prevent overidentifying with the child's progress. It gives the child a good enough example of the benefits of becoming an adult, and improves the emotional climate in the home.

A child's well-being also depends on the quality of his parents' relationship – especially how they respond to each other when the home atmosphere is emotionally charged. John Gottman, Emeritus Professor of Psychology at the University of Washington, monitored infants' heart rates and neurological responses as their parents talked about issues that had previously sparked disputes. Conflict between parents was reflected in the babies' responses. Babies born to troubled couples tended to fuss, whine and cry more than those born into a happier relationship. Babies cannot yet read books but they are adept at reading anger and hostility (subtle as well as overt).[33]

Consciously and unconsciously, children absorb from parents the atmosphere of the adult relationship, and the pent-up energy of all that the adults so sedulously ignore or avoid in themselves. Moods can be as thin as ether or as thick as tar. Children feel the family atmosphere as if it were part of themselves, a factor which can manifest in psychosomatic illness.

Grow up!

Various forms of demographic change contribute to the instabilities of our time. Every year, both boys and girls are reaching puberty earlier. A century ago, the average age a girl entered puberty was 14. Today that age is 12. The young are losing precious years of childhood, and have to cope with huge hormonal changes long before they are emotionally prepared.

At the same time, more and more of the iPod generation are delaying full entry into adulthood because of further education, extended periods living with parents while they pay off student debts, longer apprenticeships, struggling to get on the property ladder and delayed first childbirth.

The curtailing of childhood has many pernicious consequences. There is increasing pressure to grow up faster because of educational systems; a culture geared to high performance; celebrity icons; early exposure to advertising; and the need to try to understand family turmoil or break-up. 1

---

[33] Summarised in Christina Hopkinson, 'How to win at happy families' in *The Telegraph*, 1st September 2005.

Corinthians 13:11 is being rewritten: 'When I was a child, I understood as a child, but I spoke like an adult, and I wanted to dress and behave like an adult.' A rising number of young people experience their first breakdown before they even start work often because of exam pressures or student debt, or failing to match the self-cramping expectations of peers, parents, siblings or teachers.

Brought up in a culture in thrall to the ten demigods of capitalist society (power, performance, prestige, success, income, image, appearance, property, possessions and popularity), children learn, from nursery school onwards, about the need to Get Ahead: psychologist Oliver James calls this the 'affluenza virus'. They will be the wealth-orientated power-seekers of tomorrow. May we help young people to see that true identity stems not from the height of our status, but from the range and richness of our humanity.

To help young people question and develop their own personal identity and ethics, education is key. A wide education (that focuses not merely on passing exams and university entrance) can help students to define worthy life-goals; clarify their values, and modes (and boundaries) of behaviour; and refine their decision-making. A robust personal ethic helps us avoid selling our soul to society's criteria of worth.

Stress from overwork

The main causes of stress in the workplace are excessive workload, inadequate managers, tension and mistrust among colleagues, organisational change/restructuring, and the pressure of unrealistic targets.[34] The Health and Safety Executive estimates that 60 per cent of absenteeism is stress-related.

---

[34] 2004 report by the Chartered Institute of Personnel and Development.

Many staff – plus their own peers and line managers – fail to see that they are on a downward slope towards buckling or collapse – partly because the symptoms of stress build up insidiously over a period, and also because we are conditioned to accept that work is by its very nature not only demanding but also personally taxing. Whereas some people refuse to admit the amount of stress in their life, others would feel ashamed if the tempo at work was anything less than hectic. The motto is, 'The more important I am to the company, the more frenetic I should be (and be seen to be). I can cope with lots of pressure.' Because stress is widely seen as a sign of status or success, some couples argue, when they get back home, about 'Which of us has the most high-octane job?'

Many people begin the day with a 'deskfast', and then at work eat 'on the go', thereby missing the benefit of being away from desk and office for a while. 'Presenteeism' is a major problem in the business world. No one wants to be the first to leave the office, for fear of being accused of lack of commitment, being made redundant or missing out on a promotion. Some people stay at work longer than necessary to avoid (or delay) facing tension and problems at home. Tension may be repressed (sometimes emerging as psychosomatic illness) or displaced on to others, such as by anger even at a minor put-down or setback.

Heart attacks occur more frequently on Mondays than on any other day of the week, leading some epidemiologists to speculate that these attacks are triggered by the pressures of returning to work. Rehabilitating stressed employees and returning them to the same environment is akin to throwing a cleaned-up fish back into a polluted lake. There is a clear need to de-stress the system as well as the individual.

In spite of all this, work gives many people more satisfaction than leisure time, and for two main reasons. First, because work is primarily active, in contrast to the thousands of hours we spend, from childhood onwards, passively stimulated (or rendered soporific) by mass-media entertainment. Second, work is more structured, with built-in rules and teamwork, targets and feedback, challenges and rewards. The workplace can be a source of friends and of recognition and respect. It gives us opportunities to make a difference. All these factors encourage our focus and our willing participation. So we cannot blame all of the live-to-work ethic on pressure from above.

Leisure time, in its raw state, is unstructured. Perhaps we fear that to give too much design to leisure time will erode its (and our) freedom. We need to question this myth. Inner and outer disciplines can enhance our free time, just as we observe them informing and improving our work. If our spare time is to be truly recreative, we have to be proactive and – dare I say it? – organising. Once we are engaged in free choice activity, we can let go, be spontaneous, and even experience the timeless.

Workaholics

Paradoxically, it is often not the weak, but the apparently strong – reliable, responsible and successful – who pay the highest price for an unhealthy lifestyle. This personality type feels excessively downhearted if they fail to achieve the highest targets. They live for work, rather than working in order to live. And they become the victim of (often impossible) expectations (their own and those of their superiors at work). They are often type-A personalities (driven, competitive, perfectionist, goal-oriented). Thus they do their best to hide their distress from family and colleagues in order to preserve their competent image.[35]

They may suffer from one or more of the classic signs of depression: apathy and pessimism, especially just after waking;

---

[35] Meyer Friedman & Diane Ulmer, *Treating Type A Behavior – and Your Heart* (New York: Knopf, 1984).

difficulty in concentrating; feeling remote and cut off from other people; loss of sleep, appetite, libido, general energy level, and/or enthusiasm. Such a person may look back on the past with regrets or shame. Tense and anxious, they cannot enjoy where they are – even in midsummer. And they look towards the future in a wary, weary way.

When stressed, the weak tend to cave in and collapse: this gives them a chance to reassess their whole lifestyle. By contrast, the strong typically react by taking on yet more tasks and submitting themselves to ever-tighter deadlines, thus driving themselves ever further from discovery of the roots of their distress.

Workaholics tend to be perfectionists, with a craving to be in control (of self and others). They have a keen wish to please others, but often put their own needs first, and communicate poorly. Perfectionists demand so much of themselves, and worry endlessly about the level of their performance – everything must be done to the nth degree. Hence they report high levels of fatigue.

> 'Now! Now!' screamed the Queen. 'Faster! Faster!'
> 'Now, here, you see, it takes all the running you can do, to stay in the same place. If you want to get somewhere else, you must run at least twice as fast as that!'
>
> Lewis Carroll, *Through the Looking-Glass*

Exhausted, such people soon become demoralised – or worse. The Japanese – self-styled slaves to the work ethic – have a word, *karoshi* ('death by overwork'), which doctors and coroners now regularly put on death certificates. If only they could see that happiness is free. No one at the end of their life ever moans, 'I should have spent more time at the office.'

Sociologists have coined the term *homo economicus*, a person motivated to maximise personal gain. Fuelled by management targets (departmental and corporate), and goaded by the incentive to earn a bonus or a share option, stress has become endemic among management. A recent survey by the Institute of Management reported that 75 per cent of UK managers stay in contact with their office while they are on holiday. They cannot cut the umbilical cord with work. Life is in hock to the personal organiser. Even their time in the hotel swimming pool is likely to be interrupted by the trill of the mobile phone, lurking on the perimeter. These executives flatter themselves that their company and colleagues cannot fully function without their constant input. In reality, they need their daily professional fix. Not for them what the Italians call *dolce far niente*, pleasant idleness.

Stress produces cortisol, which makes managers, at all levels of seniority, feel even more competitive and territorial – a soil for conflict, jealousy and bullying (even cruelty). Many (perhaps most) managers respond to a performance challenge by tightening control, not loosening it. Having turned up the pressure, they then try to mitigate its worst effects. The new technology gives managers so much more control over their staff – as to performance and targets, use of time and productivity, and the ability to monitor communications, including personal ones. What would George Orwell make of that?

Autonomy

Jobs lower down in organisations can be just as stressful, in their own way, as those at the top. This is because staff in a micromanaged office have less choice or control over the work, as to content and amount, and how and when it should be done. Less scope for initiative leads to less fulfilment and more frustration.

More autonomy helps to buffer some of the effects of pressure. Hence the enthusiasm for flexitime, shift swapping, a better work–leisure balance, and working from home. Some staff opt to downsize, trading income and prestige for more control and personal satisfaction. Among the happiest workers are craftsmen and artisans. They work in their own studio, at their own pace, to make items that speak of their own skill, taste and chosen quality.

Success in any form of human enterprise follows a chain reaction:

carefully chosen activity → enjoyment, relish → success.

> To business that we love, we rise betime
> And go to't with delight.

Antony and Cleopatra, IV iv

We experience flow when we do what we enjoy, and so as a by-product this is the job or work or enterprise most likely to bring material – as well as personal/emotional/intellectual – reward. If my intentions are sincere, then whatever fulfils me will often benefit others and my whole human/material environment, and set up the best chances for happiness.

Pseudo solutions

Some people try in vain to drink or eat or comfort-buy their way out of stress. Cocaine and alcohol are among the greatest dangers: cocaine can boost alertness, enabling managers and staff to work longer hours; then in the evening, along with colleagues at a nearby bar, they rely on alcohol to help them unwind from the relentless pace of the day.

> And if I drink of oblivion for a day,
> So shorten I the stature of my soul.

George Meredith, *Modern Love*, XII

Recognising the huge cost (personal and financial) of absenteeism and lowered productivity owing to stress, some larger companies call in a phalanx of stress therapists, on-site masseurs, yoga teachers, personal development trainers and lifestyle coaches, to reduce strain in the workplace. In some countries, a post-prandial lie-down is well established, even sacrosanct. Some Japanese companies provide recharge rooms for a short after-lunch relaxation or sleep. In the heart of Tokyo's bustling financial district, the dormitories of the Good Sleep Salon are full every lunchtime; a refreshing whiff of pine oxygen costs an extra 500 yen. But such solutions will do little more than palliate (and sometimes exacerbate) the effects of our shared problem.

Solutions

What will fundamentally ease the strain of all this restlessness? No cure for a stressful and hectic lifestyle is more efficacious than prayer. Ring-fence time for yourself every day to retire within.

The second antidote to stress is the healing effect of nature. Closeness to nature can profoundly affect our pace, our view of time, our expectations, and even our endurance of pain or difficulty. Are we listening to her personal messages? Love of nature and respect for environment give me a sense of belonging.

> And whether it be hill or moor
> I feel where e'er I go
> A silence that discourses more
> Than any tongue can do.

John Clare, 'Pastoral Poesy'

The third solution (which flows from prayer) is to find your vocation. The true bottom line is not how much I earn, but the quality and range of my life, inner and outer. No sum of money can compensate, no level of prestige can ever begin to satisfy, if you are not doing your life's creative fulfilling wish: not what the marketplace necessarily prizes, but what is authentically yours, true to your own voice and vision. Be mindful of God's hope in you. Yours is a corner of His kingdom which can be filled only by you.

To find our destined direction (at least for this stage of our life) we need to listen deeply to every prompting from our psyche, and read (using our peripheral vision) the symbols – of dreams and our surroundings – that keep speaking to us. When you are faithful to your God-givenness, when you think, work, speak, behave and love, with and from your integrity, then every project and relationship is infused with power, drive and stamina far stronger than your own. Service and vocational work are His holy love made visible and tangible. 'For this purpose I have come to this hour' (John 12:27). What or who do you ache for? Do you dare to seek what your heart longs for?

Prayers

Of Your mercy, O God, grant me the graces of joy and balance and peace of mind, and such other blessings as You know I have need of, that my life may show forth a few of the wonders of Your glory.

At rest in the sure foundation of Your presence, I entrust all of myself to Your care. Your arm from age to age endures, strong to heal and save and lead.

May I dodge all diversions and byways along my spiritual journey: any likely dispersion or dissipation of all-precious love-energy. May I maintain my sense of true direction.

May my recollectedness keep all distractions, both inner and outer, at a distance – so as to preserve all the energies of my body and being for the real work, in communion with You: fortifying souls, and in all possible ways promoting Your Kingdom here on earth, in preparation for eternal life with You.

III
Time

She gave a flower into my hand,
And all the hours of eve went by.

G. K. Chesterton, 'Vanity'

Subjective time

In *Don Quixote*, Cervantes observed, 'Not all times are the same.' Hence we speak of time as 'racing along' or as 'standing still'. We all experience a gap between clock time and subjective duration. This can be a function of age. To the young, time – fortunately for them – can seem unlimited. This is because a youngster's brain is at its photographic peak; and because growing up provides so many unforgettable firsts: every day heralds new sights, new people, new feelings (and words to describe them) and first attempts. Time appears to us – whether we are in youth or adulthood – to be slow or quick according to how many special memories we form. 'Live as long as you may, the first twenty years are the longest half of your life' (Robert Southey, *The Doctor*).

As one gets older, the days seem to pass very quickly. This is partly because of less novelty (of both attitude and forms of activity) and also because each passing year is a smaller fraction of the lifespan: because of a reminiscence effect, we store less and reflect more on the past.

As the body slows down, the river of life – in relation to one's increasingly slow pace – seems to be moving ever faster. But this is an illusion. The river of life *is* getting faster, but not by as much as the difference between one's young and older self. This pattern points up the difference between actual time and psychological time: time as it *is*, in contrast to time as it is *felt*.

> Put your hand on a hot stove for a minute, and it
> seems like an hour. Sit with a pretty girl for an hour,
> and it seems like a minute. That is relativity.

Einstein

Our perception of time is also conditioned by the nature or tone of the hour and our mood, our emotional state. Intense work seems relatively short while it is being done, but long in retrospect. Boredom, joy, recreational drugs, near-death experiences: they each alter our sense of the tempo of time.

Two hippies, high on pot, were sitting in San Francisco's Golden Gate Park, where my father and I, summer and mild winter, used to play baseball. A jet zoomed overhead, soon vanishing across the sky. One hippie turned to his friend and said, 'Man, I thought he'd never leave.'

Joy, in any form, is all the more treasured not in spite of transience, but because of it. We are compelled – we desire – not just to drink but to sip and savour. Not only to make the most of the day, the precious hour, but also to set the memory-gem in gold. Let Keats be your mentor:

> She [Melancholy] dwells with Beauty – Beauty that
> must die;
> And Joy, whose hand is ever at his lips
> Bidding adieu; and aching Pleasure nigh,
> Turning to poison while the bee-mouth sips:
> Ay, in the very temple of Delight

Veiled Melancholy has her sovran shrine,
Though seen of none save him whose strenuous tongue
Can burst Joy's grape against his palate fine;
His soul shall taste the sadness of her might,
And be among her cloudy trophies hung.

'Ode on Melancholy'

During a near-death experience, many people, within seconds, make a rapid review of significant life events. In such cases, people have wide and quick access to personal history – a necessary part of scanning the memory – while also knowing that they have to make the most of every available second. In these straitened conditions, time feels both expansive and compressed.

A fighter pilot described how after the launch from an aircraft carrier was bungled, he could recall within seconds all the actions needed to recover flight altitude. Faced with the probability of imminent death, a few seconds seemed like minutes. The survival instinct mobilised memory and rapid astute action. After the ordeal he collapsed, emotionally spent; but in the cockpit, he was relatively calm – he had to be – even as death hovered ominously, tapping his shoulder.

The relish of sporting challenge enables star players not only to raise their game at key moments – the killer touch when the opponent is floundering – but also to play at a high level of speed, grace and power for several hours (as in tennis) or four or five days (as in cricket).

In his thirties, Danny Blanchflower, midfield maestro of White Hart Lane, always seemed to have enough time. His legs no longer had the speed-off-the-mark of a 20-year-old, but as he received a pass and prepared to make an equally precise one, he read team formations more quickly, more acutely and more comprehensively than any of the younger players yet could.

Sporting champions are adept in the art of pacing themselves – necessary on the spiritual path as well as on a football pitch. True to their own pace, rhythm and style, true champions stay on the safe side of the thin hazardous borderline between confidence and arrogance. It is vital for an aspirant to nourish his vitality, and then carefully deploy all faculties, all the gifts bestowed on us by God, bringing us safely home to Him – with courage (even boldness) and triumph at the last.

Attitudes to time

How does society – and how do you and I as individuals – regard time? My first boss used to ask me, 'Robin, how is the enemy?' The name of the old television quiz-show *Beat the Clock* symbolises our current tussle with time.

Our view of time is not just about daily practical issues: it is far more than efficient time management. It is a relationship, profoundly self-defining. During the day we need Sabbath moments in order to gauge and question our pace, our direction, and to appreciate this particular part of our day, and our life journey. In these pauses, even if brief, we can reconnect with God, and prepare, practically and emotionally, for our next activity, our next encounter.

We are proprietorial (yet also apprehensive) about time, thus we think and speak of 'my time'. We speak glibly of time, as if it were just another throw-away item of our consumer society. Our stock phrases about time reveal our values. We talk of 'using' time or 'spending' time, or even – may we be forgiven – 'wasting' time. We speak of 'filling in time' or 'marking time'. And this of one of God's best gifts!

Like our talents and our material goods, time is meant to be shared. Time in solitude and time with others – both are sacred because of God's companionship.

The Industrial Revolution and the use of the stopwatch in factories gave time a dominant script: it is used to raise output, maximise efficiency, beat the competition. The overseer speeds up the conveyor belt. The First World War accelerated the use of watches: they were issued as standard equipment to the Forces. The Battle of the Somme began when hundreds of platoon leaders each blew a whistle, their synchronised watches having pointed to 7.30 in the morning. The wristwatch is now one of the world's most mass-produced items. The irony is that we all have a watch, but we never have time.

As long ago as 1726, Jonathan Swift was satirising the preoccupation with clock time. The Lilliputians conclude that Gulliver's pocket watch is his god because he consults it so often, and – like an oracle – it dictates the time for every action in his life.

Pace of life

Modern technology makes information, people and products available to us at a click any day, at any time. Moreover, the greater our choices the bigger our frustration at not being able to buy all we desire, nor perhaps fulfil all of our ever-increasing aims. We refuse to delay, shorten, cut back or cut out. Hence we are ever-more impatient and anxious, fearing – and perhaps at last admitting to ourself – we shall never, can never, have enough time until we retire. Will we reassess our relationship with time even then?

So many are trapped on a cobweb which they themselves have mindlessly spun. For they are in a love–hate relationship with time, and all the products of time. To change the imagery, it is they who are being driven. They are strapped down and in the back seat. 'From time to time, in the towns, I open a newspaper. Things seem to be going at a dizzy rate.' That was written by Flaubert in a letter to Louis Bouillet, dated 14th

November 1850. Consider how much our life has accelerated since Flaubert's day.

The media inculcate a short attention span. The emphasis is always on specific payoff and guaranteed progress, with the minimum effort – a trend perfectly exemplified by the slick, seductive titles of two American bestsellers, *Enlightenment in Ten Easy Lessons* and *You Too Can Change Your Life in Seven Days*. You can now buy a copy of *The 100-Minute Bible*.

Paradoxically, the more time we save – thanks to our time-saving devices and better time management – the more harassed we feel. We run instead of walk. We gabble instead of talk. We gobble instead of eat. We collide, we interrupt. We tap our feet while we wait for the microwave to ring. We keep clicking the mouse. We pummel the steering wheel while we wait for the traffic lights to turn green. We keep jabbing the call-button for the hotel lift, seemingly oblivious to the fact that the lift has a fixed speed and is already on its way to our floor. We boil and fume at supermarket checkout staff. And all to what ultimate purpose? In these moods of impatience and irritability, we become more and more distracted, less and less related to the present.

We know not what the race is for, nor what the finishing line represents. Addicted to speed, are we in fact not running towards, but away from? Fleeing from sad memories, and anxiety about the future. Fleeing from aloneness, and worries about old age. Fleeing from fear of death.

Goal orientation

Rushed meetings and hurried work are seldom well done. The hasty stumble (Proverbs 19:2). When we focus more on aim and goal than on road (or route), more on our plan than on what *is* now, we miss the present unfolding moment and introduce strain. St Vincent de Paul famously said that 'he who is in a hurry delays the things of God'.[36]

If a person hurries too often or for too long at a time, they are liable not only to harm themselves, but also to discomfort and hustle other people, such as by finishing their thoughts and sentences. They do harm to themselves by making impulsive decisions, being accident prone, and straining the intricate body–mind system. Still more, their impatience puts undue pressure on others. Never more than now has it been so vital to preserve the still centre. The art of a fulfilled life is to be energetic without tension, dynamic without agitation, serene but not aloof.

We hate to admit we have time on our hands. Status is symbolised not only by a big car, a huge office and a wide desk, but also by a full diary. Being always busy, or pretending to be, feeds our self-esteem. All actions come to be seen as urgent. We endow almost everything we do with a bogus tone of semi-crisis. Every hour is a rush hour.

Many executives often rush, or skip, lunch; if they have a business lunch, they are so focused on clinching a lucrative contract that they fail to relish the vintage wine, and the taste and texture of the gourmet food. Always pressing forward to meet a never-ending series of deadlines – a modern-day Sisyphus – they have no, or scant, time to spare for the social intercourse which makes hard-edged working life civilised.

Many people come to the end of each day feeling gloomy and frustrated, because so much has had to be left undone. They have been galloping, in vain, to cram more work into less time. Never for them the evening ease of Longfellow's The Village Blacksmith:

> Each morning sees some task begin,
> Each evening sees its close;

---

[36] Quoted in Jacque Delarue, *The Holiness of St Vincent de Paul* (P. J. Kennedy, 1960) p.42.

Something attempted, something done,
Has earned a night's repose.

In 1970 the economist Staffan Linder offered an original and plausible explanation for our hyperactivity. We derive our value of personal time from what our employer pays us for working time. As incomes rise, so too does the cost of forgoing the chance to do an extra hour of work. Because our free time thus feels more valuable – and also because we work so many hours each week – we want to increase its yield by using it more productively.[37]

We crave instant cure, fast food, prompt satisfaction. This trend is well illustrated by speed dating: single people arrive at a bar or hotel, are matched with a series of potential partners, and then have three minutes (for each encounter) to try to impress each other before the bell rings. If both then tick their scorecard, indicating a wish to meet again, then the organisers pass on email addresses. There are events for speed dating on a ferry, dating in the dark, naked speed dating and silent dating: men and women try to woo each other through body language or written notes only. Speed dating is symbolic (or symptomatic) of our current Western tendency to want quick answers and complete solutions to major life issues. Can we not simply be open to love's wish to surprise us?

Erich Fromm argues that the capacity to be alone is essential to being able to love.[38] Conversely, the anxiety produced by an inability to bear one's separateness lies behind the compulsive escape into drugs, alcohol or orgasm. It is – Fromm argues – a false solution, since sex without love never bridges the gap which separates two people in any real or lasting way. Yet the one-night stand has replaced (or upstaged) the wise gradations of courtship. Love and each relationship have their own pace and originality, their own plateaux – if only

---

[37] Staffan Linder, *The Harried Leisure Class* (New York: Columbia, 1970).
[38] Erich Fromm, *The Art of Loving* (London: Unwin Books, 1962) pp.14–16, 22.

we will keep listening and respect the gift of each emergent moment.

The basic features of romantic love are evolutionary in origin, thus they are archetypal and fundamental, not disposable without harm. Courtship rituals give (women especially) more time to assess the suitability of a potential mate. And the exclusive – and often idealised – tone of the first phase is needed for the formation of a strong pair-bond – an intimacy of being as well as of the body.

Happiness is to be found not in striving for more and more new satisfactions, but in deriving deeper joy in those people, and aspects of life, already available. People whose life is a non-stop scud and hustle can never keep up with their multiplying desires and ambitions. Gasping for breath, they are always chasing the clock, or – more correctly – feeling that they are being chased by the clock. St Francis de Sales, sixteenth century Genevan bishop, observes:

> Work done with too much eagerness and hurry is never well done. ... Drones make more noise and fuss than bees, but make only wax, and no honey.[39]

Trying too hard hinders, stifles and may even prevent; non-striving frees, releases, allows to be. The way to reach a goal is to be fully mindful of each step on the way to the goal. This quality of watchfulness is not only the means to an end. In its highest manifestation it is illumination. When I am centred, I am authentic, more generous and more spontaneous – because I am more fully in the moment. Slowness increases enjoyment, and in turn, relish enhances achievement and recollection:

---

[39] St Francis de Sales, *Introduction to the Devout Life* (London: Longman, Green & Co., 1891) chapter X.

When we are busy, we ought (as often as we can) to
cease for a few moments, in order to worship God
in the depth of our being.[40]

Gratitude – not just occasional, but as a joyous attitude of
the heart, the favoured way of seeing and responding – is the
ultimate in graciousness. We would all do well to concentrate as
much (or even more) on what we have already found as on
what we seek or desire.

Our pace defines how we relate

Beckett's *Waiting for Godot* and Pinter's *The Caretaker* represent
on stage our lack of real, vital communication. Conversation
nowadays is often a race, a pressure, a procedure, verbal
sparring, a competitive event. The so-called listener is on edge,
longing for the other person to stop talking, waiting for the
briefest pause so as to be able to have their say. While the other
person is speaking, they are silently rehearsing their next
intervention. Instead of encouraging, instead of enjoying the
speaker as they round off an idea or share a concern, we are
signalling for him to finish, urging him, patronising him with
staccato phrases: 'Yes, I know', 'Well, of course'. This is at best
a conversation with oneself. There may be limited forms of
exchange (often of fixed positions), but lacking the two core
elements of true encounter – mutuality and sensitivity.

Sensitivity – to God, to this moment, to this person and to
my self – is a litmus test for the depth of our inner life. Some
people are so off-centre that they cannot even receive
sensitivity from other people, let alone bestow it. A person
with really low self-esteem has four typical ways of relating –
placate, distract, blame, patronise. Note that they are all cold,

---

[40] Brother Lawrence, *The Practice of the Presence of God* (London: Burns & Oates,
1931).

not warm; closed and defensive, not open and responsive. Sensitivity entails being open to the sad as well as the cheerful – first in oneself and then with others. A caring and empathic person has a quick and sure awareness of what is tender in another person.

Our capacity for sensitivity reflects, and depends on, our degree of integration. But, ultimately, it flows thanks to a loving, heightened awareness of God's grace and presence. Let us acquire the main virtue – love. Fasting is nothing, a vigil is nothing, without *love*.

Confucius likened dialogue to a wheel. The spokes hold the structure together; the empty spaces in between – the pauses, the moments of reflection, the tense or relaxed atmosphere – tell us about the essence of the encounter and the relationship. Good conversation owes as much to listening and silence as to words and ideas, but for most of us listening is a difficult art to learn – first of all because of the pace of our lifestyle.

If we are tempted to be self-satisfied during a dialogue, we can inwardly or outwardly thank the other person, whose quality of attention – and perhaps affection also – is encouraging us, willing us, to be lucid, warm and wide-ranging in conversation. In the same way, when we write a good letter – if we still make time to write letters at all – much credit is due to the recipient, who is silently inspiring us to give our best.

Early conditioning

The voice of the internalised parent constantly orders us to 'Hurry up'. We obey automatically – just as we were forced to do when young – but at continuing cost: the body is being used relentlessly as a machine, a thing for getting things done, and fast. Sooner or later we may find – will need to find – better and kinder ways of seeing and enjoying it as an agent of the soul.

The forces and patterns of history have their own – often sudden and unpredicted – ways of imposing balance (or retribution). The higher the see-saw rises, or the wider the pendulum swings, the bigger the adjustment. Manic behaviour of an individual, a group or a society – our consumerism, our relentlessly fast pace of life – cannot long continue unabated. Far better that the correction is anticipated and made by us, and in time, than to be exposed to forces often largely out of our control.

In the meantime, untold numbers of children go to school every morning made tense by their parents' frantic pace as they get ready to leave for work. I grieve when I see the short legs of a whining toddler, hurtling forward in a vain effort to keep up with a fast-striding parent. They are holding hands but the adult's hand is not a comfort: it is tugging, forcing, yanking. The child is invariably in a state of acute distress – a symptom of the current misery, a sign of twists in the parent–child bond, and an omen of a price to pay, in physical and emotional health, in later life.

Craving

Rushing is a form of aggression – a violation of the value of time, and an act of self-alienation. Thus we hear people say, 'I've been working non-stop all day, and I'm still trying to catch-up with myself.'

Whenever you feel an urge to hurry (or notice yourself in the midst of hurrying), stop and ask why. Whether the rush is for food or entertainment, you may find that the underlying emotion is craving. Equally subversively, rushing may have become a deeply ingrained habit. And many people are dependent on the surge of adrenaline it produces.

The lust for getting causes many people to forget the pleasure of anticipation. An advert for one of the first generation of credit cards tempted us to 'take the waiting out of wanting'. But Freud said that one feature of civilisation is the capacity to defer the gratification of instinct. We may even find that anticipation not only heightens the longed-for event, but in itself gives us pleasure.

Surfeit dulls the finer edges of our receptivity, and the natural joy of lightly experienced sensations. We can only wonder what depths of insecurity are goading this craving for instant gratification. Excess, craving and demanding, wanting everything this very moment – these are symptoms of an inner void. As ever, the first step on the road of change is patient, honest, radical self-observing.

In the West, the life of so many people centres round getting and trying to keep: money and possessions, looks and image, knowledge, success, power and control. So long as the focus is all on 'I' and 'mine' and 'me first', a person is driven by a sense of want or craving: always something is missing. Any satisfaction derived from getting what your lower nature wants is always momentary. Hollow desires keep multiplying.

> There are two ways to get enough:
> one is to accumulate more and more;
> the other is to desire less.

G. K. Chesterton, *The Crimes of England*

Dom. Lorenzo Scupoli concurs:

> Our desires are our chains. To be entangled by them is to be a slave. *To have far fewer desires* – and not to be subject to them – is to be free.[41]

Fulfilling a desire only fuels ever-more desires. Only a replacing of acquisitiveness by a radical letting go and sharing

---

[41] In Lorenzo Scupoli, *Spiritual Combat* (Mesa, Arizona: Scriptoria Books, 2014) chapter V.

will bring true freedom, lasting change and lightness of heart (Luke 12:15).

St Cyprian observed, 'He does not see that his life is a gilded torture; that he is bound fast by his wealth; and that – rather than owning his money – it owns him.'[42] Only up to a certain point do material goods help us to feel freer and more independent. Beyond that point (our best instincts will tell us when it is reached), possession becomes lord; the possessor, an abject slave.

'Hoarding is idolatry,' warns Bonhoeffer.[43] Craving, compulsive buying and hoarding may – as well as being idolatry – be a way of avoiding: a defence against anxiety and inner emptiness. What am I afraid to face – in my self, my past or present or future? Many of us define our self by what we own. Gandhi, by wise contrast, said, 'The more I have, the less I am.'

Gandhi's maxim points up the need we all have to simplify – to discard, diminish, or, at the very least, become less reliant (inwardly and outwardly) on trappings of any kind. When we have the courage to do this, we are exposed to deeper layers of the self, with its highs and lows, its darkness and light. The hard part is to face and become acquainted with the less congenial sides of who I am. The main benefit is that I can come to enjoy my wholeness, perhaps for the first time.

By seeking most of their satisfactions in the outer world, people are skewing their personal centre of gravity, making it one-sided; the inner richness, with its potential to heal and be healed, waits relatively unheeded.

> The men where you live, said the little prince, grow five thousand roses in a garden ... and still they do not find what they are seeking ... And yet what they are looking for could be found in one single rose.

---

[42] St Cyprian, Epistle I (to Donatus) in A. Roberts and J. Donaldson (eds) *Ante-Nicene Fathers*, Volume V (Massachusetts: Hendrickson, 1994) p.279.

[43] Dietrich Bonhoeffer, *The Cost of Discipleship* (London: SCM Press, 1959) p.175.

The physical eye is blind. To see you have to look with the heart.

Antoine de Saint-Exupéry, *The Little Prince*[44]

Ontological anxiety

Any form of compulsion or excess suggests denial; and repression of a fear causes endless disorder to self and others. Many people use every ploy and dodge to try to escape from ontological anxiety – the inevitability of their own death.

Mankind's innate fear of death has been altogether distended in the last 100 years. Two World Wars, the Cold War, the nuclear threat and fear of terrorism are now part of the collective psyche, and this fear ripples down – some of it overt, and some below the surface – from one generation to another. In the past few days I have, quite by chance, read an article about cryonics and the Life Extension Foundation in the USA, and also the review of a book, *How to Live Forever or Die Trying*. Then, in the TV listings, I noticed a documentary entitled *Do You Want to Live Forever?*

Fear of loneliness is a proxy, a diluted version, for the threat of death, which is the final separation from human contact. As Tillich reminds us, the courage to die is the ultimate test – and fruit – of the courage to be.[45] We can meet this test by seeing our self as belonging to – and simultaneously engaged in – both realms, the temporal and the eternal.

This inner attitude or perception needs to be lived. We cannot really begin to understand the meaning of death until we find our own unique lived-out version of the full life, *sub specie aeternitatis*.

---

[44] Editor's translation.
[45] Paul Tillich, *The Courage to Be* (London: Fontana, 1962) pp.50–53.

God is Lord of death as well as of birth and life. The fuller and more devoted our life, the more serene our last days are likely to be. Awareness of eternal life ennobles and sanctifies our time on earth. What we long for is within, as is what we are desperate to escape from.

Too many people miss the breathtaking splendours of life, all that helps us to endure and persevere, all that can enrich and enhance our life: religion, friendship, the arts and nature. Without being fully aware of the fact (so habitual has it become), they live on the run, in the twilight zone, in the narrow confines of a self-built prison, doomed never to be 'Surprised by joy – impatient as the Wind' (Wordsworth, title and first line of 'Sonnet XXVII'). Francis Thompson is eloquent about our hurrying as evasion of God:

> To all swift things for swiftness did I sue;
> Clung to the whistling mane of every wind …
> Still with unhurrying chase,
> And unperturbèd pace,
> Deliberate speed, majestic instancy,
> Came on the following Feet,
> And a Voice above their beat –
> 'Naught shelters thee, who wilt not shelter Me.'

'The Hound of Heaven'

Slowing down

Being always in the fast lane is a one-way trip to burnout – for one's self, for family, society and the whole planet. We are rapidly depleting the Earth's natural resources in order to travel through life ever faster. Most of us sprint to catch a bus or underground train – even though another is due in two or three minutes. We seem to be losing the art of varying our tempo to suit the occasion. Every event, every meeting has its own *tempo giusto*.

If only we could dare to face and work with the insecurity fuelling our vain panting after shallower forms of satisfaction, we would enjoy a range of benefits to work and family life, and to physical and emotional health. Slowing down leads to mental clarity, creativity, wiser decision-making, more relaxed encounters, deeper friendships, safer driving and better digested meals.

Darwin described himself as a relatively slow thinker. Slowness in decision-making creates space for a wide range of options to emerge, time to make connections, think laterally, be inventive and intuitive. It gives perspective and facilitates discourse between conscious planning and the wisdom of the unconscious.

Instead of being ruled by reactions and impulse, we are now creating space for a wider range of options to emerge: each can be carefully and quietly and soberly consulted, respected and weighed in the scales.

Working in a calmer way usually produces more reliable results, with fewer mistakes or accidents. We can do things relatively quickly and also more efficiently if we maintain a calm mind, a focused eye and deep breathing. We enjoy the pleasure of working to our own best standards.

> Poor hare! Tired and in disgrace, he slumped down beside the tortoise who was smiling at him. 'Slowly does it every time,' the tortoise said.[46]

Instead of always living at full throttle, we will have a richer inner life and more time for deeper encounters, with real enjoyment of the present, and alert but relaxed anticipation of the future. A slow pace gives more inner space to be sensitive to other people: to respond to, or anticipate, their needs. We

---

[46] Aesop, 'The Tortoise and the Hare', in *Aesop's Fables*.

first (and best) show that we like someone by giving generously of our time – in frequency, duration and depth of attention.

In encounter, a slow pace enables both people to be more watchful – of self and other, and of the dynamic between them. The more watchful one is, the more careful (or judicious) one is in balancing silence and verbal response. Moreover, a relaxed atmosphere elicits – from each of us – apt timing, apt tone, aptness of glance, gesture or word.

If we see and learn the value of slowing down in one area of our life – such as being calmer while driving – we soon want an *adagio* pace at other times and places.

Slowness helps us listen to the still centre while in the midst of activity: the participator is joined by our observer side. It is like swimming and at the same time sunning ourself on the riverbank. Of Brother Lawrence, a seventeenth-century French Carmelite lay brother, it was observed, 'He was never hasty, nor loitering. He did each task at the appropriate time, with an even, uninterrupted composure, and tranquillity of spirit.'[47] His skill was in matching his pace to each specific task.

Watch for the balance point – so vital in spiritual life – between silence and speech, rest and action. To attain this delicate point of balance, keep refining your awareness of it. Our safety is in our vigilance.

We cannot shift our habits until we realise what a serious trap we are in. The pace of modern life is so fast and fierce, so toxic, that most of us will have to reorder our life radically if we wish to find and establish a personal rhythm that will favour the life of prayer.

---

[47] Preface to Brother Lawrence, *The Practice of the Presence of God* (London: Burns & Oates, 1931).

Time hallowed

Some people enjoy themselves wherever they are; others are bored, or soon feel satiated, even in pleasurable situations. After allowing for time spent at work, in leisure activities and socialising, we spend about 50 hours a week in maintenance activities: commuting, DIY, correspondence, cleaning and tidying up, laundry, mowing the lawn, shopping, cooking, eating, shaving, showering and so on.

What is our mood during this substantial part of our waking hours? Is our attitude *de haut en bas*? Do we consider these as merely routine activities which are not worth much of our attention? Is our concentration on the present, or on past or future? Being playful (in spirit and action) keeps us in the present, focused and full of innocent joy. We can infuse a tone of play into almost everything we do, by being curious, taking appropriate risks, and using imagination, experimentation and variety. By doing a task slightly more slowly, we can be more inventive, and also more graceful and generous:

> You can praise Him – as Mary the mother of Jesus did – with all the daily work of your hands. You can also praise Him with all the fun and laughter that come your way, if you receive all daily activities as a love-gift from Him to you ... Learn to see every action and event in the light of the eternal present.[48]

Mother Teresa concurs:

> To show great love for God and our neighbour we need not do great things. It is how much love we put

---

[48] Gerald Vann, *The Divine Pity* (London: Collins, 1956).

in the doing that makes our offering Something Beautiful for God.[49]

True mysticism is to discover the extraordinary in the ordinary.

A core feature of a dedicated spiritual life is to dignify and honour time, which God has already made holy and eternal (Psalm 39:4). The Almighty designed time to be cherished: to be embraced, not escaped. If only we can learn to see each moment as *kairos* (2 Corinthians 6:2). This very day we can gaze up at the heavens, mindful of the vastness of the universe. If its history were compressed into an hour, the existence of the human race would scarcely fit into the last split second.

> A thousand ages in Thy sight
> Are like an evening gone.

> Isaac Watts, 'O God, our help in ages past'

To value divine time within clock time gives longer perspectives; it gives shape and value to life (both personal and collective); and will colour and deepen everything we do (1 Corinthians 3:13,14).

Awareness of the eternal dimension helps us to see earthly life in its true, God-endowed stature. Our loving relationships bring us nearer to the Godhead: they tell us, reassure us, that eternity is real, and that the divine is not just to be enjoyed in the afterlife but is with us – in us – right here and now.

'To fill the hour – that is happiness' (Emerson, 'Experience', *Essays*, Second Series). To fill the hour? It all depends on what we fill the hour with. In any case, do we really need to fill every hour? Does my busyness, all my activity, allow space and time

---

[49] Mother Teresa of Calcutta, ed. Malcolm Muggeridge, *A Gift for God* (London: Collins, 1975) p.77.

to pray and be with God – the *fons et origo* of my life and of all life?

Prayers

I dedicate to You all use of time. May I see the eternal within the heart of the transient.

May I do nothing (even the tiniest of daily tasks or duties) in a rushed or superficial way, or in a mood of routine. May I do everything with awareness and calm simplicity, in a spirit of offering back to You all that You are constantly giving.

Please guide me, protect me, in Your light. May love and blessings shine in me and radiate through me, with undiminished brightness, in all my encounters, respecting all people, revering their soul. As I become more patient with myself, may I be more gentle with others. May I view interruptions as invitations.

VISION

I
Return

*The man who teaches me to see with new eyes what I
see every day – that man is my benefactor.*

Paul Valéry, Bad Thoughts and Not So Bad[50]

Consider for a moment the fascination of visiting a foreign
country. You bring your baggage – inner as well as outer – but
few assumptions. Nothing is taken for granted. You even need
to be careful of every word you speak and hear, and the
meaning of every gesture. For the period of your stay, you
cease thinking, 'I already know that...'

Temporarily free of deadlines, competitors, mortgage
repayments, performance targets and 'little enmities'
(Wordsworth, *The Prelude*), we are sure we will feel better (both
calmer and more buoyant) as soon as we are in new territory.

We hope that the climate and the setting will widen our
mental and emotional horizon: we long for the holiday to be
also an inner voyage – of renovation and self-discovery. We
want to shed certain habits, even if only for ten days.

As soon as we have recovered from jet lag, we have a surge
of energy and purpose: we are no longer adrift on a raft which
we have named 'Inconsequence'. The air we breathe seems
(and probably is) cleaner, even scented. The light irradiates

---

[50]In Stuart Gilbert, trans., *Collected Works of Paul Valéry*, Volume XIV (Princeton:
Princeton University Press, 1970) p.475.

long-dark corners of our psyche. Each day seems, as it were, bigger – so much richer in potential – when compared with daily life at home.

Our receptivity is heightened: every detail – of sea, sky and landscape – reaches out, speaks to us. You and your hosts and companions – and life itself – are all of a sudden more eloquent. 'Expectancy' is our watchword now.

But even in this favoured place (where *kairos* seems to have no counterpart or rival), *chronos* ticks. And we may never come here again. We are compelled – we are gladly compelled – to delight in (and make the most of) every moment, every sight, every encounter. Whatever is brief is thereby all the more precious, an inspiration to be more attentive. This is why we speak of 'poignant' beauty.

Why does beauty pierce? Why does the stem of a rose have thorns? Why did the mystics – when proclaiming their love-bond with God – write of the 'wound of love'? Because – in the very moment of joy or ecstasy – happiness has an undertow of regret (or even despair). The lovely moment is transient; it can never be fully described (even by a Keats), and the ideal teases and eludes us.

The encounter is living and life-giving, it is real and yet ephemeral. As soon as it starts, it begins to slip away. A special moment (or embrace) captivates and fades, loosens its hold: seemingly lost in the river of time, but now lodged in the memory forever.

This moment, this tone or ambience, this glance or gesture or touch – each is unique to the occasion and can never be repeated exactly. Indeed, the very longing to enjoy a replica can lead to dashed hopes, unrealistic expectations. Moreover, in our pursuit of a regained past we often miss the full impact of new unfolding beauty.

How can the art of travel teach us to maintain a quality (and attitude) of first-time seeing? Picture yourself back home, coming each day to your own surroundings with this same steady alertness: quiet and watchful, and also intensely alive. You will see the usual people, you will hear familiar sounds. But you will see and hear in a new way. You will allow all facets of life to come to you, each with its own nature, individual and distinct. This is the way of non-controlling, total acceptance, letting people and things be, leading to a spirit of oneness. Instead of striving and controlling/contriving, we let the moment of beauty (such as from nature or from relationship) unfold in front of us, in its own way and time. Our role is to be ready, with open hands and an open heart.

The art of travel consists of three stages: preparation and anticipation, journey and return. The third and last stage – return – is the least emphasised. First, because most people do not consider the return as part of travelling. Second, because the glow of a holiday soon dims when you find a stack of bills in your letter box. Then, on Monday morning, the alarm rouses your reluctant body from its jet-lagged slumber. At the office the boss will be pounding the desk about 'the bottom line' before you have taken off your jacket.

If – by minor miracle – you can stay upright, unbowed by these pressures, you may feel more disposed to seek the best in (even familiar) life and other people:

> Old friends, old scenes, will lovelier be,
> As more of heaven in each we see.

John Keble, hymn, 'New Every Morning is the Love'

The art of returning means being like a newcomer in your own country – even in your own home, and then maintaining this mode of alert/expectant daily living, and first-time seeing.

A few years ago, a friar returned to his monastery after a 30-day Ignatian retreat. While they were eating porridge the next morning, he was interrogated by a grumpy member of the community. He complained, 'We've been working flat out while you've been swanning around for a month, doing nothing. And just look at you – you don't look any different!'

'You're right,' the newly returned friar replied, 'but all the rest of you do.'

On holiday, the mind is relatively uncluttered with minutiae, the myriad mundane preoccupations of daily life. Another place – another climate, culture, language and people – becomes a mirror in which one sees one's self with a new clarity, even innocence; a refreshing, releasing honesty, attending to what *is*. The art of return – indeed, the art of spiritual life – is to maintain this clear seeing throughout the day, in any place or setting.

Thus it is not only on returning home from holiday that we can feel more vital. When we awake, we are no longer exactly who we were the day before. God's style is heuristic. Daily we have a chance to see people – and experience the world around us, and our relations – in new ways.

First-time seeing mobilises our creativity, and gives new, rich life to our capacity for love. Our own hopes and needs are placed second (but by no means neglected). God's will, the joy of the moment, and the wishes of the beloved, are given primacy. Thus first-time seeing enables me to be more fully present to my loved one.

Prayers

May I interpret the world in the only way it can be seen truly: in the light of Your lustre, and as antechamber of Your throneroom.

May my ears be more sensitive, my eyes more expectant, my heart and mind more receptive, to meet You as present Reality in small, everyday events, encounters and tasks, my Friend and Companion, always walking by my side.

May the clouds on this earthly horizon never hide from me Your light, pure and life-giving, immortal and unchanging: my home, my refuge, my everlasting comfort, bread for my body, sustenance for my soul.

II
Seeing

To see a world in a grain of sand,
And a heaven in a wild flower,
Hold infinity in the palm of your hand,
And eternity in an hour.

William Blake, 'Auguries of Innocence'

Sacramental living

Sacraments make the invisible more visible, reminding us of
God's constant presence. They help us to see the Unchanging
in the very midst of our life of flow and flux (Job 19:25;
Revelation 1:8,17,18). Due time and reverence needs to be
given to these entries into the heartbeat of God.

Van Zeller observes, 'In England our cathedrals are fronted
and flanked by lawns of cut grass which are called a "close".'
We never see a cathedral wedged in between rows of houses.
This keeps the traffic and the town at one remove. In the same
way, he encourages the priest (and all of us) to:

> place a 'close' round his Mass: no traffic, no
> business. Before and after Mass – silence. The
> alternative is spiritual suffocation ... With the
> eucharistic part of his day safeguarded, and allowed

to give impetus to his charity, the priest will be able
to meet the demands made upon him by his parish,
by his studies, by his correspondence. Steeped in the
spirit of his Mass, he will be able to take the Mass
with him into his work.[51]

This attitude of preparation and post-reception savouring
can be applied to all our encounters. Eucharistic living enlarges
your awareness of God's presence, and your thankfulness for
His being here with you. Then you cherish, not only what life
reveals and yields, but also (and especially) the very fact of your
existence.

Distinguished scientists – such as the physicist Freeman
Dyson, formerly an agnostic – have highlighted the number of
nuanced chemical conditions necessary for the universe to be
hospitable to life: too many to be explained just by chance. Sir
Martin Rees, the Astronomer Royal, has written about the
extraordinary combination of factors – each in itself a miracle
of creation – which together make the Earth 'fine-tuned for
life'.[52] There are more than 30 major criteria that are all
necessary for life to be possible on a planet: for example, the
tilt and speed of the planet's rotation, its distance from its star,
and the ratio of oxygen to nitrogen in the atmosphere.

The constants of the universe – which enabled the Earth to
form and life to evolve – were set at the very beginning of time
– in the earliest fraction of a second. The explosive forces of
the Big Bang were very finely balanced. If the explosion had
been 1 part in 1,000 too powerful, then the atoms would have
gone on travelling into space and could not have congregated
into galaxies. If gravity had been slightly stronger, after a few

[51] Hubert Van Zeller, *The Gospel Priesthood* (London: Burns and Oates, 1956) pp.
52-3.
[52] Martin Rees, Just Six Numbers: The Deep Forces That Shape The Universe
(New York: Basic Books, 2001) p.4.

million years these atoms would have collapsed back into the centre.

But the immensity of the universe does not diminish the stature of the minds capable of contemplating it (Psalm 8). 'The chief aim of man is to glorify God and to enjoy Him for ever' (*The Shorter Catechism*). Wonder inspires praise; praise leads us to pray. Then we are mindful that we inherit the earth from our ancestors. We enjoy the present, holding all the world's riches as a sacred trust. Then – as good stewards – we hand the baton (of what was our inheritance) to future generations.

Sacramental living depends on a less often considered virtue: sacramental seeing – with eyes that see deeply, poetically; eyes that see below the surface to the Centre. When Jesus saw bread or water or wine, He saw symbolically, in a spirit of contemplation, and He was moved to teach in parables. When He looked at a flower, its beauty and simplicity spoke to Him of the Provider, He who 'paints the wayside flower, and lights the evening star'.[53] Each of us has the choice of seeing a flower with the eyes of a botanist or the eyes of a poet or artist; but especially blessed are the eyes that see all of creation as the handiwork of God (Psalm 19:1).

'We are as much as we see', Thoreau wrote in his *Journal* (10 iv, 1841). One form of enlightenment is to have a new, clearer and joyous vision of what is already here. Sophocles asked, 'Do we have to wait until evening before we register how glorious the day has been?' Wonder is a result of all that one holds to be of ultimate value and meaning in life. Thus Goethe said that wonder is the highest state that humans can attain – the most elevated moment, attitude or state of being. Writing of Wordsworth's early poetry, Coleridge relished its value:

> To give the charm of novelty to things of every day
> ... by awakening the mind's attention from the
> lethargy of custom, and directing it to the loveliness

---

[53] Matthias Claudius, hymn, 'We Plough the Fields and Scatter'.

and wonders of the world before us; an inexhaustible treasure, but for which in consequence of the film of familiarity and selfish solicitude we have eyes, yet see not, ears that hear not, and hearts that neither feel nor understand.

Samuel Taylor Coleridge, *Biographia Literaria*, chapter XIV

Only by slowing down can we notice (and value) the gem at the core of the familiar. Let music be our model. In the Adagio theme of the slow movement of Beethoven's Ninth Symphony, the harmonies are rich, and the melodic ornament intricate. Only an atmosphere of breadth and reverence – created by the conductor – can reveal the inner transcendently beautiful tensions of the score.

Consuming creation

We live in a cut-flower culture, severed from its roots in the soil. People in Western society have few more pressing needs than to renew their relationship with nature, hearing 'the tinkling knell of water – breaks with grateful heart'.[54]

In a relatively short time (two or three generations), we now meet youngsters who know all about the latest laptop computer, but who can identify few flowers and no birdsong. A class of primary school children was asked to draw a cow and colour it in. Several produced a square shape. One young boy, who had never been near a farm, used a purple crayon because this was the colour of the hide he had seen in an animation for a TV advert for a well-known brand of milk chocolate.

---

[54] William Wordsworth, 'The Unremitting Voice of Nightly Streams', *Poems of Sentiment and Reflection*, XXXII.

We focus on what nature provides, and we neglect what she can teach. When we lose our intimate contact with the rhythms of nature and the cosmos, we become neurotic and ungrounded.

Observe and contemplate the interdependence of all life (John 15:5): human beings rely on each other, and humans rely on nature and the material world. For example, forager bees fly about 25,000 hours and visit 1.5 million flowers to collect enough nectar to make a 1lb jar of honey. When we spread honey on a piece of toast, we use about ten grams. What we eat (or gobble down) in five minutes or less, took about 1,000 foraging trips, totalling 500 hours (about three weeks) of bee work.[55]

If we mistreat or damage nature, we ourselves will soon (or ultimately) be harmed. The exploiter becomes the exploited:

> You may drive out nature with a pitchfork,
> Yet she'll be constantly running back.

Horace, *Epistles*, Book I, 10

Humanity estranged from nature: humanity estranged from itself – the most precious parts of the self. The symptoms of this condition include:

- being able to name only a few flowers, trees or birdcalls;

- not giving enough care to the body (by wise diet, sufficient exercise and watching the balance between activity and rest);

- overindulgence of body, mind, feelings/emotions or the senses;

---

[55] For the above calculations I am indebted to Dr Francis Ratnieks, one of the world's foremost professors of apiculture.

- reaching for a packet from the supermarket shelf, temporarily unmindful of whether this item of food was plucked from a tree or grown in the soil; and

- not finding time to greet the dawn and admire a sunset.

With infinite modes of expression at His disposal, God reveals Himself in daily life. And so your religious quest can begin or continue – in prayer and in love – right where you are now (Psalm 27:4). St Ignatius, in a letter to Fr Antonio Brandão of 6th June 1551, said that the Jesuits in formation should learn to seek:

> God in all things: in their conversations, their walks, in all that they see, taste, hear, understand, and in all their actions, because His Divine Majesty is truly in all things – by His presence, power, and essence.

Love of the Creator entails a love for all creation and His creatures, in their myriad forms. Then you will be a true and wide-seeing materialist, treasuring and safeguarding the environment, by handling earthly goods with purity of heart.

First-time seeing

A virgin eye sees the thisness and thatness, the precious particularity, of all that God creates – *as if seeing it for the first time*. One of the most moving descriptions of first-time seeing has been given to us by Sheila Hocken in her autobiography, *Emma and I*. Emma was her guide dog, a chocolate-coloured labrador who never left Sheila's side. Sheila had congenital cataracts. When she was a child, people and the outdoors were only blurred shapes to her, 'as if gauze was over them'. By the age of 19, she was totally blind. Ten years later, an operation enabled her to see fully for the first time.[56] Her story – her courage and the joy of seeing her husband for the first time – is perfect material for contemplation.

The disciples on the road to Emmaus were very much like we can be: spiritually blind. Though the risen Christ was walking with them their eyes were kept from recognising Him. It was only at the breaking of the bread that 'their eyes were opened', they recognised Him and he vanished from view (Luke 24:13–35).

When we focus on ourselves – when we are self-absorbed – we don't know how to see life or the depths of others:

> Standing in front of a shop window, what [or who] do I see? The glass – or the raindrops on it? The goods on display? Staff and customers inside? Probably I give most attention to my reflection in the glass. So it all depends on what I want to see. Sanctity is like that.[57]

Seeing as a poet, child or artist

D. H. Lawrence's widow, Frieda, wrote of his grateful eye:

> His bond, his relationship, with everything in creation was so amazing – no preconceived ideas, just a meeting between him and a creature, a tree, a cloud, anything. I called it love but it was also saying 'Yes' – *Bejahung* as we say in German.[58]

This extract from Lawrence exemplifies this rich, appreciative way of seeing.

[56] Sheila Hocken, *Emma and I* (London: Ebury Press, 2012) pp.201–256.
[57] Dom. Hubert Van Zeller, *Considerations* (London: Sheed & Ward, 1973) p.30.
[58] Quoted in Geoff Dyer, 'Lawrence, a Letter and me', in *The Guardian*, 15th September 2010.

Instinct makes me sniff the lime blossom and reach for the darkest cherry. But it is intuition that makes me feel the uncanny glassiness of the lake this afternoon, the sulkiness of the mountains, the vividness of near green in thunder-sun; the young man in bright blue trousers, lightly tossing the grass from the scythe; the elderly man in a boater stiffly shoving his scythe-strokes, both of them sweating in the silence of the intense light.

'Over-earnest Ladies', *Evening News,* 12th July 1928

In *Everything and Nothing* (the title of a letter to the dead, yet still living, Shakespeare), Borges writes of the need we all have to 'recover the trees and rivers of childhood'. Watch how children become immersed in the timeless moment, totally absorbed in a world of their own ingenuity. Enjoyed hours seem like only a few minutes; pleasant moments feel as if suspended in time. Children are entranced by whatever they see because for them everything is new: like the artist and the mystic, the young live in The Eternal Present. Even (especially?) the brief experience, the fleeting impressions, of childhood delight will linger in the psyche. They vanish and return, flickering like fireflies to illumine the darks of a lifetime. A poet's most characteristic images – personal, powerful, passionate – found a lodging in mind and heart before the age of puberty.

We rightly praise a poet's *mot juste*, we laud his insights, and the original fine phrases, but expression is not the first art to be actualised: first admire the all-seeing eye and the refined sensibility. Virginia Woolf wrote of Tolstoy, 'His senses, his intellect, are acute, powerful, and well nourished. There is something proud, superb, in the [grasp] of such a mind and body upon life. Nothing seems to escape him. Nothing glances off him unrecorded.'[59]

> If we had a keen vision and feeling of all ordinary human life, it would be like hearing the grass grow and the squirrel's heart beat, and we should die of that roar which lies on the other side of silence.

George Eliot, *Middlemarch*

In order to see fully, you must pause. We do pause in front of an obviously attractive sight – a person, a painting, a landscape; but, as with music or wine, our capacity for delight – in the simple, the familiar, and the relatively small – can be a lifelong cultivation. So much lies waiting – longing to reveal itself to you:

> Life is the rose's hope while yet unblown;
> The reading of an ever-changing tale;
> The light uplifting of a maiden's veil;
> A pigeon tumbling in clear summer air;
> The laughing school-boy, without grief or care,
> Riding the springy branches of an elm.

Keats, 'Sleep and Poetry'

Be like the poet who 'beholds intensely the present as it is; and discovers those laws according to which present things ought to be ordered' (Shelley, *A Defence of Poetry*). To attain such an outlook – keep connected: we are warned that if our 'heart turns away from the Lord' we may not see, or fully appreciate, good and beautiful people, things, places and events (Jeremiah 17:5–6).

---

[59] Virginia Woolf on Tolstoy, 'The Russian Point of View', *The Common Reader*, Volume I (London: Vintage, 2003) p.181.

The skill of an artist is not only manifest in how well he draws or paints: the first attribute is the quality of his seeing: its range and depth and alertness to nuance. When we have been to an exhibition of paintings by a favourite artist, we walk out of the gallery as a person transformed: faces, landscapes, colours, shapes and shadows – all are now seen, during our daily life, with the painter's eye. Every hour has its own contours, its own medley, as Cezanne appreciated: 'A minute in the world's life passes! To paint it is reality, and forget everything else for that! To become that minute, to be the sensitive plate … give the image of what we see.'[60]

Observation

Both lovers and healers – if their intent is pure – have extra insight, feeling, caring and compassion. Specialists in many fields of work and life can perceive (and process) what most of us would not notice:

- a musician's ear for nuances of sound;

- a diagnostician's eye for symptoms;

- a stockbroker's foresight for global currency fluctuations;

- a mother's precise reading of her baby's cues;

- an Eskimo's ability to distinguish dozens of types of snow.

Hardy, like Lawrence, was a poet and a novelist: his prose writing shows the poet's highly alert senses, which – let us always remember – predate and inspire memorable language. In her essay, 'The Novels of Thomas Hardy', Virginia Woolf writes of him as 'a minute and skilled observer of nature; the rain, he knows, falls differently as it falls upon roots or arable;

---

[60] Cézanne, Letter to Émile Bernard, 23rd October 1905.

he knows that the wind sounds differently as it passes through the branches of different trees'.[61]

> To dwellers in a wood, almost every species of tree has its voice … At the passing of the breeze, the fir-trees sob and moan no less distinctly than they rock; the holly whistles as it battles with itself; the ash hisses amid its quiverings; the beech rustles while its flat boughs rise and fall. And winter – which modifies the note of such trees that shed their leaves, does not destroy its individuality.

Thomas Hardy, *Under the Greenwood Tree*, chapter I

Sherlock Holmes chides Dr Watson: 'You see, but you do not observe. The distinction is clear' (Conan Doyle, *A Scandal in Bohemia*). Could Holmes say the same of you and me? A religious person is one who is devoted to broadening the field of his vision. What does it mean to observe? To be in the presence of, simply and humbly, without motive or manipulation, without the movement of thought, without trying to get something, *anything*, and not trying to change who or what you are seeing. Just watch, clearly and closely, with charity and all due reverence.

Each of us has the capacity to develop our quality of seeing: the scope is infinite. The secret lies in softening how we look, and seeing with a wider angle. When we see more widely and at more depth, we not only observe more (in quantity and in detail), we also notice more links and patterns: our vision becomes unified, leading to a coherent view of life:

> All things by immortal power,
> Near and far
> Hiddenly

---

[61] In Virginia Woolf, *The Common Reader*, Volume II (London: Vintage, 2003) p.246.

To each other linkèd are,
That thou canst not stir a flower
Without troubling of a star.

Francis Thompson, 'The Mistress of Vision'

Like an artist, an aspirant delights not only in the current object or person of his attention, but also in the full range of his subjective responses. His exhilaration is in the very moment of experience, and continues in later reflection and assimilation: as St Ignatius pledged, when writing about prayer, 'I shall reflect upon what presents itself to my mind' (*Spiritual Exercises*).

How often do we view the sky mainly (or only) in terms of weather, rather than enjoying the sky *as sky*? Do we notice the face and demeanour of passers-by? They are individuals, not just bodies to be swerved past. This requires inner space and a weekly rhythm with enough time to be alone.[62]

Reduce, diminish or eliminate all activities that are not really necessary (Psalm 55:22; Matthew 11:28), not to renounce the world, but to see everyone and everything on their only true basis: literally by the Light of God's countenance. 'To see God only.'[63]

The first stage of mindfulness is to notice when you are not noticing. As a one-week exercise in pure observing, you could walk each day to the site of a favourite tree. Sit in silence, and contemplate without ulterior motive. No defining, no analysing – just experiencing. On each return, you will notice more: the bark, the fluttering leaves, the shape of trunk and branch, shades of colour, the surrounding area alive with flowers, birds, squirrels and insects. Mind and limbs may rebel. Half an hour

---

[62] 'Let me thy [Solitude's] vigils keep
'Mongst boughs pavillion'd, where the deer's swift leap
Startles the wild bee from the fox-glove bell.'
(John Keats, Sonnet 'O Solitude! If I Must With Thee Dwell')
[63] John Donne, 'A Hymn to Christ, at the Author's Last Going into Germany'.

of sustained concentration is likely to test the stamina of even an experienced meditator. You will probably learn as much about your self as about your favourite tree.

> One impulse from a vernal wood
> May teach you more of man,
> Of moral evil and of good,
> Than all the sages can.
> Sweet is the lore which Nature brings …

William Wordsworth, 'The Tables Turned'

A businessman or contractor, on seeing a tree, converts its bulk into so many planks of wood or reams of paper. A spiritual aspirant sees with affection: *con amore*, as a composer would note on his manuscript score. How can we begin to delight in nature unless we slow down, do not rush our fences, and cease the daily gallop?

In Dostoyevsky's novel, *The Possessed*, Kirillov tries to explain to Stavrogin the joy and delight, and the newness, of contemplating a leaf:

> 'I saw a yellow one recently. It was a little green. It was decayed at the edges. It was blown by the wind …'
> 'What is this? An allegory?'
> 'N-No', Kirillov replies. 'I am not speaking of an allegory, but of a leaf, only a leaf.'[64]

We miss full perception when we categorise: to categorise is to limit. Even a piano concerto by Mozart can be pigeon-holed as composed in a certain key and year, conducted by maestro X, and the solo part played by Y. All this factual information

---

[64] Fyodor Dostoyevsky, trans. Constance Garnett, *The Possessed* (First Edn. 1916) (London, Barnes & Noble, 2004) IV.

sets up expectations, which (depending on the performance) may not fit with the 20-minute experience itself. Instead, we could allow ourselves to be drawn into the very essence of his music, 'poised as it is between joy and heartbreak' (Daniel Barenboim).

By generalising, by thinking in terms of stereotypes, even by just naming, we miss loveliness of detail – whether in nature or in our neighbour. We reduce a complex organism – quivering with life, radiant with colour – to a single word: 'flower' or 'friend'.

> We shall see but little way if we require to understand what we see. How few things can a man measure with the tape of his understanding!
>
> Henry David Thoreau, 'Winter', *Journals*, 14th February 1857

Beauty is truth speaking to the senses and the soul, pointing us to the source of all beauty, all love, all goodness (Matthew 6:22). When a listener or a performer is in love with a particular piece of music, he may, during a peak experience, merge with the music, become one with it. 'You must feel this light, have it within yourself' (Matisse).[65]

The divine undergirding

An artist sees creation enlivened. A mystic sees (or senses) the Enlivener of creation, 'the master-light of all our seeing' (Wordsworth, Ode, 'Intimations of Immortality', IX). Only by a life of pure contemplation can we glimpse what Tillich called 'the Divine Ground of all reality'.[66] In *The Stones of Venice*,

---

[65] Matisse, 'The Eye': Interview with André Marchand, 1947 in Jack Flam (ed.) *Matissse on Art* (California: University of California Press, 1995).

[66] Paul Tilllich, *Systematic Theology* (Chicago: University of Chicago Press, 1951).

Ruskin declared that 'the whole visible creation is a mere perishable symbol of life eternal'. As Ruskin points out, we see through the physical eye, but true sight is a spiritual phenomenon.

Samuel Palmer, a visionary artist and a disciple of William Blake, said that to walk with him in the countryside was 'to perceive the soul of beauty through the forms of matter'. Blake's vision always takes him beyond surface appearance:

> When the Sun rises, do I just see a round disk of fire somewhat like a guinea? O no, no. I hear an innumerable company of the heavenly host singing 'Holy, holy, holy is the Lord God Almighty'.[67]

Contemplative seeing lifts the veil of mystery; encounters the sacred in the familiar, and consecrates – makes gentle – every word, every action. But the lifting of the veil is only partial: our vision will only become spiritually 20/20 in the kingdom of heaven where our eye will be eternally young.

What do we see when we look with love – and look for love? We see the humanity in a face: the laughter lines and worry wrinkles. We see a flower in the innocence of springtime bud, and we allow its charm to point beyond itself: 'even Solomon in all his glory was not arrayed like one of these' (Matthew 6:29).

The more often you observe God at work, and the more closely and deeply you observe, the more does all of life yield up its bountiful store. The readiness-to-embrace is all. The whole of life (both the living and the material world) is sacred and thus full of meaning: all things are created by Him and for Him (Colossians 1:16–18). 'He is so great that all things give Him glory if you mean they should' (Hopkins, *The Principle or Foundation*).

[67] William Blake, Descriptive Catalogue, *A Vision of the Last Judgment*, 1810.

Prayers

Everywhere and every day, may I see and relish and rejoice in the abundant evidence of Your presence – Your beauty and power, Your wisdom and voice, Your goodness – in refreshing rain, in river, flower and tree. May this avid seeing and hearing aid my remembrance of You.

Please guide me to see all people, all choices, all material things, from the angle and perspective of eternity.

Oh God, help me to see and hear with senses innocent, new, original.

III
Enlightenment

Even forms and substances are circumfused
By that transparent veil with light divine,
And, through the turnings intricate of verse,
Present themselves as subjects recognised,
In flashes, and with a glory not their own.

Wordsworth, The Prelude, Book III

Diatropism

Carl Rogers, an eminent American psychotherapist, saw
something which he found symbolic: potatoes whose slender
shoots seemed to be stretching towards light (coming from the
one small window in a cellar). This is an example of diatropism:
the tendency of a plant, or part of a plant, to grow at right
angles to a stimulus.

Existence is far more than just living and surviving. As the
Latin origin tells us, it is 'ex-istence', the stepping forth to fulfil
one's potential: to *stand out* in existential space as the unique
person God is even now creating, 'until we fully and finally
enter into the joy, the complete unclouded beatitude, eternal
day'.[68]

Love has its own forms of diatropism. Every relationship
(even – perhaps especially – the most intimate) knows the

---

[68] Gerald Vann, *The Divine Pity* (London: Sheed & Ward, 1945).

sorrow (and poignancy) of incompleteness: poems and love songs down the ages have expressed the longing for ever-deeper union with the beloved, or sadness at lost or unrequited love.

There is also spiritual diatropism. This forward-urging (initially often in the form of restlessness and disharmony, because of a gnawing realisation of not yet having reached full stature) is the call of the Transcendent.

There is a high cost if – for whatever reason(s) – we do not rise to our God-given destiny to become our true, full self. Anaximander wrote in a proverbial fragment: 'Every individual does penance for [his] separation from the boundless.' And Matthew Arnold, in Anti-Desperation, asks a rhetorical question: 'Hath man no second life? Pitch this one high!'

The gaze of Jesus

The Christian mystics speak of enlightenment. St Teresa of Ávila and St John of the Cross chart the long journey towards awakening in great detail, drawing on their considerable personal experience.[69] For them, the process is very much led by God and involves profound purification of the soul and an eventual coming into the light which illuminates one's vision and the whole of one's day, though the consciousness of one's limitations is always present.

In the Christian tradition, enlightenment is understood in a profoundly relational way, since the Light is a Divine Person (Psalm 27:1). Jesus said of Himself, 'I am the light of the world' (John 8:12). St Teresa of Ávila calls her Sisters in their life of

---

[69] See, for instance, St Teresa of Ávila, trans. A Discalced Carmelite, *The Interior Castle* (London: Sands & Co., 1945); St John of the Cross, *Spiritual Canticle* in Kieran Kavanaugh and Otilio Rodrgiuez (trans.), *The Collected Works of St John of the Cross* (Washington: ICS, 1998). St Teresa and St John were the two principle reformers of the Carmelite Order in the sixteenth century, responsible for founding the Discalced branch.

prayer to an experience of mutual gazing: 'I am asking you only to look at Him.'[70] St Augustine attributes the following words to the good thief, dying beside Him on the Cross: 'Jesus looked at me and in that look I understood everything.'[71] God's gaze summons us to life. It 'enriches, makes beautiful, cleanses and enlightens the soul'.[72]

In *The Interior Castle,* St Teresa of Ávila speaks her realisation of the Blessed Trinity dwelling within her in the very centre of the soul. In this experience of mystical espousal to Christ she describes a mutual exchange.[73] For St John of the Cross, the soul surrenders herself to the Bridegroom, 'keeping nothing back'. She empties herself of all she possesses other than Him, and God gives Himself entirely to her.[74] All her attention is directed towards pleasing Him. Christ has become the soul's life. St Paul says of his experience, 'It is no longer I who live, but Christ who lives in me' (Galatians 2:20). Her mode of relating to God is simply love.[75] Her prayer is simply to love Him, who loves her.

A ninth-century bishop, St John of Naples, describes the effects of this relationship in a surrendered soul:

> The man who is enlightened neither stumbles nor strays from the path; and he knows how to stay the course. He who sees his native land from afar bears adversity; he is not cast down by the things of this world, but is strengthened in God; he humbles his heart and endures, and by his humility has patience. ... This salvation fears no sickness, dreads no fatigue, sees no pain ... Though the mists of temptation rise up, ... they can assault our hearts,

---

[70] St Teresa of Ávila, *Way of Perfection,* chapter 26.
[71] The above quote comes from a series of reflections by Canon John Udris.
[72] St John of the Cross, *Spiritual Canticle* 33.1.
[73] St Teresa of Ávila, *The Interior Castle,* p.106.
[74] St John of the Cross, *Spiritual Canticle,* in *Collected Works,* stanza 28, pp.583–586.
[75] Ibid, stanza 28, pp.583–586.

but are not able to overcome them. Though the blindness of lust comes upon me, 'the Lord is my light'. So the Lord is our strength, he who gives himself to us; and we give ourselves to him. Hasten to your Physician while you can, lest when you wish to do so, you are no longer able.[76]

The goal will never be reached during earthly life because God's life in the soul is capable of infinite growth and expansion: it is a lifelong, grace-filled movement towards more light, more beauty, as St Gregory of Nyssa explains:

> The soul that looks upwards towards God, and conceives that good desire for His eternal beauty, constantly experiences an ever-new yearning for that which lies ahead, and her desire is never given its full satisfaction. Hence she never ceases to stretch herself forth to those things that are before, ever passing from her present stage to enter more deeply into the interior, into the stage which lies ahead.
>
> The soul, having gone out at the word of her Beloved, looks for Him but does not find Him. She calls on Him, though He cannot be reached by any verbal symbol; and she is told by the watchmen that she is in love with the unattainable, and that the object of her longing cannot be apprehended ... but the veil of her grief is removed when she learns that the satisfaction of her desire consists in constantly going on with her quest and never ceasing in her ascent, now seeing that every fulfilment of her desire continually generates a further desire for the Transcendent.[77]

[76] Bishop John of Naples, Sermon 7, in *The Divine Office*, Vol. I. (London: Collins, 2006) p.455.
[77] Saint Gregory of Nyssa, trans. C. McCauley, *Commentary on the Song of Songs* (Brooklin: Hellenic College, 1988).

For the Christian, mystical experiences are less important than the transformation effected in character: growth in love and humility, which is an ever-receding goal. Always more:

> Real virtue has no limits. It always goes beyond. This is especially true of love, which is the mother of all the virtues. Having an infinite goal, love is capable of becoming infinite if our heart is worthy, steadfast, ardent. What a magnificent favour He gives our soul that it can expand more and more, endlessly, in love for God. Even in this mortal body, we can climb from virtue to virtue towards eternal life.
>
> St Francis de Sales, *Treatise on the Love of God*, Book III

In order to prepare for a moment of change, we may need to let go in some way or form. St John of the Cross depicted this 'clearing of space' by means of a sketch of a mountain, which he distributed to the Carmelite sisters whom he directed. He drew many paths going up it, containing spiritual and natural goods, but not getting anywhere. Only one short path leads directly to the top, and on it are written the words '*Nada, nada, nada*': 'Nothing, nothing, nothing'. And at the top: '*Nada*' (no intervening image of God). In short, the soul is to detach herself from everything that would separate her from the love of God, from everything that deprives her of His presence, even though it will cost her considerable dryness.[78]

This separation from all that is sensual, from all false notions of God and all attachment to spiritual sweetness, is so painful to the soul that it is best described by the metaphor of darkness: the 'Dark Night of the Soul'.[79] God deals with each soul differently, and for souls such as Mother Teresa of

---

[78] Crisógono de Jesus, *The Life of St John of the Cross* (London: Longman, 1958) p.243.
[79] St John of the Cross, *The Dark Night of the Soul*, chapters 2 and 3.

Calcutta and St Thérèse of Lisieux (a French Carmelite nun, 1873–1897) we learn that this dryness and darkness was a virtual constant.

The bright blithe voice of our hope in growing towards this goal needs to listen to its shadowy counterpart – self-doubt. Most of us have a number of self-imposed limitations droning in our inner ear, tired sounds from a deeply worn groove: 'I just can't;' 'That's not for me... That's just for holy people.'

God, the giver of increase, sometimes (or often) wants to stretch us beyond – even far beyond – our previously assumed limits of strength, skill and creativity. May we each do whatever we can now so as to be ready for His call, His holy touch. In every person – whatever the surface appearance, and whatever the past or present lifestyle – some part, prompted by divine discontent, seeks light; and reaches for wholeness, fulfilment, maturity, completion – perfect cadence. This aspiration, in every human being, comes from God's prevenient action. The desire for a holy life stems from God's longing for each of us to return home to Him (Acts 17:27) – starting right now, in this stage of our earthly existence.

How can we seek or know His light, unless the light is already shining in us? We have the assurance that 'the kingdom of God is within you' (Luke 17:21, KJV). One of the signs of a saint is the high degree of longing for God, expressed in Psalm 42:1 (KJV): 'As a hart longs for flowing streams, so longs my soul for thee, O God.' Endeavour to see the world, and all people, with one eye on the transcendent (1 Samuel 16:7), resolved to do only and always what will be pleasing in the sight of God.

Contemplative living is a threefold daily path: regular and informal periods of *prayer*; and a personal revolution in *behaviour*, stemming from a *deepening* of the inmost self. The life-expanding power of prayer beckons. The precise meaning of God's name, YHWH, is 'He who causes to become'. Each day God also deepens and lengthens our spiritual sight, readying us to serve both Him and our neighbours. Every act of spontaneous kindness pleases and celebrates the Source of all goodness. It is our acts of love which will outlive us.

> Free-heartedness, and graciousness, and undisturbed trust, and requited love, and the sight of the peace of others, and the ministry to their pain. These, and the blue sky above you, and the sweet waters and flowers of the earth beneath; and mysteries and presences innumerable, of living things. These may yet be here your riches, untormenting and divine: serviceable for the life that now is; and, it may be, with promise of that which is to come.

John Ruskin, Introduction, *The Crown of Wild Olives*

Prayers

How sweet, how vital, is Your shining: it is as a lamp to my feet, a light for my path, and a call to hasten unto You.

With Your grace and in Your mercy, I devoutly pray for more light, so that – with a fuller, richer life, and by being more loving – I may leave deep 'footprints on the sands of time'.[80]

May I live in You, by and from You, beside You, and only for You.

---

[80] Longfellow, 'A Psalm of Life'.

GOD

I
Triad: God, Self and Others

A threefold cord is not quickly broken.

Ecclesiastes 4:12

When you read about the spiritual life – still more, if you both study and follow this way of life – you will find a fundamental triad: (1) seeking and adoring *God*, leading to (2) *self-awareness*, which flows into (3) loving and serving *others*. It is important to give each of the three points (or pillars) of the triad a more or less equal share of our energy and attention (Matthew 22:36–40).

We are called and destined to evolve ever nearer to His likeness, in Whose image we are made (Genesis 1:26). But before we can live from our centre, we must first break the spell (or slavery) of the heavily conditioned self. We seek freedom from rancour and the desire for retaliation and revenge. Negative habits of thought and/or behaviour are blinkers, hindering our quest, our reaching out, for new skills, new possibilities, new encounters.

The more we move on the vertical plane – towards God, and inwards, to our real, true self – the more we are able to give on the horizontal plane in fellowship. Thus the three pillars can be likened to the horizontal and vertical stakes which form the cross: we seek God above (God is, of course, not only above, but also within and omnipresent); we seek to understand our self, thus we dip down into our own depths, and with both arms, we reach out, in love, to other people. The triad can be expressed, summed up, in three words: *uplook, inlook, outlook*. Uplook consists of prayer and an ever-alert sense of God's presence. If uplook is pure and constant, inlook and outlook will have a sure foundation.

Balance

The three points of the triad are related as closely as a well-knit family, as intimately as the workings of nature. Work on the three areas ensures an integrated life, each facet harmonised into one whole.

Spiritual life is always a rich blend of contrasts – social and personal, awe and tenderness, desire and surrender, discipline and freely given love, peace at the heart of action (Romans 8:6; 2 Corinthians 6:9–10). Spiritual life involves combining and weaving, composing and harmonising, and finding affinities.

> I sought my God:
> My God I could not see.
> I sought my soul:
> My soul eluded me.
> I sought my brother,
> And I found all three.

> (Source unknown)

It is vital to work on all fronts. Neglect one or two points of the triad, and personal development will be lopsided. This can lead to extreme positions: aloofness, withdrawal, isolation if inner life is overemphasised; or, with excessive activism, a scattering and dissipating of restless energy. This could be reckless, and ultimately self-defeating, even if many of the activities are in themselves worthwhile.

St John of the Cross wrote about people who are intensely active:

> They would be much more edifying to the Church, and more pleasing to God — setting aside the good example they would give — if they would spend at least one half their time in prayer. ... Certainly they would do more, and with less trouble, by one single good work than by a thousand.

Spiritual Canticle, 28

Note the order: God, self, other people. Inner leads to outer. What we do stems from who we are. If we are to do good, we have to *be* good – with no hint of self-satisfaction. For fullness of life, we need to love our Creator–Redeemer with our whole body and being, and care for our neighbour as diligently as we look after our own interests. The degree of my closeness to God – intense and constant – is the central feature and determinant of the quality of all my relationships.

Union with God enables us to love other people without imposing conditions or having undue expectations. Mature loving does not depend on what others do or fail to do. Mature loving does not depend on their personality, their (perhaps fluctuating or diminishing) appeal, nor on the way they treat us. Thus the basis, the very essence, of pure love for others is to love God in them and them in God. A heart turned to God will have a deep understanding of whoever is nearest, friend or stranger.

Trying to love someone when you do not yet love and own your whole self seldom, if ever, works: you soon become dependent, jealous, possessive or controlling. When you really and radically begin to accept and respect your self – including your vulnerability – then you become warmer in your humanity, and full-hearted in your acceptance of others.

With a joyous conformity to God, bring out the best in other people. Help each to feel special: a *person*. Prayerfully honour other people so that they will accord more value to themselves. 'Live among people as if God beheld you' (Seneca, *Epistles*, 10, 5). It is in serving our neighbour that our best God-bestowed gifts are evoked. At any moment or place, and in any encounter, we can ask ourself, 'How can I be true to You, to myself, and to the other person? Please show me how, right now.'

Prayers

Ever-ready to love You and my neighbour, may Your every wish be done, in me and through me, my will merged with Yours.

May I love the uniqueness of each individual, and see other people as persons. And let them see that I regard each one as brother or sister, and – whatever the outer appearance – as precious in Your sight and Your all-loving heart.

May it please You to enlarge my heart, heighten my sensitivity (to You and to my neighbours), and widen my outreach.

II
God

*The King of kings and Lord of lords, who alone has
immortality and dwells in unapproachable light,
whom no man has ever seen or can see.*

1 Timothy 6:15–16

Baggage: false notions of God

Most of us are prone to projecting our fears and needs on to
God, so that – to our limited sight – He is seen either as judge
or rescuer. But 'A God all mercy is a God unjust' (Edward
Young, 'Night', iv, *Night Thoughts, The Complaint*).

We have to avoid drawing a polarised picture of God. God
is not only our divine Companion, but a Source of wonder –
steadfast and unchanging, timeless (Psalm 90:4) yet ever new.
God is all-transcending, as well as near and comforting. If we
dwell mainly on the immensity of God, the danger is to
depersonalise, and to underplay the activity and the presence of
God incarnate. The scrupulous 'magnify His strictness with a
zeal He will not own'.[81]

At the other extreme, we should not anthropomorphise or
oversentimentalise the Almighty – however understandable is
the attempt to reduce His scale to a size which our limited
faculties can comprehend. A balanced view is to see God both

---

[81] F. W. Faber, hymn, 'There's a Wideness in God's Mercy'.

as mysterious, 'the King of ages, immortal, invisible' (1 Timothy 1:17) and as intimate friend. His dual nature is summed up in Rudolf Otto's phrase: *mysterium tremendum et fascinans*.[82] The Awesome One is approachable. He is high soaring and also indwelling. The Ancient of Days is also our constant companion: 'Closer is he than breathing, and nearer than hands or feet'.[83]

Michaelangelo's fresco-depiction of *The Creation of Adam* on the ceiling of the Sistine Chapel in the Vatican, in which the forefinger of God meets the forefinger of man, is symbolic of the divine–human intimacy, a love-bond of mutual delight.

To try to define God is to limit His reality. The nearer Jesus came to the cross, the less He said. Silence is our best response to the mystery and majesty of God: a calm, deep, expectant silence in which heart and soul are alert to hear the beloved voice. All of our notions and images of God – however lofty and refined, and however helpful they may be at various stages of our maturing in spiritual life – will always be limited, in their inevitable falling short of God-beyond-form, ineffable, God in His spaciousness and grandeur. The mystery – of a God who is within and beyond us, the immanent Transcendent – can disconcert or delight: 'and yet dearer for its mystery' (Shelley, *Hymn to Intellectual Beauty*).[84]

We do not even know how large the universe is. Astronomers estimate that it contains 100 billion galaxies – each tens of thousands of light years across, and each with an average of 100 billion stars. At the most recent count!

Brain and intellect know by thought and imagination, but only ever just so far. The God-filled heart knows primarily by *experience* (Luke 2:19). If our rational side cannot comprehend

---

[82] *The Idea of the Holy*, trans. John W. Harvey (London: Pelican, 1959) pp.26–56.
[83] Anon., trans. Clifton Wolters, *The Cloud of Unknowing* (London: Penguin, 1978) pp.134–135.
[84] In *Rosalind and Helen: A Modern Eclogue with Other Poems* (London: C. H. Reynall, 1819).

God in His immensity – matchless in purity and goodness, mysterious and yet of unsullied simplicity – then we shall have to live the mystery: watchful, fearful and yet hopeful.

God's self-revelation

By being active in our daily life – in His creative, revealing and redeeming acts – God enables us to enjoy a direct relationship with Him. Sometimes declamatory, He tends to reveal Himself and His glory subtly, discreetly (1 Kings 19:12):

> I heard among the solitary hills
> Low breathings come after me, and sounds
> Of undistinguishable motion, and steps
> Almost as silent as the turf they trod.

Wordsworth, *The Prelude*, Book I

God's apparent wish – for us to seek and find the drama (and colour) within the seemingly undramatic – shapes and sharpens our looking and our listening, prompting us to search for Him in the face of a stranger, and in the needs of the anxious and the troubled.

We cannot know – should we even guess – what the rewards of our service may be. Sometimes the so-called coincidences – 'That power which erring men call Chance' (Milton, *Comus*) – turn out to be so beneficial. Are His rewards chosen so that we will not readily link them with our own input? Perhaps His intention is to invite our participation, as more and more we come to discern the Eternal at work in Time.

Along with Eli and Samuel, we say (or pray) 'Speak, Lord' (1 Samuel. 3:9). And it is only natural that we hope God will speak to us personally, loudly and often. May we, instead, trust God to give of Himself when and how He, for the best, chooses.

Coming sometimes like fearful claps of thunder,
Or the low rumblings earth's regions under;
And sometimes like a gentle whispering
Of all the secrets of some wondrous thing
That breathes about us in the vacant air.

John Keats, 'Sleep and Poetry'

For our sake, and knowing just how much we can accept and absorb at any given time, the majesty and might of God (Psalm 36:5–7) are often revealed in careful stages (Isaiah 45:15). God revealed Himself to the people of Israel gradually, under names denoting ever-greater intimacy. First to humanity (in the persons of Adam and Noah), He was *Elohim* – the general name for God. To the Patriarchs He was *El Shaddai*, the exact meaning of which is unknown, but may mean 'omnipotent', 'God of the mountain', 'mother's breast', 'my guardian spirit' or 'God of the field'.[85] To Moses He revealed the divine Name, YHWH, meaning '*I AM WHO I AM*': a name so holy that Jews never pronounce it, and omit the vowels when it is written (Exodus 3:13–14).[86] What respect (bordering on awe) we should show for the divine Name (Proverbs 18:10). After all, God placed honouring His Name as the second of the Ten Commandments.

Just as the name of a loved one gains in depth and resonance as we share life's experiences together, so also our use of God's name becomes richer as our relationship with Him grows in awe, insight and companionship.

When we revere His name, God is not just spoken about; He is directly addressed: He is spoken *to*, by my words (which

---

[85] E. Maly, 'Genesis', in R. Brown, J. Fitzmyer and R. Murphy, eds., *The Jerome Biblical Commentary* (London: Geoffrey Chapman, 1962) p.258. The name is used in connection with the promise of posterity, so may be connected with blessing and increase.
[86] Exodus 6:3 in *Navarre Bible: The Pentateuch* (Princeton: Sceptre Publishers, 1999) p.100.

He inspires) and by my love in action. Everything done to honour His name (Hebrews 6:10) thereby gains its ultimate meaning and purpose. Then all aspects of life make even more visible (and vivid) God's presence, and reflect the divine beauty.

> Dear name! the rock on which I build:
> My shield and hiding-place,
> My never-failing treasury filled
> With boundless stores of grace.
>
> John Newton, 'How Sweet the Name of Jesus Sounds'

Jesus' name in Aramaic, 'Yeshua', is an abbreviation of 'Yehoshu'a' (יְהוֹשֻׁעַ). It means 'YHWH saves'. In this name is held Christ's identity and His mission (Matthew 1:21). He is a living icon of the Father's heart ('He who has seen me has seen the Father', John 14:9). Through the cross He manifests the fullness of the Father's love and mercy. In Him we receive the grace to call God, 'Father' (*Abba*). This adoption is summed up by St Paul in Ephesians 1:4–8:

> He chose us in him before the foundation of the world, that we should be holy and blameless before him. He destined us in love to be his sons through Jesus Christ, according to the purpose of his will, to the praise of his glorious grace which he freely bestowed on us in the Beloved. In him we have redemption through his blood, the forgiveness of our trespasses, according to the riches of his grace which he lavished upon us.

God's presence

A formula of ancient theology holds that God is naturally present in things by 'presence, power and essence'. Frank Sheed observes that we say, quite properly, that God is omnipresent, that he is everywhere: 'Do I not fill heaven and earth?' (Jeremiah 23:24). This implies that He is in everything, though because God is greater than creatures, it might be more precise – Sheed argues – to say 'everything is in God'.[87] St Paul said to the Athenians, 'in him we live and move and have our being' (Acts 17:28) and to the Colossians (1:15–20) 'in him all things hold together'. Ephesians 4:10 tells us, 'He who descended is he who also ascended far above all the heavens, that he might fill all things.' Being infinite, and pure Spirit, He is transcendent to things, yet at the same time intimately present to them.[88]

It is perplexing to ponder *how* God is present since He does not occupy physical space, and is certainly not identified (identical) with creatures.[89] Frank Sheed offers this explanation: that Spirit is where it operates, namely 'in the things that receive the effects of its power'.[90] The point at which this is experienced in creatures is at the point of their being (or existence) which is most intimately within them. For God's unique attribute, St Thomas Aquinas teaches, is that His essence is His existence: God is pure Being itself, *ipsum esse*

---

[87] Frank Sheed, *Theology and Sanity* (San Francisco: Ignatius Press, 1948), 'The Mind Works on Infinity', pp.62–65.

[88] *Catechism of the Catholic Church* (London: Geoffrey Chapman, 1994) paragraphs 290–311.

[89] To identify creatures with God leads to the error of pantheism (the creature as God, which is distinct to seeing God in creatures and creatures in God). Nor are the traits of humanity's fallen nature in any way reflections of God – for 'God is light and in him is no darkness at all' (1 John 1:5). Though, by some pale semblance, creatures can point us to attributes of God (to the extent they are good, true, beautiful, wise, one – attributes God has to a superlative degree, and in a quite different order), God for His part is never like creatures.

[90] Frank Sheed, *Theology and Sanity*, pp.62–65.

subsistens ('I AM WHO I AM', Exodus 3:14). He bestows being (existence) on creatures, who *receive* their being in a participative, secondary, contingent manner. And God continually exercises moment-by-moment causality by upholding creatures in existence. If this essential union – God's intimate presence in the fact of a creature's being – were to be lost, the creature would instantly perish.[91]

Besides the essential union which exists at the natural level, St John of the Cross describes a 'union of likeness' which occurs at the *supernatural level* in a soul in grace. Jesus says, 'If a man loves me, he will keep my word, and my Father will love him, and we will come to him and make our home with him' (John 14:23).

The soul receives the grace – never by its own efforts – to be transformed in God by love, and to become a child of God, when born again of water and the Holy Spirit (John 3:5–6). This grace is capable of infinite development in proportion to our surrender of the will to the infinite God, desiring nothing but what He desires.[92]

Is God hiding?

Despite His omnipresence, God sometimes hides His saving action behind a veil of seeming absence. We may miss (or botch) what seems like a good opportunity; or we are rejected; or we are not granted the fulfilment of a long-cherished aim. We then toss and turn in our doubt about God's goodwill towards us. Later events often show how God prevented embarrassment, *débâcle* or defeat. Oh, that we might have more faith in His benign intentions!

It is often only years later that we can see the negative consequences we were spared: likely outcomes which, at the

---

[91] St Thomas Aquinas *Summa Theologica* Ia, 8, 1.
[92] St John of the Cross, *Ascent of Mount Carmel*, Book 2, chapter V; Wisdom 11:24–26; CCC 301.

time, we had denied, or not foreseen; or, having sensed them, we overruled our ally, intuition. *Deus Caritas est.*

Now any taint of disbelief vanishes, faith is strengthened, and tossing and turning give way to a bowing of the head, seeking forgiveness for doubts, and thanking God for His mercy and tolerance (Matthew 28:20) and design:

> For thine own purpose, thou has sent
> The strife and the discouragement.
>
> Henry Wadsworth Longfellow, 'A Village Church'

Even (or especially) when hit by the mystery of suffering, we can be drawn closer to the presence of God, 'Soothing with placid brow our late distress' (Keats, 'On Peace'). And – by increase of compassion – we are more open to hear the deepest needs and longings of other people. By being especially close to us during times of trial, God is giving armour to our courage, emboldening us, perhaps making us more equipped to face future tests of our skill, character and maturity. Thus pilgrims discover, in the words of Camus, 'in the midst of their winter an unconquerable summer'.

> Hast thou not seen
> All that is needful hath been
> Granted in what He ordaineth?[93]

The life of St Josephine of Bakhita (c. 1869–1947) (affectionately known by the children of her Italian neighbourhood as 'Black Mother') offers a heroic example of trusting in God, even amidst barbaric human cruelty. She was kidnapped from her family in Senegal at the age of seven and sold into slavery. At the hands of her traffickers she suffered physical battering, humiliation, unkindness, starvation,

---

[93] Joachim Neander, trans. Catherine Winkworth *et. al.* 'Praise to the Lord, the Almighty, the God of Creation'.

degradation. One of her owners, in a fit of anger with his wife, took it out on Josephine, beating her to within an inch of her life. Another had her tattoed with 114 cuts on her chest, arm and belly, as a sign of his own status, and had salt placed on the wounds to keep them open – a torture which left her in agony for months. She was ultimately sold to people from Italy, and as part of caring for one of the owner's children, she ended up receiving instruction in the Christian faith from the Canossian Sisters, whose order she ultimately joined.

When people heard her story they would say, 'Poor thing, poor thing.' This distressed Josephine because they failed to see how these circumstances had given her her life's work, and brought her by a safe path to the kingdom where she hoped to enjoy eternal communion with her Spouse. 'I'm not a poor thing because I belong to the Master, and I'm in his house. People who don't know Our Lord – they're the ones who are poor!' she said to the children. 'If I were to meet those who kidnapped me, or even those who tortured me, I would kneel down and kiss their hands. Because, if those things had not happened, I would not have become a Christian and would not be a Sister today.' She could trust and see that God can bring good even out of human evil, as through the cross: 'where sin increased, grace abounded all the more' (Romans 5:20).

How nobly she lived the heart of the Gospel message – to forgive enemies. When one Sister spoke out against 'those wicked slave-owners', Sister Josephine placed a finger on her lips: 'Sshh … Poor things, they weren't wicked. They didn't know God. And also, maybe they didn't realise how much they were hurting me.' On another occasion she smiled and said, 'I pray for them a lot, that Our Lord who has been so very good and generous to me will be the same with them.'[94]

---

[94] Jean Maynard, *Josephine Bakhita: The Lucky One* (London: Catholic Truth Society, 2002) pp.33, 68. See also C. S. Lewis, *The Problem of Pain* (London: Fontana, 1957).

Attending to the upside and the downside

The service of God is a path pitted with outer and inner ordeals – all designed to strengthen our growth and our trust in God. How sobering to realise that we are much readier to discern the work of God when things are going well: 'And May was all the year' (John Clare, 'Song', *Prison Amusements*).

If 'every cloud has a silver lining', it is also true that every boon or benefit, even every miracle, has its downside, its own undertone of sadness and shadow. In the big moments, the major events, the life-changing phases of our life, the art is to attend to both the upside and the downside. What courage this needs, what clear sight, rather than denying doubt and avoiding conflict (actual or potential) with manic behaviour; or by focus on externals, to-do lists and filling the diary; or, sadly, by any form(s) of addiction.

A closer look at the whole picture may reveal, slowly or suddenly, glints of light even in our darkest moments and most gloomy moods. It is therefore vital at the very start not to stick a single label or name on a person, a relationship or an event. Each should be seen and heard not as an aria, single-voiced, but as a string quartet, with rich inner voices that will repay deep listening.

> That which we've learned from sorrow shall increase us
> ... Thou canst illumine even our darkest night.[95]

Three months after he wrote these lines, Dietrich Bonhoeffer was on the way south from Buchenwald. On 8th April 1945, the prisoners celebrated Low Sunday in the school at Schönberg, a small village in the Bavarian forest. Bonhoeffer took the service. He preached on the reading for the day, so

---

[95] Dietrich Bonhoeffer, trans. Reginal Fuller, *Letters and Papers from Prison* (London: Fontana edition, 1959) © SCM Press, New Year 1945, p.175.

poignantly apt for their plight – 'By his wounds we are healed' (Isaiah 53:5, NIV) – reflecting on the spiritual maturity that prison had wrought in them: God's presence in their last helpless days strengthened their hopes for eternal life.

They arrived at Flossenbürg concentration camp in the late evening. After a brief trial, the SS summary court pronounced the death penalty – for high political treason – on Bonhoeffer and six other members of the Resistance. They were hanged the next morning, a grey dawn outside:

> On the morning of that day [9th April], between 5 and 6, the prisoners were taken from their cells, and the verdicts of the courts martial were read out to them.
>
> Through the half-open door to a room in one of the huts, I saw Pastor Bonhoeffer, before taking off his prison garb, kneeling on the floor, and praying fervently to God. I was most deeply moved by the way this lovable man prayed, so devout, and so certain that God heard his prayer. At the place of execution, he again said a prayer – a shorter one and then climbed the few steps to the gallows, brave and composed. His death ensued after a few seconds. In almost fifty years that I worked as a doctor, I have hardly ever seen a man die so entirely submissive to the will of God.[96]

This is the camp doctor's narrative, written ten years after the execution. At the time he did not recognise one of the foremost theologians – perhaps also one of the noblest human beings – of the twentieth century. He could not put a name to the face, but he was quick to measure the stature of Bonhoeffer's faith, secure amid barbarity. V-E Day (8th May) was only four weeks later.

---

[96] Eberhard Bethge, *Dietrich Bonhoeffer: Theologian, Christian, Man for His Times: A Biography* Rev. ed. (Minneapolis, Fortress Press, 2000) p.927.

To Payne Best, an English officer and member of the British Secret Service, and a fellow prisoner, Bonhoeffer confided his last recorded words: 'This is the end; but, for me, the beginning of Life.'[97]

From his very first days in prison, Bonhoeffer had continued the daily disciplines: meditation, intercession, thanksgiving, Bible study and praying the Psalms. What inspiration his epitaph gives us: to follow his example of life-giving regularity in our own spiritual journey, however hard or tragic. Those final hours of his earthly life – in the fullness of his stature, so human and so devoted – form a living monument of universal reach. Bonhoeffer was 39.

Divine companion

When you are in a time of doubt or darkness, trust in God and stay yourself on Him (Isaiah 50:10) and His saving grace. He is not aloof, not indifferent. He cares about human suffering far more than we do – so much so that He did not withhold His Son, but rather willed that Christ take upon Himself all human misery and sin, at the point of the cross, and transform it into redemption. As Abraham prophesied, before the angel held him back from sacrificing his son Isaac, 'God will provide himself the lamb' (Genesis 22:8). God transfigures the hour of agony by giving us the assurance of His comforting presence. Thus does suffering on the pilgrim path become one way of deeper communion with Him.

> Yes, in spite of all,
> Some shape of beauty moves away the pall
> From our dark spirits.

> John Keats, 'Endymion', Book I

---

[97] S. Payne Best, *The Venlo Incident* (New York: Skyhorse, 2010).

On the spiritual path, we mature primarily by becoming more dependent on grace – readier to entrust our entire life and self (inner and outer) to the safety of God's arms, to His farsighted design, and the comfort of His companionship. 'No pain is unendurable with God' (Joseph Roux, *Meditations of a Parish Priest*).

St Thérèse of Lisieux – at a time of spiritual wandering and distraction, even anguish and near-despair, when she felt the foundations of her faith quaking (Isaiah 54:10) – scratched five words on a wall of her cell: 'Jesus is my only love.'

The way to seek healing is never by trying to manipulate God, or bargain with Him, or be ever on the hunt for specific results – and within a self-set timeframe. Trust that God is nurturing us at all times, in the hidden deeps of our psyche as well as our currently manifest/outer life. The initial or cumulative results may not begin to show for months or years or even decades. Faith is the core requirement (Hebrews 11:1). From faith comes acceptance (Roman 8:28). The enduring of doubt, difficulty, loss or pain (physical or emotional) may be part of the healing process: 'There's a divinity that shapes our ends' (*Hamlet* V, ii). Constantly ask yourself: 'He gave me this… He took that away… What is God trying to teach me?' (Job 1:21).

Faith may also bring increase of wisdom: the wisdom to see that, at this particular time, the experience and bearing of any form of hurt may be God's way for us to grow (1 Peter 1:5–7). St Ignatius saw times of struggle as a test of our fidelity and our trust in God's long-term plans and purpose. How it must please God to see us – when in the midst of storm or confusion – staying true to our commitments, both to Him and to our neighbours. 'Say not the struggle naught availeth' (Clough).

If we listen deep within our self, we may find that God is already providing us with strength – for coping, trust and patience (1 Corinthians 10:13; Ephesians 6:10–17).

Rely on, accept and respect the wisdom, the perfection (often seen only in hindsight) of God's choice of what is the best timing and pace for your growth, and that of all human beings. Above all, trust God for the balance of content in your life. Many aspects of life can only be learned through suffering, personal or vicarious. The whole pattern of our existence – with colours sombre as well as bright – is a unity. After all, beautiful music for the keyboard is composed by using the black keys as well as the white ones. If only we could trust His benign intentions and His longer perspective.

Most of us know people who persevere in the face of awkward hurdles, severe setbacks and long (or seemingly impossible) odds. By health of attitude and strength of character and *Deo gratias*, they maintain a level of personal satisfaction and deep-down contentment, *whatever their current circumstances* (Philippians 4:11). They do not try to avoid, delay or deny challenge: 'The real adventure does not begin until we enter the forest' (Gide, *Journals*).

People such as these emerge stronger, often wiser and sometimes transformed. Resurfacing from a time of unrest or struggle can bring wider perspective, be a spur for personal growth and creative change, and increase confidence in the ability to cope with future challenges and life in general:

> A frame of adamant, a soul of fire,
> No dangers fright him, and no labours tire.

Samuel Johnson, *Vanity of Human Wishes*

These inspiring individuals tend to share a cluster of attributes: to a greater or lesser degree, they are integrated, positive, focused, flexible, and they enjoy being stretched. They have a sure instinct for when to peer at detail and when to stand back so as to see the whole picture. Lastly, and most vitally, in the moment of experience they *combine the maximum of involvement with the maximum of observation.* Thus they can adapt while they participate.

The endeavour to avoid pain and suffering reduces our capacity to contain and manage anxiety and challenge. We have created a new kind of tension: the fear of future adversities which may never befall us.

The graph of a spiritual life is seldom, if ever, an unbending upward curve. We grow also – perhaps especially – from the scare of scarring experiences, when we are most dependent on God (2 Chronicles 20:12). Proof of this is shown by the inner and outer sorrows and joys of the saints (2 Corinthians 6:10), and their tolerance of risk and ambiguity, which are among the signs of psychological and spiritual maturity.

'We may not look at our pleasure to go to heaven in feather-beds: it is not the way.'[98] By seeming indirections, God teaches and fashions us so that – with trust in our vocation, and with a faith that shines in dark times – we may become loyal witnesses in all our encounters.

God's design

One aim of spiritual life is to be fully and creatively engaged: accepting every event from the hand of God, in trust, and thanking Him constantly – not just retrospectively (though after-the-event gratitude has its own worth) but *in the very moment* of experience.

> Not thankfull, when it pleaseth me;
> As if thy blessings had spare dayes:
> But such a heart, whose pulse may be
> Thy praise.
>
> George Herbert, 'Gratefulnesse'

---

[98] Quoted in William Roper's *Life of Sir Thomas More* (Leopold Classic Library, 2015), part I.

Through prayer, people and events are seen in a clearer light, and in their true proportions, because they are known to be part of God's wise design and loving intent. Cultivate a spirit of acceptance of God's designing of your life (Proverbs 3:6).

Embrace each person, each circumstance and God-chosen setting – including the awkward and the painful – as His way of strengthening you for your pilgrimage of faith, love and service: 'That which purifies us is trial, and trial is what is contrary' (Milton, *Areopagitica*). Observe how a jolt or a severe test of your character will – if you respond with maturity, skill and prayer – often teach you far more than placid periods. Above all, trust the balance of conditions and the sequence of events which God, in His wise vision, provides for your growth, ever-nearer to His likeness.

William Cowper wrote the following hymn in June 1773 during a solitary walk in fields, while in dread of another bout of mental instability. In these verses he expresses his resignation to, and confidence in, God.

> God moves in a mysterious way
> His wonders to perform.
> He plants his footsteps in the sea
> and rides upon the storm.
> Deep in unfathomable mines
> Of never-failing skill,
> He treasures up his bright designs
> And works his sovereign will.
>
> Ye fearful saints, fresh courage take;
> The clouds ye so much dread
> Are big with mercy and shall break
> In blessings on your head.

Judge not the Lord by feeble sense,
But trust Him for His grace ...
Blind unbelief is sure to err
And scan his work in vain.
God is His own interpreter,
And he will make it plain.

William Cowper, 'God Moves in a Mysterious Way'

Faith

Faith is the entrance to reciprocity – relationship with the mysterious yet ever-present Being from whom all rich meaning comes. Faith gives us a new and wider angle of vision, from which to see all the ups and downs of life in proportion, and from a more spiritual perspective: in the cleansing light of God, who is within and beyond.

'Do you see yonder shining light?' Evangelist asks Christian in *The Pilgrim's Progress.*

'I think I do,' Christian replies.

'Then keep that light in your eye.'

The most surprising facet of faith is not our trust in God – at best, this is flickering and fragile – but rather, and despite our daily backsliding and fallings-short, the regal consistency of *His confidence in us.* In time, we realise that God Himself is the seeker, and we, His people, are the lovingly sought.

Faith restores hope (Hebrews 6:18), transfiguring all experiences, and giving meaning and coherence to everything we do, everything we see. *Faith is the supreme unifier – of person with person, of people with God, of Earth with eternity.* Faith as unifier means the adherence of the whole person, listening to God's voice in our inmost soul, always ready to do 'the one thing needful', yielding our heart and all our faculties to God's will and purposes. 'An enduring faith means patience with the lamps lit' (Tertullian). To the eye of faith, this world is on the very fringe of the everlasting shore:

> The angels keep their ancient places,
> Turn but a stone, and start a wing!
> 'Tis ye, 'tis your estrangèd faces,
> That miss the many-splendoured thing.

Francis Thompson, 'The Kingdom of God'99

Soon or late, we shall rest for ever in His abode, and meanwhile we rejoice in the reappearances of God's benign countenance. He was always present but we saw Him seldom: did not trust that He was all the while with us, working in soul and life, for our return to His always available embrace. If we sincerely seek entry to the kingdom of heaven, faith is the key, and constant prayer opens the door.

Prayers

May my one aim, my sole desire, be You and only You, and what will meet with Your pleasure. I bow before You, God, our ever-present Reality, transcending as well as intimately involved, sovereign and also personal, Who has with each of us a special and individual bond.

The deepest longing of my soul is that – even at great cost to myself – Your holy name shall be everywhere revered, Your standard of honour adhered to, and Your way of unself-seeking love adored.

---

99 D. H. S. Nicholson and A. H. .E. Lee, eds. *The Oxford Book of English Mystical Verse* (Oxford: The Clarendon Press, 1917).

May I preserve my living faith, O God; and my alertness to Your presence. May Your will, and only Your will, be done – both in my life and by the whole world.

III
Prayer

Father of Jesus, love's reward,
What rapture it will be
Prostrate before Thy throne to lie,
And gaze and gaze on Thee.

F. W. Faber, 'My God How Wonderful Thou Art'

The language of faith is prayer. And prayer is the renewal of faith. When we pray, we pledge our will, uniting it to God's actions and design (Hebrews 11:6) – allowing change and our evolving to come at the right time, as part of the organic pace of self-growth:

> Being an artist means, not reckoning and counting, but ripening like the tree which does not force its sap and stands confident in the storms of spring without the fear that after them may come no summer. It does come. But it comes only to the patient ones, who are there as though eternity lay before them, so unconcernedly still and wide. I learn it daily, learn it with pain to which I am grateful: patience is everything![100]

[100] Rainer Maria Rilke, trans. M.D. Herter Norton, *Letters to a Young Poet* (London: W.W. Norton, 1934), Letter to Franz Kappus, Viareggio (near Pisa), 23rd April 1903.

Prayer is not just for the safe footfall of our next steps, nor just to heal and hallow the past: so that one day we may hear as plangent music what today we feel as undiluted pain. Prayer is an act of adoration of God *now*.

St Teresa used an image of four ways of watering a garden to depict stages in prayer life. First there is a bucket, involving filling, lifting and pouring – a lot of effort and activity. Then a waterwheel and conduits. Next a stream, and finally (on the lucky few) rainfall, which she sees as symbolic of deep prayer and a transcendent experience of the Infinite. Conscious effort is gradually reduced between stages one and four, the ultimate in prayer being a state of silent attention and adoration. St Teresa writes:

> When you pray, you proceed by a royal highway – which leads to heaven – because the King of Heaven has prepared it for you.[101]

Anything that inspires you can be considered a form of holy company: Scripture; a candle, a cross or a Rosary; a Handel aria; a stroll in a park on a summer evening. Choose whatever – on this particular day of your life – will arouse a sense of the numinous. The ideal holy company – available to us at any time or place – is constant grateful remembrance of the presence of God.

Neither St Teresa of Ávila nor St John of the Cross advocate any particular method of prayer, rather they focus on the conditions (including purity and detachment) that make prayer possible. St Teresa's approach to prayer was to represent Christ within herself, and then to keep Him company. 'I remained with Him as long as my thoughts would allow.'[102] 'I

---

[101] St Teresa of Ávila, *The Life of St Teresa of Jesus*, chapter 11.
[102] Ibid, chapter 9:4. 'If you become accustomed to having Him at your side, and if He sees that you love Him to be there and are always trying to please Him, you will never be able, as we put it, to send Him away, nor will He ever fail you. He will help you in all your trials and you will have Him everywhere. Do you think it

think that if I had understood then as I do now that this great King really dwells within a little palace of my soul, I should not have left Him alone so often and never allowed His dwelling place to get so dirty.'[103]

Our relationship with God must be practised – otherwise we shall not find the right tone when He comes to us unannounced. This relationship is developed by faith, by seeking everywhere His face and listening for His voice, by vocal prayer and psalmody, meditation[104] and recollection, communal worship, and *lectio divina*.

Lectio divina

Lectio divina (or 'divine reading') is a way of entering into the Scriptures – the narrative, the meaning and symbolism, and the Spirit that impelled the writing – so that the very marrow of the text touches both one's heart and one's whole life.

Aloofness is the pitfall to avoid: to fail to give enough to a book of Scripture that could be life-changing. 'Books must be read as deliberately and reservedly as they were written … How many a man has dated a new era in his life from the reading of a book' (Thoreau, *Walden*). The art of reading is to sympathise, to work together, become the writer's partner:

> Books are not absolutely dead things, but do contain
> a potency of life in them to be as active as that soul
> whose progeny they are; nay, they do preserve as in a

---

is a small thing to have such a Friend as that beside you?' *Way of Perfection*, Start of chapter 26.

[103] St Teresa of Ávila, *Way of Perfection*, chapter 28.

[104] Older Christian writers use the term 'meditation' to refer to pondering a Gospel scene or a mystery of the faith. When 'meditation' is referred to in this book, it means a naked intent to love God, harnessed (if helpful) to a single point of focus (e.g. a prayer word or phrase), rather than 'meditation' of the imaginative or discursive type.

vial the purest efficacy and extraction of that living intellect that bred them.

John Milton, *Areopagitica*

The timeless content and quality of a book is shown by its scope: it speaks to each succeeding generation. A spiritual classic also offers more of itself on each rereading, enabling us to grow during and after the revisit.

The return to a book can cause shock: it seems as if the text has been rewritten while you were not looking. But it is the reader who has been rewritten by time and by experience. When rereading we are richer in our humanity, and so we see deeper into its intention and prism of meaning.

One enriching form of prayer is to choose, each morning, a psalm or a favourite hymn. Pause after each line or verse and reflect on what you have just read. What is its personal message to you – on this particular day, and at this time of your life? At the end, make practical resolutions, and then follow through – act on what you have read and learned. Return to a verse or contemplation that has consoled or challenged you.

> If your spirit finds enough relish, light and fruit in any of these meditations, stop there without going further, doing as the bees do, who never quit a flower so long as they can suck any nectar from it.

St Francis de Sales, *Introduction to the Devout Life*

Lectio requires an unlearning of conditioned modes of study: the motive for the enquiry is not primarily intellectual but personal. The reading becomes relational and invitational. The book of Scripture is now a kind of mirror or enlightener: the reading of the text – the absorbing of its spirit and message – teaches me about the texture of my deepest self.

Petition

In one of his homilies, St John Chrysostom says that prayer is for the soul what the nerves are to the body, walls to a city, wings to a bird. But not all prayer is so lofty, in motive or in expression. Shopping-list prayer is a one-sided 'conversation', in which specific items are selected by the caller, and the supplier is told when the goods – all of them, and in the required quantities – need to be delivered, on unlimited credit. And then the caller rings back, with a reminder about what the shopkeeper forgot to send last week...

How would you and I really feel if life obeyed, and almost exactly replicated, our plans and self-prescriptions? God smiles on those who concede to Him both the first and last word – when we pray and in all our daily communion with Him.

If we kneel humbly before God, with purity of intent, we do not try to coax Him to grant, and promptly deliver, our wishes. Rather, we seek to bend our will to His will, which is our peace, secure in the knowledge that He will provide grace and strength for all our journeying (Philippians 4:13). True prayer is a loving dialogue: a conversation in which we listen more than speak – or try to!

> We humbly tender a blank into the hands of Almighty God. Write therein, Lord, what Thou wilt, where Thou wilt, by whom Thou wilt.

Thomas Fuller, *Poems and Translations in Verse*

May we increase in certainty of faith that God knows us and our needs far better than we do (Matthew 6:8, 32; Philippians 4:19). 'O Lord, thou hast searched me and known me! Thou knowest when I sit down and when I rise up; thou discernest my thoughts from afar' (Psalm 139:1–2).

Vocal prayer

There are many anthologies of prayers, and many helpful manuals with suggestions about how to pray. Both can be useful aids. But no prayer – however fine and lofty – can be allowed to displace those of your very own, when you are moved, guided and inspired by the Spirit.

One central guideline is worth mentioning: better a short prayer said slowly, with care and understanding, deeply felt. This approach is better by far than trying to rush through a series of long prayers, and, in the process, merely skimming their depth and richness of meaning. Always, always, *put quality before quantity.* 'Little and often' is deeper, more lasting and of longer reach than 'much but seldom'. And a shorter prayer can be very helpful, even consoling, when we feel tired and/or low in spirits.

When you say (not recite) the Lord's Prayer, or any set prayer, contemplate every word and phrase, find new personal messages, new depth and meaning. The most important aspect of prayer is your attitude, your state of mind and soul. Prayer is above all an activity of the heart, and thus a form of love. With love, faith, trust, joy and calm expectation, place your prayer life, your whole self, in the safety of God's affectionate arms (Psalm 95:6). When praying, a loving attitude produces loving words or affectionate silence.

Preserve a sense that the main initiative, and the inspiration, are both coming from God, as to prayer content, intensity and duration. He will endow your prayers (after we allow for inevitable dips of mood and attention) with continual freshness and creativity. If you wait, watch, listen, for the sublime voice of the Almighty, and allow for this degree of spontaneity, you will often be delighted and surprised by the quality of your prayers.

However, God surely does not wish us to be too fastidious about the words we use (or receive) in prayer: one day we are fluent; another day we are much less articulate. If only we could see and accept how much God appreciates our endeavour to pray during times of test or challenge, dryness or impoverishment. After all, these attempts – though frail and fragmented – cost us far more than the heaven-gazing praise and warm gratitude of our spiritual summers. When you cannot pray as you wish, pray as best you can.

God wishes to be your guide, so let Him lead. Your role is to be so at peace that – even when most busy – you will work with extra efficiency: productive and fulfilled because focused. Action by itself is short-sighted; thought (or even faith) by itself is impotent (James 2:17). Faith and works need each other; they support each other.

Relational

It is only because God first loves us that we are able and inspired to love Him, our self and our neighbour. This is the heart and essence of the Christian message. The depth and quality of our prayer depends on the depth and quality of this divine/human relationship. Trust the vast often silent work of His infinite love to warm and irradiate the deepest parts of the self – calling forth all your heart's natural affection, widening your love for Him and your neighbour, filling you with even more desire to return, again and again, to drink from the wellspring of eternal life.

Prayer centres on our dependence and response – in that order (Psalm 1:1–3). Prayer, from its very first stirrings, is God's gift – stimulated (or tailored) by God, robed by our desire, and then crowned by Him. The mystery of God, the as yet partially known, compels and propels. He 'leads the eye a kind of chase' (Hogarth, *The Analysis of Beauty*).

Praise

Seven whole days, not one in seven,
I will praise thee ...
E'en eternity's too short
To extol thee.

George Herbert, hymn, 'King of Glory, King of
Peace'

The religious vocation is to *praise* – with a steadfast and
unflinching gaze on God, the all-enhancing. To praise and to
thank (Psalm 69:30) is to acknowledge the priority of God, and
His sovereignty in your life. Just as God loves a cheerful giver
(2 Corinthians 9:7), so also He welcomes a grateful heart
(Ephesians 5:18–20). Perhaps the more we render thanks (2
Corinthians 4:15), the more He gives us to be thankful for (2
Corinthians 9:12). As Bonhoeffer said, 'The heart sings because
it is overflowing with Christ'.[105]

A delight in observation – in-the-moment savouring – is the
essence of gratitude. We praise what we first *ap*praise. What we
appreciate we 'see as precious'.

I once had a sparrow alight upon my shoulder for a
moment while I was hoeing in a village garden, and I
felt that I was more distinguished by that
circumstance than I should have been by any
epaulette I could have worn.

Heny David Thoreau, Winter Animals, *Walden*

The first great reality of God's nature and divine being – for
which we should always be thankful and in awe – is His ever-
Presence. Praise steadies the focus of attention. Praise inspires

---

[105] Dietrich Bonhoeffer, trans. John Doberstein, *Life Together* (London: SCM
Press, 1949).

that impassioned gaze of love which adores – at the heart of outer ceaseless movement – the throb and beat of the Unchanging (Psalm 73:25):

> Half an hour's roaming about a street or village or railway station shows so much beauty that it is impossible to be anything but wild with suppressed exhilaration.
>
> And it is not only beauty and beautiful things. In a flicker of sunlight on a blank wall, or a reach of muddy pavement, or smoke from an engine at night, there's a sudden significance and importance and inspiration that makes the breath stop with a gulp of certainty and happiness.[106]

A good starting point is to be quite specific about who and what you are thankful for. Constant thanksgiving makes you more alert and attentive, and thus more responsive: to see and feel the warmth of His hand, in every circumstance and in all encounters (1 Corinthians 1:5).

Whenever you see beauty, praise God for this sign of Him, a bloom from His endless garden (Matthew 6:29). In stillness, savour, relish and appreciate. And modulate from praise to a wish to please the Beloved. The only real experiences are those lived loyally and with a virgin sensibility.

Praise also widens inner vision: you come to see how – in everyday life, wherever and with whomever He places you – God is always listening to your needs and responding to your prayers (according to His own wisdom and perspective about what is best for you, at any given time). God not only presents us with new gifts, surprising us with His love; He also helps us to be more receptive/responsive – so that now we thank Him for people, or any aspect of life, hitherto not fully appreciated

---

[106] Rupert Brooke, Letter to F. H. Keeling, 20th–23rd September 1910.

by us. Praise – like love itself – is cumulative: it generates compound growth.

The livelier your vocation – and the more you do for and with God – the more energy He gives. When you are enjoying companionship with God – hearing and heeding His voice, seeing the work of His hands, rejoicing in His omnipresence – then praise gives birth to ever more praise. He is the life of my being and the subject of my song. Happy are they who rejoice in His presence day and night.

Contemplation: waiting on God

> Contemplation is nothing else but a secret, peaceful, and loving infusion of God, which, if accepted, will set the soul on fire with the spirit of love.

St John of the Cross, *The Dark Night of the Soul*

Prayer should be seen as an invitation from Almighty God: a banquet lovingly prepared for the benefit of the soul. How then could one dare to be cavalier about regularity and reliability in prayer life, forever making excuses for being neglectful or forgetful?

Prayer is the breath of God giving grace to human breath (and our use of it) – and to the soul, which is immortal. Prayer changes the atmosphere of time. When you pray, you have a chance to turn aside from the duties and demands of the day. By shedding many of these preoccupations for a while, you restore the balance of your focus, as between outer and inner life. Your mind, your breathing and your sense of time slow down. Then you can recollect. You remember what you already possess – or, more correctly, what (or Who) possesses you. You remember that God *is*, and that you are filled with His presence now.

No matter how short the clock time available, enter prayer with a sense of spaciousness: you are crossing over into an infinite timescape. Move the attention away from time in order to attune yourself with the Timeless. Greet Him, welcome Him. And let the Ultimate welcome you, embrace you. Remain open to be startled and in awe – of the process of prayer, and the work of God.

When Blessed Paolo Giustiano was asked how he prayed, he summarised his approach in six words: 'I thank, appeal, adore, honour, desire and await.' First of all, attune your whole self to God's wavelength, and determine anew to walk in His ways (2 John 4), maintaining communion with Him by constant love-conversation: hearing and seeing a world in the holy Word. Begin brief devotions when you are inwardly still, silent and receptive.

Attend initially to the body: slowing and softening the breath; untensing neck and shoulders; ensuring that the spine is upright, with neck and back in line; and providing, with the lower body, a firm and stable foundation – the whole body, the whole person, poised, in balance and oneness. When you meditate, wait without plan or picture; without thought or expectation.

> What if I bade you leave
> The cavern of the mind?
> There's better exercise
> In the sunlight and the wind.

W. B. Yeats, 'Those Images', *New Poems*

Recall your mind and attention to God's presence. Then wait – in moment-by-moment stillness and pure awareness – and allow prayer to arise: 'Keep your desire steadily and simply towards God' (*The Cloud of Unknowing*).

When you wait upon God with purity of desire – wishing to attend to Him and become attuned to Him, seeking to live in accordance with His will and way, yearning to become all that He wants you to be – you regain your spiritual poise (Isaiah 40:28–31), *thanks to God's waiting for you*. He is patient about the pace of your growth: forgiving, and steadfast in the outpouring of His Love.

Peter of Alcántara – the Spanish saint who was such a support to St Teresa – gave this guidance for prayer: 'Let a person return into his own self; and there, in the centre of his soul, let him wait upon God ... knowing he has God in his heart.'[107]

Instead of starting from where they are, many people begin each time of prayer in a state of desperate need, with expectation of a truly transcendental experience. Such high expectation – indeed, any expectation which does not have a dialogue with what *is* right now – is usually self-defeating. All pressure to 'pray well' is sour, unripe fruit. Beware of leaning into the future, instead of feeling now the floor beneath your knees. Every moment can be the prime occasion for a life-changing breakthrough: more reliance on God, and becoming readier to follow His way, not ego driven paths.

Stay with the paradox (to the ambitious Western mind) of waiting without expectation. 'Waiting for what?' you ask. This – the goal or the next plateau – is as yet unknown to you. God will reveal His message, and His route, when He judges you are best ready. Wait for Him to guide. Wait for Him to give. Only a quality of total innocence has a chance.

A person who cannot wait for the harvest does not know the expectant glow of the sower. How content are we with the natural pace of the ripening of love (or of any form of personal growth)? In the love dynamic between two people, God's kingdom in their midst is waiting to be entered and enjoyed:

---

[107] E. Allison Peers, *Studies of the Spanish Mystics*, Volume II (Sheldon Press, 1927) p.115.

And since my love doth every day admit
New growth, thou shouldst have new rewards in
store.

Donne, 'Lovers' Infiniteness'[108]

So much of what we long for in the deeper aspects of partnership will never come to us by push, pressure or demand. It emerges quietly, naturally, freely:

When a beloved hand is laid in ours,
When, jaded with the rush and glare
Of the interminable hours,
Our eyes can in another's eyes read clear;
When our world-deafen'd ear
Is by the tones of a loved voice caress'd –
A bolt is shot back somewhere in our breast,
And a lost pulse of feeling stirs again.
The eye sinks inward, and the heart lies plain,
And what we mean, we say, and what we would,
    we know!
A man becomes aware of his life's flow,
And hears its winding murmur, and he sees
The meadows where it glides, the sun, the breeze.

Matthew Arnold, 'The Buried Life'

We can apply the tone and spirit of these verses to our meditation. Look and listen with purity and wonder – no memories, no expectation, no pre-notion, just the vastness of solitude. For our prayer life, and to each fragile aspect of our being, God gives what we need and more – more than the mountain-peak of imagination can envisage or desire (Isaiah 64:4):

---

[108] John Donne, *Donne: Poems Selected and Edited by John Hayward* (Harmondsworth: Penguin, 1950) p.31.

Who would not love Thee,
Loving us so dearly?[109]

To pray is to dwell in that secret shrine and chamber of the soul – secret and also portable (Exodus 3:5). Here you are alone with God – trusting, confiding and safe – in delighted awareness that the unspeakable majesty of God deigns to talk with you, and knows you better than you know yourself (Psalm 139):

> God is nearer to us than our own soul, for He is the ground in whom our soul stands.

Julian of Norwich, *Revelations of Divine Love*

The All-Transcending is offering you the intimacy of His presence, as the sure foundation of your inmost self (Acts 17:28). Only God – infinite, incarnate – can fully warm the heart. The prayer style I imagine to be best loved by God is semi-continuously said (or proffered). In Arabic there is a word that means both repetition and remembrance. Remembrance of God begins with repetition (by the tongue) of His holy name. Then prayer descends, to become repetition in the heart.

Finally, heart-felt prayer deepens and becomes remembrance in the soul – a state of recollectedness, constant mindfulness of Him. At first you say the divine Name. In time, you allow God Himself to pray and sing in and through you: you are the choir; He is both the composer and the cantor.

Prayer should end with a promise. The fruits of prayer need to be shared, in intercession, and in love (John 15:16). Goodness can never be a single or final attainment: it is a daily divine gift to those who loyally follow His call.

It is vital to emerge calmly and gently from prayer or meditation:

---

[109] 'O come, all ye faithful', translated by F. Oakeley, W. T. Brooke, et. al.

As you go out from this heart-prayer you must take care not to give your heart a jolt, lest you spill the precious balm it has received by means of the prayer. I mean that you must if possible keep silence a little, and gently remove your heart from prayer to your business, retaining, as long as you can, a feeling of the affections you have conceived. ... Do not turn your attention at once to other things, but look simply before you.

St Francis de Sales, *Introduction to the Devout Life*

On a day (or in an hour) when we are struggling to pray, it takes much faith and a lot of courage to maintain our flickering concentration. But prayer can be a moan or a sigh (Romans 8:26). A groan or even a whisper can be of great worth. 'Prayer and love are really learned in the hour when prayer becomes impossible,' says Merton.[110]

Peace

Peacefulness is the sterling hallmark of the life of prayer. Jealously, decisively, guard the peace of your soul. The whole edifice of the triad – your relationship with God, self and others – depends for its safety on this watchfulness, this *vigilance*. To be at peace, your life has to be consistent, in the same key, all of a piece. Without virtuous living – purity of mind and heart – there cannot be serenity in prayer (Isaiah 32:7). Peter of Celle, a French bishop of the twelfth century, put this graphically: 'He who snores in the night of vice cannot know the light of contemplation' (*Free from Sufferings*). Outer and inner peace depend on constant fidelity to a wholesome, rhythmic lifestyle.

---

[110] Thomas Merton, *New Seeds of Contemplation* (New York: New Directions, 2007) p.221.

The purpose of prayer and meditation is not to *get* peace, but to uncover our living core of inner stillness. What we seek we already have by the grace of our baptism. God's presence in the soul is the destination of our journey.

From time to time (amidst duties), briefly stop what you are doing. Relax. Observe your pace and your posture. Watch the depth and length of your breathing. Unknot any body tensions. 'Rest, rest, perturbed spirit' (*Hamlet*, I v). Recommit yourself – your current work and your entire life – to God. And resolve not only to do His work, but also to do it in His way – graceful because grace-full. Later – whatever the outcome – end with praise and adoration (Ezra 9:5).

Unceasing prayer

The literal translation of St Paul's 'pray constantly' (1 Thessalonians 5:17) is 'come to rest'. The Greek word for 'rest' is *hesychia*. A hesychast is a person who seeks silence and solitude as pure ways to attain a state of unceasing prayer.

Prayer – in its fullest and widest sense, and ultimate meaning – is not a single action at a specific time, but an all-life, all-governing state of being. Prayer must not be separated from life: it *is* life. We should pray always but we also have to work, so we pray while we work. We have to eat, so we pray while we eat. While filing and writing, digging and sawing, sewing and cooking and baking, say 'This is for you, O God.'

Prayer helps to set a right stance: open, alert, expectant, disposed and available to obey God's will and, perhaps above all, ready to be surprised: by new learning – about God, self and others; by new opportunities for service; by the unfolding of the unexpected. Prayer sanctifies all actions, all encounters. Resolve to be always sensitive – and responsive – even to God's *sotto voce*. Then remind yourself of God's constant wish for you to come to Him, and be embraced by Him, and find your eternal home in and with Him:

The most necessary practice in the spiritual life is the practice of the presence of God, whereby the soul finds her joy and contentment in His companionship, talking humbly and lovingly to Him always ... During our work and other activities ... we ought to stop for a moment, as often as we can, in order to worship God in our hearts, to touch Him as it were by stealth as He passes. Since you know that God is with you in all your actions, that He is at the very depth and centre of your soul, why not then pause an instant in your external occupations, and even in your prayers, to worship Him inwardly, to praise Him, to petition Him, to offer Him your heart and to thank Him?[111]

Unceasing prayer means to pray before, during and after every activity: *before*, as preparation – a readying of body, mind and soul; *during*, as reminder of God's sustaining hands; *afterwards*, in songs of praise and trust – whatever the outcome. Prayer transforms work into worship: by purifying motives, by making more constant our recollection of God, and by making ardent every love-offering to Him.

Prayer invites us to enter and embrace life as it is – the one Reality, a God-composed blend of discord and harmony. Observe, remember, that harmony is all the more beautiful, and welcome, when preceded by discord.

Communing with God, absorbed in the vast and generous silence of God – beyond petition, beyond words – we experience a mysterious emptiness-fullness (John 3:30). The paradox is that *from self-emptying (kenosis) comes self-finding*. Renouncing (or, better, not identifying with) the lower self, you are free to find Him within you (John 12:24). Observe how your inner stillness is always present, always available: it was

[111] Brother Lawrence, trans. D. Attwater, *The Practice of the Presence of God* (London: Burns & Oates, 1977), Maxims: Necessary Practices for Attaining to the Spiritual Life, I and IV.

there waiting before you paused to become aware of its presence; it will remain deep within until the next time you tune in to its vibrations. Stillness comes first and last. Regard stillness as your inner landscape.

Distractions

How do you deal with distractions while praying or meditating? How not to be downcast? By reminding yourself that the very observing of inattention (on this occasion the movement of the mind, not the content of the thoughts) is itself a form of attention. Prayer is the art of patience.

The encounter with silence needs daring and courage, emulating the trust of a high diver in the water's buoyancy. To switch your attention from outer sounds to inner quiet can leave you feeling exposed, like a long-term drug addict suffering withdrawal symptoms. Wordsworth gives us another image when writing of the chastening loneliness when one can feel chased by inner demons:

> Oh! At that time
> While on the perilous ridge I hung alone,
> With what strange utterance did the loud dry wind
> Blow through my ear!

The Prelude, Book I

When outer distractions are reduced, inner distractions may arise – with force:

> The mind is its own place, and in itself,
> Can make a heav'n of hell, a hell of heav'n.

Paradise Lost, Book i

Like a window, the mind can be dirty or clean, closed or open. D. H. Lawrence describes our minds as 'crammed waste-paper baskets' ('All-knowing'). Without regular periods of silence and the experience of actions emerging from a bedrock of silence, we soon lose contact with our soul. Then we become the plaything of fugitive fears, thoughts and emotions; easily submerged in – and smothered by – the ups and downs, the coming and going, of daily life; and as fraught, in body and mind, as Grand Central Terminal in rush hour.

This is Lawrence's description of the troubled Siegmund:

> When he seemed to be going to sleep, he woke up to find thoughts labouring over his brain, like bees on a hive. Recollections, swift thoughts, flew in and alighted upon him, as wild geese swing down and take possession of a pond.

The Trespasser

Shakespeare, on going wearily to bed after a day's travel, speaks for the daily experience, and the meditation travails, of most of us:

> But then begins a journey in my head
> To work my mind, when body's work's expir'd:
> For then my thoughts (from far where I abide)
> Intend a zealous pilgrimage to thee.

'Sonnet XXVII'

At the heart of contemplative prayer is the need to be gentle with all my detours and deviations. Annoyance with distractions gives them more status, power and energy than they deserve. If I fight them, they will not let me leave the mind's boxing ring.

When we observe our thought patterns closely, we find how our preconceived notions, of all kinds, hinder our seeing what really is. When you have a troublesome thought, a haunting memory or a compulsive desire, hold the idea or feeling for an instant and then breathe out – silently, slowly, smoothly. Distractions are teachers of humility. They can be met with patience and quietness – of body, mind and emotions – as when waiting for the return of sleep after waking in the night. The best response is no response. The best mode is a spirit of not minding. 'Not minding' means not analysing distractions, not dwelling on them, not fighting them nor trying to suppress them. Resurface in a self-lenient way, without judging or blaming yourself, or cringing with a sense of failure.

By focusing on a carefully selected peace-giving object, such as a phrase from the Psalms, we screen out, ward off, the battalions of thoughts and memories that invade us, day and night. Our breathing becomes slower, our whole being deepens, and our chosen subject (restful and congenial) becomes for us a sign of God, a manifestation of His incarnate glory, and focus for our yearning.

Allow your prayer word or phrase to arise with the gentleness of the unfolding of a rosebud. When you begin your time of meditation, be and feel like the rejoicing of Zechariah, described by St Luke (1:78–79), in poetic prose of charm:

> Through the tender mercy of our God,
> when the day shall dawn upon us from on high
> to give light to those who sit in darkness and in the
> shadow of death,
> to guide our feet into the way of peace.

Picture your prayer word or phrase as a chain on a rowing boat that is anchored in harbour. Whenever the tide tries to coax the boat out to sea, the chain is a firm (but friendly) restraint. Keats gives us another simile for our prayerword:

Like a bell
To toll me back ... to my sole self!

'Ode to a Nightingale'

Is there any hardness in your concentration? If so, cast your mental/emotional focus into the middle distance. Be a relatively uninvolved observer – not excusing, not justifying, not condemning. What remains is what is true. Without effort or striving, you become more present to what *is* – both within and all around you.

We identify – can even become one with – whatever (or whoever) really attracts and captivates us. Keep observing how rapacious, how lustful, the mind can be. Ask yourself how much of your thinking is creative, productive, God-led and God-directed. Assess how much of your mental/emotional activity is leeching your vitality from peace-founded love and warm, wholehearted service.

Except for the privileged few, the diminishing (or temporary elimination) of thoughts is a hard school, but has potential to be the best reward of all. Watch thoughts as if you are on a riverbank seeing the water flow past; or lying on a grass verge watching clouds scud or wander across the sky. Say to every thought, 'You too will pass by.'

Letting go (in the wider sense) means relaxing control, eliminating power games, curbing the urge to manipulate. Then you see how much your *perceptions are being shaped by your expectations*. And only then will the silence of meditation (Isaiah 33:2) take you to gardens of unimaginable beauty. The attainment of inner silence frees you for a while from the claims of feelings and emotions, conflict and confusion, desires and plans, unresolved problems (inner and outer), and all forms of distraction.

The very watching of the movement of the mind, and the restlessness of the body, in itself calls for a high quality of attention. This attention and listening – mainly inside oneself, but also to some extent outside – is the core and essence of a contemplative mind.

Thought dissects and discriminates. Thought is the fetid soil of like and quick dislike. Thought forever chatters and analyses; selects, judges, criticises:

> Our meddling intellect
> Mis-shapes the beauteous forms of things:–
> We murder to dissect.

> Enough of science and of art;
> Close up these barren leaves;
> Come forth, and bring with you a heart
> That watches and receives.

William Wordsworth, 'The Tables Turned'

Fruits of prayer

God 'by the power at work within us is able to do far more abundantly than all that we ask or think' (Ephesians 3:20). Those who have travelled farthest on the path of prayer tend to be the most humble of people, the most awestruck in their wonder (Psalm 8), the readiest to acknowledge that they start each morning as beginners, and the most gentle in all their relating to others.

St Teresa of Ávila's test for true prayer – and indeed for all spiritual experience – poses three questions, simple yet searching: Am I more humble (in the creative, not the self-abasing sense)? Am I more loving? Do I have a more vivid sense of the holy character of daily work and daily life?

A sign of authentic prayer is to regard other people as they are in the sight of God – of high potential and infinite worth. The more you allow His hand to touch and guide you, the closer you come to other people with the core of your being stable, simple, silent (Psalm 46:10).

Prayer can help us reach that realm or dimension where our contact with God is purest. Here we rejoice in God not so much because of what He does, but because *He is*. Frivolous thoughts and minor concerns burn out, in the flame of meditation, and give way to words 'from the Soul's eternity' (Rosetti, Introduction, *The House of Life*, part I).

The eternal is like a rainbow: arched over the Earth, and yet also touching, blessing, the world of time. The timeless – if only we can let go, and open ourself to receive – can heal our past, make our present rich and full, and give hope for what is to come.

Meditation is a revelation – often a first disclosure – of your God-given essence. If you listen deeply, meditation brings a message of warning and advice about all forms of body use: facial expressions, breathing, gesture and posture, tension, diet, sexual life and the balance between rest/sleep and work/exercise.

The more often, and the more acutely, you observe yourself speaking and behaving with ease, calmness and modest efficiency, the more you will enjoy living from this relaxed and skilful state – even in conditions that are noisy, tense, testing or combative. When we are criticised, do we pause or retort? When kicked emotionally, do we kick back? Do we act or react? How often do we respond from the silent centre within, in a serene, sovereign way?

If you sense that your annoyance or anger is rising – or an argument is brewing – watch and gently curb the impetuous motion of mind and emotions. Stay still, stay supple and easy, natural and relatively loose. Locate your truth and your strength in the stillness and poise of your centre. Then find areas of compromise, reciprocity and mutual concern.

Observe your self in action – soul, body, mind and emotions – being free and effortless, alert and responsive. Live your whole life with this degree of God-centred awareness. Pause and peace give poise. Keep asking yourself which part of you is prompting a word or an idea, an action or a reaction. Is it a desire to defend or control or defeat? Is it a craving?

Meditation is like the regularity and rhythm of the sea: wave after wave, washing smooth the sand on a shore. In this simile, sand is symbolic of the mind's impurities. In the relaxed state of meditation, the restless and agitated and wandering surface-mind becomes relatively quiet and peaceful. This space allows for repressed material to emerge from the unconscious: previously unfaced negativity, such as envy, guilt, regret, resentment, fears, conditioning, distortions, defensiveness. Obstacles (both inner and outer) are our teachers:

> Your defects to know,
> Make use of every friend – and every foe.

Alexander Pope, *An Essay on Criticism*

We become swifter to recognise our true motives for any choice or decision. Once observed and worked with, a stuck and self-blocking mindset can be loosened: old, deeply ingrained patterns can be reassessed; outdated mental/emotional furniture discarded.

Self-fantasy gives way to self-facts, resulting in a genuine sense of self-worth. Formerly entrapped by its own grandiosity, the posturing false self can now be seen for what it was – self-limiting. This letting go allows the whole personality to breathe more deeply. As yet unrealised potential, which was waiting in the unconscious beneath the buried murk, emerges (Genesis 26:15–22).

Meditation can lead to a rebalancing, a new quality of feeling: sadness without morbidity; weeping without abject despair; a longing for intimacy without greed, craving or undue dependence; passion without lust. Gradually (or in a sudden awakening), separate strands of the self form a harmonious whole – your body, your heart and soul, your still mind, the observer side and the participator side all coalesce to function as a unit:

> Dust as we are, the immortal spirit grows.
> Like harmony in music: there is a[n] ...
> Inscrutable workmanship that reconciles
> Discordant elements, makes them cling together
> In one society.

William Wordsworth, *The Prelude*, Book I

Faithfulness to daily practice of meditation – at regular times, if possible – clears the way for continuous meditation-in-action. Reliability, continuity, will bring ample reward.

Meditation is, ultimately, the purest state of being, the final surrender, as you relax and rise to who you really are – the full stature of your humanity. You come to an apprehension of God dwelling within you. You recover your innocence – and by doing so you discover your innate oneness with your neighbour and your Creator.

Innocence is not to be aimed at but preserved, so that one is as unselfconscious of the impression one is making on others as trees are of their reflection on the surface of a lake.

In that innocence, love is born. 'Innocence' means, literally, not to harm oneself or others; not to plot, scheme or ensnare; to think the best of people unless shown otherwise. To protect this innocent core, be on your guard against shadow: any form of negative energy including – starting with – one's own, and yet retain a spirit of open-hearted delight and discovery.

We are not earthly beings seeking spirituality. We are already spiritual beings, here in temporary residence. The early Christians referred to themselves as *paroikoi*, sojourners, citizens of heaven on their way home. Can we, too, learn to keep our eye on the Eternal? Prayer makes us aware that, in our earthly life, we are simultaneously in time and in eternity. With this sense of both *chronos* and *kairos* – *chronos*, time as flow and *kairos*, fullness of potential, a deep-felt sense of the right/favourable/propitious time – every encounter, every moment of life, becomes charged with vitality and new opportunity.

Prayers

I consecrate myself to You: Joyful self-spending, with You and for You, answering Love with love.

May the whole of my life be worship, a constant celebration of Your constant presence. May I ever praise and proclaim Your glories: the countless gifts You grant to us all, Your unfathomable depth, and Your grandeur. May gratitude never depart from lips or soul.

Please grant me continuous awareness of Your continuous presence. The aim of my life, my entire being, is eternal union with You.

O, for grace to love You more. Heaven and earth are full of the majesty of Your glory: Your Love bountiful, measureless, ineffable.

IV
Contemplatives, Solitude and Silence

I already feel my solitude again a little, and suspect it will deny me nothing if I hearken to it with new strength.[112]

Contemplatives

One of the younger men asked someone of longer experience: 'What is a monk?'

He received this reply: 'A monk is someone who asks himself every day, "What is a monk?"'

Monks and nuns have much to teach and remind the world about belonging and commitment, stability and loyalty. For them, each morning is a recommitment. They pray that time and experience will deepen their relationship with God. And they pray that, in the adventure of faith, they may continue to grow into their vows.

Monastic communities have a leading role – of ever-expanding importance – as protectors of a life-balancing archetype that is under threat: the archetype of silence and solitude.[113] Religious communities also provide a priceless model by their sanctifying of the way time is perceived and used. They sanctify time by prayer, by regularity and stability,

---

[112] Rainer Maria Rilke, Letter to his wife, Clara, Spring 1903.
[113] An archetype is a fundamental human experience that keeps recurring – to most generations and in most cultures. An archetypal experience is prismatic: it engenders ever-new feelings and reactions, descriptions and interpretations.

and by recollection. For them – and potentially for us also – prayer is not just one part of life: prayer gives life and *is* life. By attending to the spiritual, the contemplative becomes more keenly aware of the needs of created reality.

We are created to find our self in God, and God within our self; and, as often as possible, to help others become the best they can be, in His sight. Prayer – our inner altar and sanctuary – is the very heartbeat of our human solidarity. A contemplative person lives the everlasting life within the world of time, and sees the Unchanging at the very heart of change, constantly 'retying the love-knot between lover and beloved'.[114]

A true contemplative is not passive or withdrawn. On the contrary – in addition to a rich interior life, they feel equally at ease in encounter. This balance between inner and outer comes from being poised – having one's centre of gravity – in God. *Contemplation is to see the world as temple, oneself as priestly, and all life as sacramental.*

Contemplation is not just for contemplatives. Contemplation is not only quietness and aloneness: contemplation is for all day. Contemplation frees you to be non-possessive, encouraging people to be true to their own individual nature and character: accepting, not correcting; receiving, not expecting; not trying to change, but allowing to be and become.

Contemplation is ultimately about how – and how purely – we see. Contemplation means *respect*, seeing into the very heart of things (1 Samuel 16:7): nothing is merely material. May all our senses regain innocence: our childlike, godly openness.

A single focus

Contemplative communities provide a witness to all of us about the powerful efficacy of directing all one's affection and creativity towards one single purpose. One-pointedness is like

---

[114] Julian of Norwich, *Revelations of Divine Love* (London: Penguin, 1998).

the searching power of sunlight through a magnifier, beaming on a single spot. Having a worthwhile goal – union with God – integrates energy and will; focuses concentration; harmonises all our desires, hopes, and values; and gives coherence to our life. 'Put the readiness for God before all other things' (Thomas à Kempis, *The Imitation of Christ*).

> He who aims at the attainment of God's love must devote all his heart and mind and energy for this single aim.

St Francis de Sales, *Treatise on the Love of God*

I find highest meaning, and I am at my best, when my actions, my skills and my psychic energy (i.e., the combination of thought, emotions, will, sense of self and direction) are directed towards my chosen goal: 'Obedient to the light that shone within his soul' (Shelley, 'Alastor; or the Spirit of Solitude').

My life is transformed into a single theme: to become more fervent in His service, in all freedom and fruitfulness. God is my coherence: all is from Him, all is for Him. This all-encompassing goal is like a magnetic field, attracting all my energy. And the more you centre each facet of your life in God, and continuously celebrate and show forth your alignment with Him, the more does He reveal His affinity with you (Psalm 145:16).

> Simplicity, simplicity, simplicity! I say, let your [activities] be as two or three, not a hundred or a thousand. Simplify, simplify.

Henry David Thoreau, *Walden*

Simplifying can inspire us to thank God for the small daily things of life as well as the more immediately obvious bigger ones. All is from His gracious hand.

Silence

The ultimate prayer is constant awareness of God's continuous presence (Psalm 16:8). To approach this goal – the bliss of the divine embrace – we need, at set times, to experience His presence – and especially in the wisdom and beauty of all-disclosing silence. God is everywhere, but silence is His special residence.

Silence is not the absence of sound. Rather, sound is the absence of silence. Silence is primary.

Silence, stillness, God's Word: each comes like the dawn, when the sky is 'pinking in' (Thomas Hardy, *The Withered Arm*). The dayspring is coy in the first disclosure of its glory; and then, second by second, rapidly more flushed. Such is the feel, the glory, of the first light of a spiritual dawn. He comes to us in the silence and stillness of our listening worship (1 Kings 19:12).

But silence and solitude put us to the test, as Pascal observed: 'Nothing is so insufferable to man as to be completely at rest, without passions, without business, without diversion, without study' (*Pensées*). If true in 1670, how much more so today! The more one's inner life is dominated – by a focus on the external; by an overload of information; rush and hurry that enslave, and lower one's sights; and the pace, noise and strain of city life – the more is silence needed.

The outer noise is an echo-effect of a prior noise: the thought-and-desire clatter of the restless mind, always manufacturing desires – which fills 'the air with barbarous dissonance' (Milton, *Comus*). If man worships false gods, lesser gods, idols, he destroys himself (Exodus 20:1–6).

[Primitive cultures] bow down to idols of wood and stone; the civilized man to idols of flesh and blood.[115]

We need to find much more time to reflect (Luke 2:19) amidst a complex, fast-moving, fast-changing lifestyle that hinders thoughtfulness and perspective. Information swamps knowledge, knowledge outruns wisdom, and outer smothers inner:

> But so many books thou readest,
> But so many schemes thou breedest,
> But so many wishes feedest,
> That thy poor head spins and turns.

Matthew Arnold, 'The Second Best'

Each of us can ask why, consciously or unconsciously, we avoid the sound of silence and the sounds of nature. A country's degree of politeness and manners depends partly on the density of population. In overcrowded cities, people crave personal space, and they walk the streets (and even the roads!) in their own private bubble. Disengaged from other people by our iPod or smartphone, we withdraw into solipsism and often feel no need to apologise when we bump into someone. It is the qualities of courtesy, consideration and restraint, which together enable people of different nations and customs to live and work productively and in relative safety.

The iPod insulates us from the daily din, but this aural cocoon, this self-administered anaesthetic, cuts out the sounds of real life. We miss the exultation of nature: what Keats celebrated as the 'little noiseless noise among the leaves, born

---

[115] George Bernard Shaw, *Maxims for Revolutionists* (Seattle, WA: CreateSpace, 2014) 'Idolatry'.

of the very sigh that silence heaves' ('I Stood Tip-toe Upon a Little Hill').

The media preach 'Input, input': this leads to indigestion of the mind and the senses. By contrast, Frank Buchman, founder of Moral Rearmament, used to exhort his colleagues to 'Absorb: absorb all that you see and hear and experience'. Virginia Woolf writes appreciatively of George Eliot's capacity to process: 'Everything to such a mind was gain. All experience filtered down through layer after layer of perception and reflection, enriching and nourishing.'[116]

An experience is not fully owned until it has been named and savoured.

> Music, when soft voices die,
> Vibrates in the memory;
> Odours, when sweet violets sicken,
> Live within the sense they quicken.

Percy Bysshe Shelley, 'Music, When Soft Voices Die'

We are in flight from silence, equating it (unconsciously) with emptiness, death and the demonic. Fear of our own shadow side has caused us to set up technology and mental noise as barriers in the way of contact with our experience.

People try to drown inner dissonance with a torrent of foamy words. Too many words, sounds, ideas, opinions and images invade us and overtax our power of assimilation. Words proliferate, are excreted, because they have lost their roots in creative silence, quiet awareness and discovery. The title of one of George Steiner's books says it all: *Real Presences: Is There Anything in What We Say?*

We share with others what was once considered private. And too much talk is usually accompanied by indiscretion. As

---

[116] Virginia Woolf, 'George Eliot' in *The Common Reader*, Volume I (London: Vintage, 2003) p.166.

George Herbert remarked: 'More have repented speech than silence' (*Outlandish Proverbs*, n. 682).

If we do not keep attuning to silence, we lose gravitas, we become lightweight. When deprived of the oxygen of silence, our true self suffocates. To a silent mind, truth and oneness are revealed. In sacred silence, the wholeness of man/woman pines for the holiness of God. The wisdom disclosed in silence is far beyond the fringes of speech.

In Hardy's novel *Under the Greenwood Tree*, there is a description of Geoffrey Day:

> 'He can keep silence well. That man's silence is wonderful to listen to.'
> 'There's so much sense in it. Every moment is brimming over with sound understanding.'

Silence is the foundation of all our meeting, connecting, conversing, communing – with God, self and our service to other people. If we have learned to be silent before the Word, we shall also balance our silence and our speech during the day.

Any action will be more creative when it stems from silence. As often as you remember, begin and end each activity with silence. And during the activity, sense the calming of deep silence. Speaking and behaving from your still point within enables you to be new and original in the living moment. In the light and sincerity of prayer, we refine our motives: pure silence leads to purer service.

Silence transforms a narrow, rational mind into a religious mind, a mind that knows where its true home is: in God. By constantly remembering the presence of God, a person is able to see and find the sacred heart of daily life.

St John of the Cross gave three guidelines for the protection of spiritual life: 'Wisdom enters through love, silence, and mortification':

> Alone and withdrawn from all forms, and in
> delectable tranquillity, the soul communes with God
> – for knowledge of Him is in divine silence.

St John of the Cross, *Spiritual Sentences and Maxims*

Silence provides a new start for this new day, and a fresh
and potentially loosening look at past and future. In prayer, we
hear our 'own past calling in [the] heart, as men far inland
sometimes hear the sea and fall weak with powerful, wonderful
regret, nostalgia'.[117]

In His goodness, God gives us potential, and scope without
limit, in silence – for the infinite refining of silence itself, and
thereby for deepening of character and the perfecting of love.
Love can be born (or reborn) in solitude. Love is the substance,
the very flesh, of the soul. Growth in the capacity to love
purifies the soul:

> Whatever comes to God is changed ... Since God
> changes such worthless things into himself, what do
> you suppose he does with the soul which he has
> honoured with his own image?[118]

Solitude

A loving relationship (or community) depends on individual
mutually treasured solitudes. Space and salvation are twins. 'I
love a broad margin to my life' is Thoreau's model for you and
me ('Sounds', *Walden*). In the Hebrew lexicon, *yasha* (salvation)
has several connotations: to be capacious; to make wide; to live
in abundance; to be placed in freedom; liberated (Psalm

---

[117] D. H. Lawrence, 'Poetry of the Present', in *Complete Poems*, p.181.
[118] Meister Eckhart, Edited by Bernard McGinn and Frank Tobin, *Meister Eckhart: Teacher and Preacher* (Paulist Press, 1986), Sermon on Acts 12:11, p.246.

18:19).[119] Isaiah 30:15 conveys the comfort of trusting, resting in God, confident in Him.

Jesus' name in Aramaic, 'Yeshua', implies wholeness; to be at one's ease; to be free to develop without hindrance; to bring into a spacious environment. Here we have a perfect summary of pure love: *To bring each other, with all gentleness, into His spacious/gracious presence.*

> We should place each action within a circumambient air of space – of leisure for the spirit of prayer. This would be like the ordering of a wise gardener, who carefully ensures that the young trees he plants have sufficient space, each from the other; and enough air in which to grow and expand.

Friedrich von Hügel, *The Life of Prayer*

At the heart of contemplation is solitude – not the solitude of isolation, but solitude as the foundation for true love. We can retain our inner solitude even when in the midst of groups or crowds.

True solitude – as an inner state – means living, loving and learning from the peace in one's soul. It unites us ever-more closely to all other people. Solitude is only genuine and truly worthy when it is inhabited (in vision, imagination, intercession, intent), and when it makes the whole world my habitation because it is His.

Like love and silence, solitude is not a once-and-for-all fixed state. Solitude is a daily encounter, living and creative; often lost and then regained after any wandering – a faithful centre (or home) to come back to. Solitude is always capable of more development: more trust, more depth, more loyalty to its vocation.

---

[119] These reflections on salvation stem from a conversation with the Reverend Paul Hunt and a follow-up letter from him.

A pure mind and heart are expressed in sincere wishes and kind actions. Each stage brings a nudge to continue: towards richer, ever-more alert loving, and responding to God's ongoing invitation (Luke 11:9–10). Solitude prepares the soul for heaven.

A mystic is at all times both a seeker and a seer: a seer, seldom as oracle or prophet, but as one who rejoices to find their Master's face in unlikely people, or in less promising events or settings. If you find it hard to love one of your neighbours or a member of your family or community, is this a sign that you need to love both God and your self more?

The purpose and goal of spiritual life is union with God, in steady awareness of His nearness and of our affinity with Him (Isaiah 26:3). By going apart, we become more 'a part of'. He who prays alone is never alone, for four reasons (John 16:32). First, God is ever available (Matthew 28:20; John 15:5). In pain or perplexity, we have Someone who accompanies us and shares our burden (Psalm 55:22), just as He bids us bear some of the burdens of others (Galatians 6:2). Second, at any hour of the day or night, millions of others will be praying at the same time. Third, our praying includes intercession: prayer can help us be more aware of the needs of others, and of how we might give support:

> If a little child's tears move you, they are windows to show you the vastness of the water: for not those tears only, but the whole world's tears, are quickening your compassion; and this child is but one who takes you by the hand and shows you the sorrows of mankind.[120]

Thus does prayer – deeply personal prayer – carry a community dimension and message. Lastly, our prayers are offered in

---

[120] Antoine de Saint-Exupéry, *The Wisdom of the Sands* (Chicago: University of Chicago Press, 1984).

concert with the one prayer of all God's faithful servants who have preceded us and prepared the way for us (Hebrews 12:1), those in heaven, singing the 'Everlasting Yea'.[121]

Those monks and nuns who make a healthy non-escapist choice to live on the margin of society do not thereby marginalise themselves. Rather, they see society with a clear eye, and are able to distinguish between the false and the true, in human needs and values. Profound simplicity: so easy to say, so hard to attain:

> A condition of complete simplicity
> (Costing not less than everything).

> T. S. Eliot, 'Little Gidding', *Four Quartets*

Community grounds us

The two core Christian commandments are that we should love God with all our heart and soul and mind; and, second, that we should love other people with as much warmth and energy as we have for ourself. There is a vital third requirement for spiritual life: that our devotion to Almighty God needs to be matched by our affection for other people. 'God gives His mercies to be spent; Your hoard will do your soul no good.'[122]

Hence true prayer does not end with an isolated person, prostrate with ecstasy because of his pious illumination. Having made wings from wax and feathers for their escape from imprisonment on Crete, Daedalus warned his son Icarus not to fly too close to the sun. But Icarus did, the wax melted, and he fell into the Aegean and drowned.

Virginia Woolf spoke about a silent retreat which enabled her to see to the bottom of the cup. For her – and for many – this was a troubling, even terrifying, experience.

---

[121] Carlyle's chapter title (9) in *Sartor Resartus*, Book II.
[122] William Cowper, hymn, 'God Gives His Mercies to Be Spent'.

For Elijah, the 'still, small voice' created such awe that he had to hide his face in his cloak.

> That sense of ruin, which is worse than pain
> That masterful negation and collapse
> Of all that makes me man; as though I bent
> Over the dizzy brink
> Of some sheer infinite descent;
> Or worse, as though
> Down, down forever I was falling through
> And needs must sink and sink
> Into the vast abyss. And, crueller still,
> A fierce and restless fight begins to fill
> The mansion of my soul.

Cardinal Newman, *The Dream of Gerontius*, I

In the spiritual life, as in all ways of living, we too need to avoid what Jung called 'one-sidedness' if we are to soar safely. This will mean a middle way – not being earthbound, nor living with our head in the clouds:

> Why didst thou leave the trodden paths of men
> Too soon and with weak hands, thou mighty heart
> Dare the unpastured dragon in his den?
> … oh, where was then
> Wisdom, the mirrored shield?

Percy Bysshe Shelley, 'Adonais', XXVII

A former supervisor of mine when I was training as a social worker said to me, 'Some of those who spend a disproportionate amount of time in the rarefied air of higher regions may be trying to dodge the need to look within … Natural before supernatural.'[123]

---

[123] Maurice Kidd, in conversation with RD, 22nd November 2005.

In order for us to keep safe and stay balanced, the flight of our spirit needs structure, foundation, roots and groundedness. Reflective Mary also needs to be an effective Martha. 'Nor strive to wind ourselves too high,' John Keble warns.[124]

The really holy person is also the most human: radiant in their love for God; worshipping Him, and also rejoicing in the poetry of life, open to life's *chiaroscuro* – light and shade, joy and sorrow, experiencing smiles and tears; not remote but, rather, generous and related; often humorous and always humane. True prayer (at set times) summons life-changing power (Philippians 4:13), and is completed when, in the spirit of Isaiah, you utter the words 'Send me' (Isaiah 6:8): to affirm others and kindle the sparks of hope. This is the ministry of encouragement: to delight in the growth, fulfilment and successes of other people.

In order to assist better in the self-realisation (or individuation) of another person, we need to see them both in their actuality and their potential. Instead of seeing them as just a sum of doubts and inhibitions, qualities and hopes, be aware of them as a God-endowed unit: affirm them in their wholeness. To an observer of such purified sight, people offer their true self.

In the triad, prayer and peace and service are all one. *Prayer* is constant communing with God. *Peace* comes from joy in His presence (Isaiah 26:3). And *service* is the fulfilment of religious vocation: to be a messenger of His love (James 1:22–25).

Thus purifying your intentions, all that you do – from waking and dressing, cleaning and shopping, until bedtime – will gain in depth and direction. And every experience (small or large) will be transformed into a special and spiritual experience. But 'special' does not necessarily equate with 'grandiloquent', as St Francis de Sales, in one of his letters, reminds us:

---

[124] John Keble, hymn, 'New Every Morning is the Love'.

Opportunities seldom present themselves for the practice of great and heroic virtues; but each day presents us with a thousand occasions for practising little virtues with a heroic spirit.[125]

Our deeds, more than our words, define us (Matthew 7:20). God will ask at Judgement Day not only, 'Did you behave?' but also, 'Were you a doer or only a talker?' For Bunyan, 'the heart of religion is the practice part'.[126]

Prayers

Dear God, may I worship You and only You. May I let no idol, however attractive – and no human being, however beautiful – distract or divert.

May I listen in prayerful silence for Your Holy Word, at each stage and each moment of the day, so that communing with You pervades my whole being, shaping every thought, every feeling, every activity.

May I be discerning: in the balance between words and silence; in my choice of words and length of speaking.

[125] C. F. Keeley, ed., *The Spiritual Maxims of St Francis de Sales* (New York: Harper, 1953) p.16.
[126] John Bunyan, *The Pilgrim's Progress* (London: Unwin Brothers, 1978) p.5.

V
Decisions

One of the desert fathers was asked, 'What is the work of a monk?'

He replied with one word: 'Discernment.'[128] This means developing a spiritual sense of good taste: discrimination in choosing only what conforms to love and to God, Who is the quintessence of Love.

For all that you are about to think or say or do, there is one sure test, one safe basis for proceeding: If I bring this to God, can I be certain that He will give His blessing? May His purposes and ours become as one. Then, and only then, are we truly free and at peace. St Thérèse: 'My God, I choose all that

---

[127] Fr Elder Mullan SJ, trans., *The Spiritual Exercises of St Ignatius*, 1909, 5th annotation.

[128] Columba Stewart, *The World of the Desert Fathers* (Oxford: SLG Press, 1986) p.36.

You will for me';[129] 'It is what He does that I love' (*Last Conversations*).

In our relationship with the Creator, our soul and our life as a whole (inner and outer) are like wax waiting for a seal: the firm/gentle impress of His will. Wax that is hard, dry and brittle is not receptive; it will not take the defining imprint of God's wishes. By contrast, wax that has melted can readily receive the stamp, the holy design.

> A voice comes yet more fleet –
> 'Lo! naught contents thee, who content'st
> not Me.'

> Francis Thompson, 'The Hound of Heaven'

May we conform to His every wish – *Fiat voluntas Tua* – devoting ourself to accomplishing His most holy will: responsive to the lightest touch of grace; matching promise with follow-through. In specific terms, this means seeing that your whole life stays on wise and godly lines: in faith and morals, in work and use of leisure time. You then translate your love of God into your love of people (John 13:34; 15:12; 1 Thessalonians 4:9; 1 Peter 4:8; 1 John 4:21):

> I ask Jesus to draw me into the refining fire of His love; to unite me so closely to Himself that He may live and act in me.

> St Thérèse of Lisieux, *Story of a Soul*

---

[129] St Thérèse of Lisieux, trans. T. N. Taylor, *Story of a Soul* (London: Burns & Oates, 1912) chapter 1.

Seeking God's will

The word 'hear' shares a Latin root with 'obedience'. Thus full hearing is both receptive and responsive – attention leading to appropriate action (James 1:22). We seek God because He is always seeking us. We need to distinguish carefully between a genuine wish to conform to God's will and a lurking or overt hope that God should fulfil our worldly desires.

To be truly free, we need to be 100 per cent obedient to every touch (or whisper) of the Spirit. Augustine calls this *tranquillitas ordinis*, the cosmic calm that comes from ordered/unified desires. Life as a single integrated act of service and worship of Almighty God. There is no other peace like this peace.

Seek God through His Word, allow it to search you and speak to you. Doing what God wishes, and in the way He wishes, together allow Him to direct and sculpt your life (Psalm 25:4–5). Pray that, even in the smallest duties, you may hear and understand and have the strength (Psalm 73:26) to obey, and manifest some glimpses of His love (Psalm 73:28). You receive grace and share grace – in that order.

Our safeguard in any action is integrity of mind and body, founded on singleness of heart (Psalm 32:11) and also on trust (Psalm 34:8). Harmony of wills, divine and human, restores us to wholeness. We can then 'look into the seeds of time, and say which grain will grow and which will not' (*Macbeth*, I iii). When we start out on the adventure of faith, we tend to ask God to support our plans. In time, we see that He wants us to listen to His call – to serve His holy purpose, and that this is where fruitfulness lies.

When making a vital decision, one sure foundation is to consult all aspects of your self – mind, feelings, intuition and soul (in prayer). Before every action we can ask in prayer, 'Will this bring me (and other people) closer to Thee?' As always, St

Ignatius – in *Spiritual Exercises* – expresses this consultation process perfectly:

> [I] ask of God our Lord to be pleased to move my will and put in my soul what I ought to do regarding the thing proposed, so as to promote more His praise and glory.[130]

Spiritual poise has two aspects: being where you are (inwardly as well as outwardly) in a balanced way, and being ready to move with ease in any direction which God indicates, ready to do what will be most for 'the glory of his Divine Majesty, and for the salvation of my soul' (St Ignatius, *Spiritual Exercises*).[131]

For decision-making, the best criterion is *peace*. According to the guidelines for Jesuits, an aspirant can imagine they have decided on a particular course of action and then try to hear a fore-echo of the future. Will this action (or friendship) bring peace – to self and others? Will it honour the trust God has in me? May I assess the whole situation and its possibilities in the light of truth, and behave with the help and guidance of grace. Rollo May points out in *Man's Search for Himself* that each choice which leads to greater freedom enables us to decide more freely in future.

Consulting all parts of self

Wholeness in decision-making depends on the range and balance of our input: from God, in prayer; from significant others, in discussion; and from all parts of one's self, in thorough inner dialogue – my hopes and my fears, my will and my values, my soul. Then in time all the factors and all the

---

[130] Fr Mullan, trans., *Spiritual Exercises*, Prelude for Making an Election, 'The First Way', III.
[131] Ibid, Fourth Day, 'Three Pairs of Men'.

sources form a Gestalt. We need to wait for this crystallising moment.

> How will you know the pitch of that great bell?
> ... Listen close
> Till the right note flows forth, a silvery rill.

George Eliot, *Middlemarch*

As we mature, our centre of gravity (moral and emotional) moves from outside to inside. We then come to see that our first and best authority is *within*. Our intuitive side is worthy of special respect. Its promptings, often indirect and allusive, may convey a vital warning or a life-changing affirmation. Listen also to instincts. D. H. Lawrence cautions us to beware haste, impulse or compulsion:

> So the only thing to do, is to keep still, to hold still at any price;
> To learn to contain ourselves.
> So that in the long pause the instincts can reassert themselves
> and our intuition can come to life and give us direction.[132]

When we set out to make a major decision, the first step is the most vital, as it is in any outer or inner journey. Here we need the discipline of pausing, so that we do not automatically select what our first impulse tells us to do.

Before we look at choice and content, we should focus on tone and pace: the calmer and more measured I am – throughout the whole time and process of exploring, and allowing for time constraints – the wiser and more original my

---

[132] D. H. Lawrence, 'What is to be Done?' in 'Uncollected Poems' in *Complete Poems* (Harmondsworth: Penguin, 1977).

decision is likely to be, and the more economical of both time and energy.

To put this in practical terms, it is best not to be prematurely extroverted about a dilemma, such as by reaching for ready-made or tailor-made solutions – or, indeed, any solutions at this early stage – in the (perhaps vain) hope that this will stop the problem from hounding the mind. No trying to resolve a challenge by a frantic rush from book to book, or door to door, before we have listened to the original question widely, with care, and with deep attention.

The longer we wait – and can afford to wait – the more coherent, the more fluent, and perhaps unexpected, the interim or final answer. Then we will have moved from solution to discovery. Live the question. Love the question.

It is vital, first, to be open to, to listen out for, all the smaller signs and signals we receive – from our inner and outer life – which may help guide a dilemma, a relationship, a choice, a decision or a plan. Then we owe it both to ourself and these ally-messengers to heed and give due weight to what they want to tell us. I long ago lost count of the number of divorced clients – in my consulting room over the years – who have moaned, 'I had real doubts about him [or her or us] right up to our wedding day, but I always ignored or overrode them.'

Intuition is visionary: it sees round the corner of our life, or round several turnings. A man's faculty can be natural or developed; a woman tends to have easier access, with more frequent pointers, more intense flashes. Neither gender has a monopoly on accuracy. Intuition comes with a warning: 'Handle with extreme care'. It can hit the bullseye or its arrow can miss the target by yards. Therefore – even at best and however worthy of our high respect – intuition needs to be seen as but one member of our inner board of management, our personal panel of consultants.

A colleague of intuition is our gut instinct, a specialist not always given its due in our culture and in these times, when education emphasises analytic left-hemisphere thinking and a rational, researched approach.

The wisdom of the body – especially in and from the mid-region – is part of our genetic inheritance, long predating our acquisition of knowledge and our gaining of life experience. Here are some guidelines for decision-making:

- Listen to gut instincts before doing systematic rational analysis.

- Limit how much information you read and assess. Too much will swamp instinctual feelings; blurring clarity and perspective.

- Listen carefully to your sense of timing. Is this the right time for this meeting, enterprise, relationship …?

- Cultivate detachment towards the options, especially early in your enquiry. We can so easily persuade ourself that the facts really do fit our preferred outcome.

- Get your own orientation before asking and sharing. If we consult others too early, we may become bemused by conflicting advice, and we may detour from our own best course in order to satisfy the expectations that others have of us. How easily we become slave to image, and how fast we run to protect it.

- Trust your unconscious. It can work and process at high speed. It helps us select major strands and criteria. It brings all data to a Gestalt.

- The more aligned you are on the vertical plane – with God the Creator and your true self – the clearer the direction of your life journey.

The spiritual value of any action is found in answering the three-part question: Will it hinder or foster continuous prayer;

my praise of God and attentiveness to Him; and sensitivity to the deepest needs of my neighbour?

Context

Willed overload blunts the quality of our discernment; it dims the clarity of our decision-making; it tapers our perspective, and gives us much less time and space (inner and outer) to learn from the lessons of the past. Good decision-making needs the consultation and the coordination of all one's faculties. It also thrives on a sure sense of direction – in love, in work and career, and in personal ethics/values/behaviour. Strategy aids clarity. We need to make a careful assessment of our actual circumstances, our personal resources and our talents before making any major decision about our direction of life. God will not ask the impossible, and He makes use of our natural gifts.

Discerning how best and where best to direct our energy and our talents is as vital as assessing our energy level. Skilled use of our powers is the ultimate in fulfilment. And when we are fulfilled (when we are feeling enthusiastic), we find we can do even more than before.

I am most likely to make wise decisions when I am feeling centred: that state of poise and relaxation when my body, my energy, all personal resources, my prayer life and my ultimate purpose in life are coordinated, in balance, heeded and respected, and thus now available – for my self, for other people, for serving Him now and in the future.

Decision-making thrives on more inwardness (*Innigkeit*). One day the Mother Superior of a religious order put a question to Pope Pius XII: 'Holy Father, I have pastoral charge for women engaged in active life. What is the main advice I should give them?'

The Pope replied, 'The interior life.' He paused. 'The interior life, a very deep interior life.'

Rilke concurs:

> Consider yourself and your feeling ... if you are
> wrong after all, the natural growth of your inner life
> will lead you slowly and with time to other insights.
> Leave to your opinions their own quiet undisturbed
> development, which, like all progress, must come
> from deep within and cannot be pressed or hurried
> by anything. Everything is gestation and then
> bringing forth. To let each impression and each germ
> of a feeling come to completion wholly in itself, in
> the dark, in the inexpresssible, the unconscious,
> beyond the reach of one's own intelligence, and
> await with deep humility and patience the birth-hour
> of a new clarity: that alone is living the artist's [or
> mystic's] life: in understanding as in creating.[133]

One of the saints – was it Francis de Sales? – was asked
how long he prayed in the morning. We can all profit from his
reply: 'At least for one hour. But when I am very busy – two
hours.' How much time would he allow for prayer were he
alive today? How long do you give? How long do you need?

Risk

The right road, the Godward road, is often the middle way of
prudence and moderation. But God sometimes points us –
strengthened by Him – to dangerous, and personally
challenging, routes.

Decision needs courage. Decision entails risk and
responsibility: to a greater or lesser extent, I am putting my self
and my future on the line. The results of my decision may

---

[133] Rainer Maria Rilke, trans. M. D. Herter Norton, *Letters to a Young Poet*,
(London: W.W. Norton & Co, 1934) Viareggio (near Pisa), 23rd April 1903
pp.22-25.

disappoint me or others, or both. We can mitigate this fear somewhat by resolving to listen and learn from the outcome so that, whatever happens, there will be some current or future gain. Deeper listening involves becoming more aware of my subliminal (and often less edifying) motives. The full life means risk. Many decisions are based on a balancing of risk.

> The trouble is: if you do not risk anything, you risk more.

> Erica Jong

Decision is drenched with pathos, because the content and implications of a commitment cannot be foreseen. During one's involvement, they positively unfold or negatively unravel. From our decisions, the self emerges and is constellated. One of the special truths of spiritual life is that real freedom comes from total commitment – to a person and/or worthy work.

Trust the sense of rightness: 'This is really *me*. This is my destined path.' Above all, we need to trust in the confirming messages of our prayer life; and the signs of our journey that speak of flow, and of cooperation with our intention and our goal. We can almost always feel safe about a course of action if it fulfils – fully meets – two tests. First, are my motives clean? Second, is my sole intention to honour, praise and glorify God's holy Name (Proverbs 18:10)? Will this action fulfil His wish? Is it in accord with eternal truth? Actions become dangerous when they are autonomous, unrelated to Spirit.

Solitude of the desert or mountain-top safeguards all our activity and experience in the marketplace (Micah 4:2): detachment gives wisdom to involvement.

Timing

Discernment helps us read the difference between what is really God's will for us and what is self-will in the disguise of being part of His plan. The secret is in the waiting. But what is the type, tone, tenor – disposition, the *complexion* – of our waiting? Is it eager yet relaxed? Is it trending, tendentious? Or are we totally at His service, poised and trusting?

In ancient times, and at all levels of society, people had a lively sense of timing. By reflection, and by consulting a sage or an oracle, they wanted to know, 'Is this the propitious moment for a potentially pivotal action, or for making a major decision?' By contrast (with the recent exception of Churchill), we have all but lost our feel for the appointed (or the auspicious) hour. We need to balance our urge to arrive with the capacity for watchful, creative waiting. 'Ripeness is all', *King Lear*, V ii. We need to await the moment when the personal and the collective intersect:

> There is a tide in the affairs of men,
> Which, taken at the flood, leads on to fortune;
> Omitted, all the voyage of their life
> Is bound in shallows and in miseries.
> On such a full sea we are now afloat,
> And we must take the current when it serves,
> Or lose our ventures.

Julius Caesar, IV iii

Instead of trying to second-guess or determine the future, focus on present realities. By being fully absorbed in 'what is now', the 'what will be' is more likely to be fruitful. This entails paying more attention to the question (or choice or dilemma) than to the possible answer. The best result will arise from our constant examination and refining of the original question. Or – to vary the imagery – focus on walking over the threshold, and allow God to reveal what is on the other side of the door. Much of life (both the pleasurable and the painful) cannot be foreseen (Psalm 31:14–15), and so God bids us be more trusting and prayerful.

A personal ethic

Our joyful yielding to Him does not rob us of our freedom; it purifies our use of it: 'The more virtue, the more liberty' (Coleridge, *The Table Talk*, 15th June 1833). Our ethics are the collective results of many large and small decisions. In one of his most uplifting poems, Wordsworth says that the Happy Warrior 'makes his moral being his prime concern'. And televangelist, Bob Schuller, counsels, 'Never take the world's minimum as your maximum.'

To be genuine, coherent and effective, ethics must be owned. We own our values, we live our insights, when we have (or are allowed) the time for testing and the space for discovery. What we do and how we do it will reflect our own style. To follow someone else's line is to fail to take account of the uniqueness of your situation, the subtle nuances and complexity of which only you are fully aware. Only by deciding on a course of conduct for ourselves will we be prepared to take responsibility if it turns out to have negative consequences, and improve our approach next time. Only a fully owned decision carries conviction in the follow-through.

The most effective precepts are the ones we believe in and fully own: because we see that they reduce suffering – to self, to other people and to God Himself, and (from a positive standpoint) because they foster peace, enhance joy and develop our bond of communion with Him.

Probity is not by nature prissy, nor need rectitude be rigid. Classical Greece saw moral goodness as the highest form of beauty. The principles of human morality, like the processes of nature, come within a universal order established by the

Creator, to be recognised by those who have eyes to see and ears to hear. Ethical precepts are to a contemplative what the North Star is to a navigator – a sign, a direction, a goal (even if never fully attained).

The framework to uphold the stature and structure of our life can be strong yet simple, like a trellis which supports a climbing rose. The purpose of the trellis is not to restrict, but to allow the rose to flourish, to be itself. Our ethics are not primarily a rod to admonish us: their purpose is to help us be free – free to learn, free to love:

> I say more: the just man justices;
> Keeps grace: that keeps all his goings graces;
> Acts in God's eye what in God's eye he is.

Gerard Manley Hopkins, 'As kingfishers catch fire'

What happens when morality/conscience/obedience sleep? In an RE class a teacher was asked about the meaning of sin. She paused for a moment, seeking a vivid example. Noticing a vase on the windowsill, she took out a lily, a perfect bloom, and showed it to the class. 'Has God made anything more beautiful?' she asked. Every child agreed. Then – in an almost operatic gesture – the teacher threw the lily to the floor and crushed the flower underfoot.

The children shrieked, 'But, Miss, *why* did you do that?'

'Because this is how we feel if we disappoint our heavenly Father.'

God makes a treble call and claim: that we contemplate His ways and obey His laws (Psalm 1:2; Psalm 19); that we behave uprightly in all our tasks, doing justice to daily life, our own needs and those of others; and that in our 'humble walk with Him' we respect – but see beyond – daily externals (Micah 6:8). How wide, how long is our perspective? We can always ask ourself, 'How much will this really matter to me next week?' 'Am I turning small matters into Big Issues?'

Morality is about fairness, respect and being sensitive, as well as codes of right and wrong. Behaving well means tone as well as text: the how is as vital as the what. A test to discern whether a potential or existing friendship is wholesome is to ask oneself, 'Will it (or does it) bring both of us closer to God?' A real friend elicits my best self and theirs. 'Will this action (or friendship) bring peace – to self and others? Will it honour the trust God has in me?'

> True friendship comes from God, and tends towards God.

> St Francis de Sales, *Introduction to the Devout Life*

Mistakes

A combination of God's indications and our own perception will point out any mistake or failure. And our God – in His love and mercy, and ever-readiness to provide healing to a soul that is sincerely penitent and contrite – wills us to make amends. He will help us regain our faith (and our foothold) so as to get back on course, and He will guide us as to the best path (Isaiah 48:17).

Even if we have taken many wrong turns, if we know where we want to go, there is a route from here to there. One of the infinite number of God's graces to us – and a sign of His wondrous power and mercy – is that, out of our mistakes, He fashions our search for truth and integrity; out of flawed and broken pieces, He mends a vessel to serve and irrigate His kingdom (Isaiah 40:4–11). Restoration brings peace.

When we look back on past experiences and our less-mature self, we see how the divine potter (Isaiah 64:8; Ephesians 2:10) repairs us in unexpected ways. Now we can see more of our main routes and their byways, all the stages by which He has led and brought us to Himself, and we bless His hidden work in us (Romans 11:33).

With acceptance, lit by grace, perplexing times can bring us closer to God's presence, and increase both our trust in His providence and our dependence on His protection: 'in quietness and in trust shall be your strength' (Isaiah 30:15).

We fall and we rise. God bids us cherish our frail humanity. Remember that the only real mistakes are those we do not learn from. Major or minor setbacks give us a chance to express our faith in Him, and manifest character by resilience and speed of recovery – emotional, spiritual and philosophical. We show our character by our patience in the face of relatively small repeated jarrings.

If we can accept this premise, we need to show those who suffer that we have faith in their dignity, their stature and their resilience in the face of adversity. May we never resort – often to ease the observer's pain – to platitude or facile palliative. We and they learn most about struggle existentially, in heart and gut, rather than by intellectualising real darkness from which there is no escape. When someone I know is being tested, I shall encourage, embolden. 'Hear, hear' to their emerging courage is far better than the lazy pat and patter of 'There, there'.

Humility means knowing your limits and weaknesses; but, at the same time, being thankful for personal gifts and talents, abilities, strengths. Indeed, knowing your own worth gives you the confidence to admit when you have bungled, and then recover your quality of attention.

I am reminded of a piano recital given by Richter. He had played four or five bars of the first movement of a late great Schubert sonata (the B flat). When he realised that his tempo was faster than he had intended, he stopped playing, paused, and then began the first movement again. Only a true master – young or mature – has the confidence to apologise, and the alertness to see so quickly the need to apologise.

In a non-egoistic way, continuously self-listen, self-accept, self-forgive, self-honour. You are then more likely to treat other people in the same way.

Prayers

Relying on both Your overt gifts and hidden graces to me, I offer at Your throne all current tasks and callings, all decisions and dilemmas, and also my future direction. May each activity be preceded by prayer and dedication: 'To proclaim Your glory.'

In loving conformity with Your Will and holy wisdom, grant me, O God, the grace to hear and to heed all of Your wishes. And may I have the strength to fulfil them.

United with You, in deep confiding intimacy – and in a spirit of complete faith, total abandonment, entire love – I now offer my whole self to You; and hearken to all that Your sweet voice shall say to me, in listening obedience.

VI
Support and Self-Examination

He who insists on being left to himself, without a director to guide him, is like an unowned tree by the wayside; however fruitful it may be, the travellers pick its fruit, and none of it ripens.

St John of the Cross, Spiritual Sentences and Maxims

When the Spirit moves you, you might consider going on a retreat. Periodically joining a group of like-minded people provides an opportunity to encourage one another and gain (or maintain) impetus in the following aspects of spiritual life:

God
Deepen faith
Spend time with God, receiving His love
Regenerate/improve prayer life

Self
Inspire you to work on developing chosen virtues
Yield your time to His time-eternity
Consider your vocation

Others
Enhance recollectedness, when in the midst of activity
Enrich witness to God's bounteous love
Renew a spirit of service to God, our Redeemer

On a long-term and regular basis, perhaps once a month, it may be helpful to find a spiritual director, someone who is both congenial and experienced, in life as well as in spiritual direction (Ecclesiasticus 6:14–16). The many benefits of having a spiritual director include deepening prayer; space to consider one's relationships with others; listening to which areas of your life give energy and life, and which, deplete, confuse; and finding out what is hindering us from grounding and incarnating our good intentions.

Spiritual direction can ensure that the totality of life is lived under God's guiding hand, with no qualification (overt or lurking): 'Of course I bow to Your holy will, O God, provided that I thereby get my way.'

Aside from speaking with your spiritual director and your confessor, it is wise to be reserved about speaking of your spiritual journey and view of your progress – careful as to when, to whom and why. Edith Wharton warns: 'Blessed are the pure in heart for they have so much more to talk about' (*John O'London's Weekly*, 10th April 1932). Prayer is both intimate (because relational) and creative (because fruitful), and so – like creativity and human intimacy – prayer needs privacy. The hiddenness of creativity is symbolised by the planting of seed in soil, the baking of bread in an oven, an egg in a nest, an embryo in the womb, a writer or composer in their study. Our best personal gifts (or attributes) need the most protection by being modest and avoiding overexposure.

Self-examination

We can ask ourselves from time to time a series of questions. The aim is to face and know reality, to learn and discover the hidden truth about ourselves: what we resist, persists. What do I hear (or see) as discordant with my true self, my home key?

> As hair which is frequently combed is untangled and is more easily combed upon all occasions, so is it with the soul which frequently examines its thought, words, and works, doing all things for the love of God.

St John of the Cross, *Spiritual Sentences and Maxims*

Here is the outline of a self-inventory (using the triad in extended form) with some of the questions you could ask yourself. Be your own diagnostician.

God

- Do I look for, and find, my rest, my relaxation, in my Saviour (Matthew 11:28)? Is my deep contentment in Him (1 Timothy 6:6)?

- How thankful am I to God for the talents He has given me? Do I express my thanks by using all my gifts in the service of God for His glory and His honour (1 Timothy 6:16)?

- How willing am I to be drawn into God's plan?

- Do I give of myself to other people in reverence – with a tone of joy?

- Do I place all my energies, all my personal resources, at the feet of the Almighty, remembering that they are God-given, and thus wishing that they be used, and only used, to worship Him, and witness?

- With purity of intention, am I doing everything for God, and with God, and solely from my love of Him?

- Do I have faith in His promise of present, and eventual, abundance (John 10:10)?

- Do I really believe – with my limited spiritual vision, and when faced with a troubled world – that God, in His good time, will work and interweave all events for our eventual good and well-being?

- In times of sacred silence, do I renew my basic attitude of being mouldable, totally abandoned to the slightest whisper of God's wishes?

- And then – when I am in the very midst of the rough and tumble, all the ups and downs of life – do I place all activities in the hands of God, working only to delight my Maker and Sovereign, and devote all that I do to His good pleasure?

Self

- Do I put all of my trust in God? And do I rely on His plenitude (1 Corinthians 2:12), as Source of strength, physical and emotional?

- Do I have a good, working balance of human will and divine grace (Mark 14:36)?

- How often do I remember to praise God for His constant generosity? And how often do I remember to thank other people?

- For how much of each day am I a well-focused person?

- Am I in tune with my own nature and innate rhythms – mental, physical, emotional and spiritual?

- Do I listen for, respect and heed my own deeper instincts and intuitions?

- How God-centred am I? Is God my first love?

- Do I give centrality to prayer life? Am I a continuous adorer of my God?

- Do I live at a self-willed pace, or at God's wished pace for me?

- How secure are my values, in both principle and practice?

- How firm, how straight, is my aim, my sense of purpose and direction (Matthew 6:22)? And how open am I to God's directing?

- God knows my intentions, both the overt and the hidden. Am I sincere? Is my motivation clear or cloudy?

- How friendly a person am I? And how warm?

- Am I a welcoming person? And am I easily approachable – especially by people in need?

- Do I show empathy and understanding?

- Do I keep a watchful eye over any negative impulses in myself?

- How open am I to appropriate risk-taking? How bold, how daring, am I? How quick in response to wholesome opportunities?

- How would I rate my basic attitude in the spectrum of pessimistic – optimistic?

- How adaptable, how flexible, am I? And how do I regard, and cope with, change? Do I see change as threat or as opportunity?

- How well do I face problems and difficulties, and loss, in its many and varied forms?

- How much importance do I give to all aspects of health and body care?

- How buoyant and well founded is my self-esteem?

- Am I ever envious of other people: their wealth, looks or abilities?

- Do I respond to the whole diversity of life: the poetry, the pathos, the poignancy?

- How rich is my humour; how wide my sense of fun?

- In short, do I (all of me: in my most secret thoughts and emotions, in my words and in all my deeds) lead a truly sanctified lifestyle – in public and in private?

Others

- Do I have a sense of the inherent delicacy of all life – human, animal and plant?

- Am I as proficient at listening as I am at talking?

- What can I do now to improve, to increase, my listening skills?

- Am I an encourager of other people?

- How open, how accepting, am I towards the uncertainties of the future? To life's ambiguities?

- How open am I to people who are different from the way I am? Do I set any limits as to who is my neighbour?

- How tuned in am I to the sensitivities (and deep – often unarticulated – needs) of other people?

- Do I give others a second chance? And a third?

- How ready and willing am I to love the less attractive: those who are offhand, unresponsive, unreliable, self-seeking, unkind (Matthew 5:44–48; Luke 6:27, 32)? Do I realise that I need the infusion of God's empowering to help me to love people such as these?

- Do I see that God, in His infinite wisdom, may be sending people to me for my greater good – my purification, and my growth as one of His love-channels?

- Do I keep in mind that every person was created in God's image (Genesis 1:26–27; Colossians 3:10), and thus that I am called to love everyone 'in God'?

- Am I anxious to rush the inbuilt pace of self-disclosure? Do I thus not allow friendships to evolve naturally, with enough breathing space?

- How do I cope with partings, separation (temporary or permanent) or grief?

- How do I cope with life's pauses, times of aloneness, ageing, ill health?

- Am I prepared to stay loyal and committed during ups and downs: the natural cycle of all relationships?

- How prompt am I to help to bear some of the burdens – practical, physical, emotional – of others (Galatians 6:2)? Do I keep in mind that a burden shared is a burden halved?

- Am I ever too proud to receive?

- Do I always remember that – in order to love fully – I shall need to maintain a vivid, and vivifying, life of prayer, and ensure that I remain always conscious of being in the divine presence?

The art of self-improvement is to take a long view and to mend or amend in stages, working on only a small cluster of issues at any one time. After examination, action – in a spirit of self-patience and prayer. Metropolitan Anthony is helpful and eloquent on self-patience:

> If you were given an ancient painting or an icon – badly damaged by time, by circumstances, by carelessness or evil intent – you can look at what is left of the original beauty. After looking at this painting very attentively for a long time, you can begin to repair the damage.
>
> When you start, be grateful for the beauty which survives. This will inspire you. The image of God cannot be destroyed – it *is* still there.

Each of us is like a damaged icon, but we are still an icon, we are still all-precious to our Creator. We are – and shall always be – significant, and of stature, in His eyes; and it is in co-operation with Him that we can begin to see the beauty which He always sees (and has created), the shining beauty of His own image.[134]

Prayers

May I not be self-contained, but more thankful to You, and more gracious and generous to my neighbours.

May I see my whole life as an offering, an oblation, unceasing in my praise and thanksgiving; with every aspect (small or large) sacramental, because inspired, produced and sustained by Your all-hallowing touch, which enriches and enhances, and makes this our life already an altar of eternal Life.

May nothing be too large for me to do this day for You. And nothing too small. May I live and work only for Your pleasure and Your glory. May I be ever mindful that You are always worthy of thanks and praise. I must take nothing for granted: even the seemingly trivial daily duties and recurring actions are to be done with You and for You.

---

[134] 'How to Live With Oneself', talk given in Effingham, Surrey, 1989.

SELF

I
Self-awareness: Facing your Shadow

Thou art like the day,
but thou art also like the night ...
for the strongest light throws also the darkest
shadow.

D. H. Lawrence, 'Climb Down, O Lordly Mind'

Costly growth

Wisdom begins with – is founded on – self-knowledge. One evening, when Socrates was expounding on this theme, a young man asked him, 'Do you know yourself?'

Socrates smiled as he replied, 'I know what I am not.'

All real progress in spiritual life is, first, an inner creation filled with joy in the Infinite. But in this life, joy is usually tinged with – and often preceded by – pain. Crisis is often a creative jolt or goad: some event or person or cramping pattern forces us to flex, test our strength and flee or battle to become *one* – integrated, free and authentic; with better focus, more energy, and our own true voice.

Every form of growth is costly – to body, emotions and soul – and none more so than the attainment of personhood. We may have to separate ourselves in some way from persons who have an emotional grip over us, from relationships of undue dependency or possessiveness. Am I prepared to give up some degree of safety and comfort in the search for truth? Am

I willing to experience darkness in the hope of light; emptiness or even rejection because of His promise of abundance?

The more single-minded our commitment to the Way of Truth, the more alert and sensitive we become to any thought, desire, word or gesture – actual or imminent – that is discordant with our best self. We each need to identify our own chromatic notes.[135] This noticing – after, during and, if possible, before (to prevent) – is accompanied by adjusting and amending, quelling and learning.

St Philip Neri, founder of the Oratorians, was often involved in quarrels. One day he decided that this tendency must stop, once for all. He ran to the chapel, fell prostrate before the statue of Christ and begged the Lord to free him from anger. More hopeful now, he walked out of the chapel. The first person he met was a brother he liked, but for the first time this brother was unpleasant towards him. Philip retaliated angrily. Now red with rage, he met another of the brothers, with whom he had also (as in the first encounter) always had a cordial relationship. But this brother also spoke to Philip in a gruff way. Philip, in despair, ran back to chapel. Again he fell down in front of the statue, and pleaded, 'O Lord, did I not beseech you to free me from my anger?'

And the Lord replied, 'Yes, Philip. And for this reason, I am multiplying the occasions for you to learn!'

Our anger can be a creative spur to self-observation, self-knowing, learning and change. When we watch the mind more closely, and the subversive stir of negative emotions, we are compelled to re-examine our habits, our defensiveness, the collusive roles we adopt and our conditioned responses – such as repression, projection and acting out.

Many of these patterns – of thought, of feeling and of behaviour – took hold in us (took hold *over* us) during the first months and years of our childhood. They erupt so fast, and are

---

[135] A chromatic note is outside the main scale, but does not imply a move away from the key for that scale. Like a chromatic note, a hindrance is a diversion.

so deeply ingrained, that they are hard to see and work with, let alone dismantle and disempower. In order to be fully in the present – in silence or in encounter – I need to be accommodated to my past, not dictated to by it. The aim is to be emotionally up to date, shored up, integrated: not carrying unworked-through luggage of the past into the living present.

If I am still in the grip of the experiences of earlier life, I behave from old/stuck patterns, and I speak from worn-out/frayed scripts. We need to incarnate our letting go, making it quite specific. Inner scripts and labels limit us, whether self-given or stuck on us by other people. A label says, 'I am this; I am not that.' An inner script says, 'I always ...' or, 'I can never...'

Self-observation of negative (and hitherto automatic) tendencies is the first step on the road of change. Maintaining a false self-concept absorbs so much valuable energy – spiritual, mental, emotional and physical. Because of the body–mind link, emotional blocks become somatised, resulting in rigid body armour. This ongoing, often subtle, self-knowing, this expanding of the God-given self, frees our mind, heart and senses to enjoy – and fully engage with – whoever or whatever is in front of us now. Our participation in life will be richer, our touch and decisions more sure.

Psychotherapy and religion

Psychological and spiritual work support and reinforce each other. Some parts of us are stagnant. Psychology unblocks, frees and opens out potential. The spiritual life gives meaning, direction, dimension, and grace for transformation. Though the journeys of psychotherapy and prayer are complementary, they are not coterminous: they do not cover identical terrain, nor do they have identical goals.

Psychotherapy can help you see why you keep repeating unhelpful patterns of behaviour that prevent you from incarnating your best intentions. But insight does not automatically translate into transformation – although it can help. The life of prayer yields insight too, but it will also train you in – and provide grace for – behavioural change (virtue), and increase in love. Psychology will help you to 'be yourself' (an important start): Christ invites you to '*Be Me*' (an *alter Christus* – to be His hands, feet and smile, and a bearer of His presence to those you meet). Paradoxically, in this surrender to God and yielding to your neighbour, you will be more your self than ever before – simpler, more unified: 'whoever loses his life for my sake will find it' (Matthew 16:25).

This fullness begins now: in holy silence – as well as in all-loving, self-spending action – we are healed and remade: 'For love uncurtained Heaven to let thee live' (Keats, *To Homer*).

Good self-esteem

The word 'ego' is widely used to describe an inflated self, with much more image than substance: a precarious state or condition, subject to sudden deflation by the pricks of fate and even by the taunt of gossip, the nudge-nudge of spite, smear and scoff.

All through this book, I use the word 'ego' (and its derivatives: ego-driven, egoistic, egotistic) in this now-usual pejorative sense. However, as a psychotherapist I use 'ego' in a wholly positive way. In its technical sense, ego is a vital part of character structure. In the consulting room I call it 'the manager (or coordinator) of the self'. The ego regulates the competing pressures of primitive *id* drives (for food, sex and satisfaction), and moderates the imperious pressures of the *super-ego* (or conscience, which contains the internalised and often exaggerated prohibitions and commands of parents, teachers and other authority figures). Thus, in this clinical usage, the stronger and more robust your ego, the less ego(t)istic you tend – or feel the need – to be.

We have a paradox here. If my ego is strong and steady enough, I have no ruling need to defend or sell my self. From this firm base, I can be more unselfish – generous in motive and altruistic in service. I have more to give – in energy and in range – and without undue fear of depletion. 'It is no longer I who live but Christ who lives in me' (Galatians 2:20). In other words, I try not to live in a narrow track or groove. More and more I live with God, and for Him and my neighbour.

In order to be authentic, I must not be overly influenced by the expectations of society, nor by friends, family, or colleagues. To whom (or to Whom) am I accountable? Where and to whom do I look for values and affirmation? How much of my satisfaction with life depends on what other people think about me and say about me? How much time do I spend in my comfort zone, my limited mindset, spouting my fixed notions, opinions and positions?

> It is great to shake off the trammels of the world and of public opinion ... and become the creature of the moment.

> Hazlitt, *On Going a Journey*

To be mature is to be selective. What I say and what I do is thus suited for *this* occasion, relevant for *this* person, and appropriate in content, tone and volume. The aim is to have a wide palette of choice: about how I think, speak, behave and relate. Then I am a free agent, alert and supple in the living moment. And I will have a surer touch – in word, gesture and manner: just as a painter, after each brushstroke, consults his own personal set of criteria for what works and what does not.

The way forward is to build a bridge across the wide – or widening – gulf that separates inner and outer life, the intention and the behaviour. In specific terms, if you wish to attain synthesis, pay more attention, much more, to your inner life (Mark 1:35). And see God as Source and Centre of all you say and all you do. Solitude, and then (relative) inner peace during activity, are the conditions necessary for being centred. Wordsworth describes his hero as he 'Whom neither shape of danger can dismay, nor thought of tender happiness betray' ('Character of the Happy Warrior').

Clarity in values and personal standards allows for flexibility of both perception and movement. One of nature's best models for flexibility is a palm tree. Certain species can survive hurricane winds of up to 150mph by bending almost to the ground. We can be both sturdy and also dynamic. Being strong and secure in my integrity, I do not need to adopt fixed or defensive positions. I can hear and receive your opinion, your truth, without fearing that mine is under threat. Disagreement can be adversarial or creative. The tone can be hostile or mutually respectful: we can agree to disagree.

Facing and integrating your shadow

We each have 'an equivalent centre of self, whence the lights and shadows must always fall with a certain difference' (George Eliot, *Middlemarch*, chapter 21). Self-awareness crucially entails facing (and working at) all parts of our self – the dark or shadowy as well as the light, the fragile as well as the strong. Only in this way, only by heroic self-truth, can we even hope to avoid (or reduce) the subversive and scheming influence of repression.

If parts of the self are split off and unacknowledged, they can become an internal (and infernal) fifth column, sabotaging our best efforts. Freud's 'return [or revenge] of the repressed' was one of his most original contributions.[136] The less we acknowledge our shadow side, the more potently it undermines our relationships. (Our shadow side contains all aspects of our

---

[136] Sigmund Freud, trans. James Strachey, *New Introductory Lectures*, Lecture 31 (Harmondsworth, Penguin, 1964) pp.88–113.

personality and experience that we have not yet accessed. But there is hope if we dare to confront these unconscious elements, for under the dark – or behind or above – is light.)

Jung always underlined that becoming fully ourselves – 'individuation' was his term – must include the integration of our shadow side. Cut off, alienated parts of our self come back to haunt us and those near us, including those we love. By allowing the darker side of our self and psyche to emerge into consciousness, we avoid a one-sided persona; only presenting to the world what we consider acceptable, and causing a rift between the outer self and the inner reality. Our freedom reflects the unity, the coherence, of our interior life, and a gradual growing oneness between what I espouse and how I live.

We need to find a working balance between various parts of the self. Remember Luke 11:17: 'a divided household falls.' This is true of a family, an institution, a nation and also of an individual person. The classic example of hypocrisy is Tartuffe, who pretended to be a saint but never had the will to become one. He played the role of a saint not because he sincerely sought truth, but in order to inherit the fortune of Orgon.[137]

I cannot be intimate with another person until I see, face and embrace the whole of my self. 'The shadows are as important as the light,' explained Jane Eyre after Mr Rochester had looked at her revealing sketch of him. The unconscious, in addition to landmines (i.e., unacknowledged, repressed and primitive tendencies), also contains flowers of unexpected and lasting vividness. Thus I need to integrate within myself:

- active and passive tendencies;

- extrovert and introvert sides;

- the masculine and feminine sides of my nature; and

- the two hemispheres of the brain.

---

[137] Molière, *Le Tartuffe ou l'Imposteur* (Paris: Jean Ribov, 1669).

Many people deny and repress the irrational forces within themselves, Eros and other passions, but in so doing deplete themselves of powerful sources of love and efficacy. This is illustrated by the powerful, snorting horses in Plato's *Phaedrus* which it takes all the charioteer's efforts to control. Being in touch with one's feelings – and the freedom to express them – is a chief part (and gain) of self-awareness. And the more self-aware, the more alert and alive I will be – and thus the more attractive to others.

Neurotics are afraid of the intensity of feelings (their own and those of other people) – especially negative feelings. But these have to be faced before the full range of positive feelings can flow. Thus Rilke writes, 'If I do not dialogue with my demons, my angels will take flight.'[138]

In Jung's formulation, neurotic people unconsciously prefer to create new tensions rather than face the raw pain of original hurts. Their biggest handicap is in not being able to affirm themselves or others. I am fully human in so far as I own my vulnerability, and hence can share that of other people.

We need to be relatively strong in order to relate to our vulnerability, and openly share it with others – at appropriate times and places, and without loss of face. It is the strong person who weeps – Jesus, Mary, Achilles, Odysseus. If only we (especially men) could see that, in a relationship based on trust and mutual respect, our frailty is one of the most endearing aspects of our character.

Deep empathy and compassion flow from a loving, living relationship with one's own wounds, 'our naked frailties' (Banquo, *Macbeth*, II iii). This triad gift – to self and the other person, in His service – comes directly from one's hurt. Remembering mine helps me to relate to yours: 'A deep distress hath humanized my soul.'[139]

---

[138] Rilke, *Letters 1907–1914*, Letter 74.
[139] Wordsworth, 'Elegiac Stanzas Suggested by a Picture of Peele Castle'.

Doubts about introspection

Some clients, early in their work with a psychotherapist, worry that talking at length about oneself is self-indulgent. They fear that introspection may make them selfish. But the usual result of self-work – psychological or spiritual, or both – is that one becomes more unselfish: *insight leads to outreach*. To be self-aware is not the same as being self-absorbed. On the contrary, the more self-aware you are, the greater your capacity for understanding other people, and the better you are able to relate. Being at ease in oneself leads to being at ease with others, and they with you. The more your self-worth, the more emotional security you will have for the affirming of other people.

As you gain in self-knowledge, self-awareness and self-respect, you cease to use other people for your own (mainly unconscious) needs: such as playing the role of entertainer because of a craving for appreciation; or of victim because of a wish to be cared for. Another gain of maturing is that you no longer adopt extreme positions, such as power-seeking or submissiveness or selfishness. By ceasing to use others to boost your self-value, emotional energies are freed: these can now be used creatively, enlarging the capacity to give.

Yet many people have mixed feelings about increasing their self-knowledge: they agree in theory, but they delay or resist the experience. In His light, we have no cover or shield from reality. The glare of this light (but God's intention is to heal) exposes all the dusty corridors and memories of the psyche (Psalm 90:8). What a task to face the truth – to discover one's closet, camouflaged, clandestine self; to see the hidden from so near.

> This silence pours a solitariness
> Into the very essence of my soul;
> And the deep rest, so soothing and so sweet,

Hath something too of sternness and of pain;
For it drives back my thoughts upon their spring
By a strange introversion.

Cardinal Newman, *The Dream of Gerontius*, II

When facing the prospect of personal growth, an early doubt is, 'If I dare to plunge into meditation or prayer, or introspection, or psychotherapy,[140] what will happen during silences? What might come to the surface from the psyche?'

The accompanying doubt is, 'Will I be able to handle and cope with shadow material which contains both known and unrecognised parts of myself – fears, regrets, repressed bitterness, unfulfilled hopes?' In effect, this is like saying, 'Here is new inner territory, posing a new kind of challenge. My fortitude and travel equipment are untested.'

The first doubt is entirely realistic: it is sensible to be prepared for shadow material to emerge during silences. Becoming one's full self will often entail bringing into awareness childhood dreads, unconscious needs and longings, and even archaic (or primitive) psychic content. We need courage to face, at a deep level, who we are and have been.

But the second doubt – and this is to be read as if underlined – may be based on an underestimation of capacities: our coping mechanisms. We may have more emotional muscle and endurance than we suppose, and these, like bodily muscle and stamina, can be strengthened by use and exercise. The prospect of a task is often more daunting than the eventual experience. 'If hopes were dupes, fears may be liars' (Arthur Hugh Clough, 'Say Not the Struggle Naught Availeth').[141]

---

[140] These journeys are not coterminous, though the resistance discussed here is a feature common to them all.

[141] Seneca adds, 'It is not because challenges are inherently difficult that we do not dare; it is because we do not dare that they seem even more difficult than they will prove to be.'

In any form of creative life – and especially on the spiritual path – doubts are inevitable and necessary. They test our resolve. They help us clarify our route, and refine our tactics. Exploring our doubts can open up new avenues, new approaches. As well as placing more reliance on our own coping mechanisms, we also need to remember that we have the constant support of God's empowering (Philippians 4:13), seen and unseen (Psalm 107:24). And His empathy: 'Tears and smiles like us he knew'.[142]

Growth involves risk: If you always stay at the shallow end of a pool, you will never find out if you have the courage and technique to swim when you are out of your depth. The pool, of course, is a metaphor for life itself. 'Look if you like, but you will have to leap' (Auden, 'Leap Before You Look').

Freedom

Freedom wears a price tag. Release carries new responsibilities: the risk of facing dark lanes and unknown wells in the psyche; the prospect of having to change unskilful behaviour, now seen with a clearer eye; and the new self-truth that comes from autonomy – I can no longer place all the blame on others or on fate.

Freedom is a mystery, an archetype. The source of freedom and the roots of evil are closer than we may realise. Freedom contains in (or near) itself the seeds of its own potential destruction, for we may use our freedom to pursue options which enslave us. He – who made, and constantly remakes, the world – has, of His own initiative, given each of us freedom for trust or betrayal, kindness or cruelty, beauty or moral squalor. Having overcome much resistance in order to become one's self, one may abuse the hard-won gain. The revenge of 'I'll show you now' gets turned against one's self. 'None can love

---

[142] Mrs Cecil Francis Alexander, hymn, 'Once in Royal David's City'.

freedom heartily but good men; the rest love not freedom, but licence' (Milton, 'Tenure of Kings and Magistrates').

To enjoy freedom without excess – especially if release (or wealth, for example) comes suddenly – is a special test of character. Berdyayev forcibly reminds and warns us that freedom – if caught up in this dangerous dialectic – can plunge head first into anarchy. The backlash can be authoritarianism and rigid, self-righteous virtue. Therefore we need education to enjoy freedom responsibly.[143]

If we are fully open to its potential, liberation means not only to become free *from*, but especially to be free *with* and free *for* – a person, a cause, service. The *for* is to fulfil our potential for creativity.

'Freedom' is an Anglo-Saxon word, rooted in the Teutonic *frei* and (earlier) the Sanskrit *priya*, 'to hold dear, to love and be loved'; as a noun it means 'my beloved'. In any culture or language, the first and last fruit or purpose is to be free for love. 'Freedom' is a sister word to 'friend': these two concepts came into Anglo-Saxon at about the same time, and they share the same twin derivation. When we look at these two words in association, we learn that one cannot be truly free by oneself. 'Freedom' is a social word. How will we respond? Will we be responsible?

Prayers

Forgive *what I was*, sanctify *what I am*, guide *what I shall be*.

Self-forgiving, may I be forgiving of others. Self-patient, may I treat others with patience. May I be like the sun – warm, light, comfortable, and showing the same face to everyone.

---

[143] N. A. Berdyaev, trans. Fr S. Janos, *The Metaphysical Problem of Freedom* (Berdyaev Online Library, 2000).

May I give unhesitating consent to Your will, in sadness and suffering, as in joy. All is Yours. I live only to glorify You.

II
Stages and Temptations

The easy, gentle, and sloping, path ...
is not the path of true virtue.
It demands a rough and thorny path.

Michel de Montaigne, Essays, Book 2

In growth of spiritual life, three testing phases are to be watched for, each with special care: (1) the resistances which accompany setting out; (2) en route, the battle between shadow and light; and (3) near-summit precipices.

1. Setting out

Resistance

We tend to be ambivalent about personal development. The start is sometimes delayed; or, if a beginning is made, it is hesitant. One of Cardinal Newman's prayers tells us how to face and embrace change:

> Oh, support me, as I proceed in this great, awful, happy change, with the grace of Thy

unchangeableness. My unchangeableness, here
below, is perseverance in changing.[144]

Some people do not realise – or will not face the fact – that
they are standing at a personal crossroads, a crucial potential
turning point. In these times we are much less adept at reading
and responding to the propitious moments of our life – of
which we may have only a handful in 70 or 80 years. But, even
if we do see the signs of pivot and fulcrum at the time, we may
burke, silence, suppress, evade or delay, so great is our awe at
the responsibility of life-changing choice. Another danger is to
take a wrong fork or route, and lack the wit or courage to
backtrack and reassess/regroup; or to do so when it is too late.

Extreme avoidance of risk – whether conscious or
unconscious – is itself a form of recklessness: this life will not
for long allow us to stay in a safety first, stuck lane. A delay, a
baulking at the struggle for self-awareness, may result in being
tripped up by one's unacknowledged shadow side: such as by
choosing unsuitable partners. Growth is costly: the price of not
growing is higher.

Sometimes we may need to ask – or, like John Donne, beg –
God to shake us from our torpor or complacency. Donne
pictured God taking the form of a battering ram, beating on his
heart. The poet depicts himself as a city under siege, wanting to
open the gates to God, but captive to his weakness and his
disloyalty:

> Batter my heart, three person'd God, for You
> As yet but knock, breathe, shine, and seek to mend;
> That I may rise, and stand, o'erthrow me, and bend
> Your force, to break, blow, burn, and make me new.
> I, like an usurp'd town, to another due,
> Labor to admit You, but oh, to no end;
> Reason your viceroy in me, me should defend,

---

[144] John Henry Newman, *Meditations and Devotions*, Part 3, IX.

But is captiv'd, and proves weak or untrue.
Yet dearly I love you, and would be loved fain,
But am betroth'd unto your enemy:
Divorce me, untie or break that knot again,
Take me to you, imprison me, for I,
Except You enthral me, never shall be free,
Nor ever chaste, except you ravish me.

John Donne, 'Holy Sonnets' (after 1609), no.10

Every spiritual director, every therapist, and those who have been on any kind of journey, outer or inner, know about the nervous stage before setting out – the moment of flinch or recoil; the dither and delay; the wince or shiver at the risk of danger or change. What jarring sides of my self will I have to face and admit to? Am I willing to yield control to God? Am I really ready to start now? This pivotal time – as one stands poised between past and potential – is full of ambivalence, yet it is an inherent part of many forms of breakthrough, minor or major. Therapists call it 'resistance': it is frustrating and very often creative, being a sign that a person is on the brink of discovery. 'To have begun is half the task' (Horace, *Epistles*, Book I, 2).

Why do we tend to resist change – especially when the change could be so beneficial? Because if we seek, as it were, a deeper centre of gravity, we will have to leave the familiar world of our current psychic life, let go of long-cherished habits and patterns, such as self-defining by what we know (intellect), what we do (activity and status), what we have (possessions), how we look (appearance), how much we earn (income), and how we behave.

The mirage of contentment offered by the enticements of work position, social status, power, wealth or fame are present-day recapitulations of the devil's three temptations of Christ – avarice for material goods, celebrity and awesome power.

If we persist in staying in a safe spot, a complacent rut, God has myriad ways – of all hues and intensity – of stirring our body and heart: some beauty, or some loss, friend or stranger recalls us to Him. To choose, at last, to face inner depths (Luke 5:4) – so long and so understandably avoided – is a brave step, but the gains will be lifelong.

Purification

Sanctity is a continuous conversion (*metanoia*), a daily refining of mind and heart based on all our choices, large and small. 'Deciding' comes from the Latin for 'to cut off'. Creative limitation and fulfilment are both part of one integral work and movement.

Surrender of self-will means being ready to give up anything (or anyone) – for God. This letting go is like the death-then-new-birth cycle of nature: when a flower withers and dies, it simply drops from the stem.

The essence of purification is constant self-simplifying. This means detaching our identification somewhat – from what we know, do, crave or have – so as to enjoy real freedom and real (because wider) choice (Philippians 3:8): the freedom to become who we innately are: *Werde was du bist.*

Mortification means a yielding of self-will to God's will (Luke 22:42): this yielding causes a major readjustment within the psyche. As we move from the dim light of lower levels of awareness to the sunny uplands where God reigns, we may be fearful of the dazzling Light (Exodus 3:6; 33:20), feeling all the more daunted because we have left the base camp where we relied on memory, mind and will. Thus the first quality needed – for a pilgrim soul – is courage: noble courage, heroic, enduring, unremitting (Galatians 6:9). One admits the fear of risk, but resolves not to be led or ruled by that fear: 'One does not discover a new land until one has left familiar shores for a long time' (Gide, *The Counterfeiters*).

D. H. Lawrence offers encouragement:

It's a different kind of happiness we've got to come through to – but while the old sort is dying, and nothing new has appeared, it's really torture. But be patient, and realise that it's a process that has to be gone through.[145]

2. Continuing the journey: shadow battles light

To continue on the inward journey, you need perseverance (Hebrews 3:14). A major test often comes after spiritual growth has begun. Ego and flesh are ranged against light and spirit (Galatians 5:17). This is one of St Paul's recurring themes. In Ephesians 4 he tells of the feud between the old and the new self, self-love and pure love (see also Job 7:1).

'The farther a soul advances, the mightier are the [inner and outer] adversaries against which it must contend' (Evagrius Ponticus). The devil always attacks the light (John 3:19–21). In the Middle Ages the devil was believed to aim his sharpest darts at the most holy people.

The doubts and tensions of this stage are all the more acute because they are in such contrast to the comfort of earlier consolations. Consolation is never a constant experience.

During this second testing, deep reserves of patient endurance are needed – an 'in spite of it all' base – and an ever-firmer trust in God: 'Roam on! the light we sought is shining still' (Arnold, 'Thyrsis'). His hand on our shoulder is always both gentle and firm, and – in times of doubt and loss and pain – has a holding quality, which is an expression of His gentleness. When the sky is dark and the outlook bleak, we need to be firm in our faith, valiant in courage: when we pray at such times, all we may be able to do is to find (or be given) hope.

---

[145] D. H. Lawrence, Letter to Ada Lawrence, 22 February 1929 in K. Sagar and J. Boulton, eds., *The Letters of D. H. Lawrence, Volume VII, 1928–1930* (Cambridge: Cambridge University Press, 2002) p.186.

Archbishop Michael Ramsey once said that, of the three Christian virtues – faith, hope and love – hope tends to be seen as the last and least of the trio, the Cinderella. Ramsey was referring not to the intrinsic value of hope, but rather to a tendency for it to be underestimated. The middle placing of 'hope' is significant: it is the bridge between faith and love/service.

Hope as a state of the soul keeps us strong and steady (Hebrews 6:11, 19), especially during times of special need. Hope is a form of light. Dark shrinks space; light enlarges space, in our inner as well as our outer life, raising morale and widening our range of choice and opportunity. God's light shows us who we really are. If even the angels have to veil their sight – as Chalmers Smith reminds us in the hymn 'Immortal, Invisible' – how much more so we still-earthly creatures.

This light cleanses, but we can take only so much Reality. The clarity of Light can cause anguish – at the exposure of our own shortcomings and need for maturity. In confusion, one may not realise that the light has a perfecting purpose. God's candid, penetrating light – which is now being allowed to shine with more intensity into mind and soul – reveals dark places which previously were not, or only faintly, seen (Ephesians 5:8–14).

Some traits (of personality or behaviour) may now feel more uncomfortable. This is not necessarily a sign that a pattern has become more florid or that a personal problem is now enlarged. Rather, an issue has been highlighted. When the glare of truth exposes pre-existing negative aspects of the self, one's self-esteem – even, for a while, one's balance – feels threatened: 'I thought I could not breathe in that fine air, that pure severity of perfect light' (Tennyson, Guinevere, 'Idylls of the King').

But this agony, this torment, is not a sign of backsliding, nor of incapacity for the spiritual life: it is the pain which is an integral, inescapable part of growth. Sooner or later, we realise that we are always standing in God's light. God's ultimate purpose is surely that we should embody the light of His truth, and thus have a constant internalised searchlight. This ongoing assessment is from inside, not outside. It is not an appraisal done *to* me, but *with* me. God is helping me to be judge to my self. He remains the final authority but wants us to share responsibility for our own moral health (John 3:16–21).

Lorenzo Scupoli's *Spiritual Combat* is a classic text. In its companion book *The Treatise of Inward Peace*, he writes:

> Be well assured that all things happen to prove [i.e., test and strengthen] you, that you may become fit to attain your chief good: to merit the crown made for you by the Lord of infinite mercy.

Seeking God and growing in self-truth may be the hardest of all climbs, but it is also the most rewarding. *Sursum corda.* The hardship and the prize are inseparable (1 Peter 5:6–10). Instead of, or in addition to, 'I feel troubled', say to God, 'Thank you for being ever-present by my side.' What cannot be cured has to be endured. 'I bend and yet I break not' (La Fontaine, The Oak and the Reed, *Fables*, i, 22).

The saints provide us with the model and inspiration for endurance: for valiantly bearing all the challenges of the spiritual life – sometimes joyful, often painful and obscure, always fertile, and in the end rewarding their courage.

They are acutely aware of their own blemishes (but they do not dwell on the shortcomings of other people), and they have the compensating gift of self-forgiveness. The saints' physical pain, as well as their inner and outer struggles and self-wrestling, makes their peace and goodness all the more remarkable – whether at one particular stage of life, or else a continuing (perhaps lifelong) need for patience, as with the unspecified affliction of St Paul (2 Corinthians 12:7). Saints are not immune from complexities, not insulated from perplexities.

They are propelled by their own passions, driven by their own idiosyncrasies.

> Our greatest honour is not that we never fall down,
> but that we pick ourselves up again each time we fall.
>
> Translation of a maxim engraved on a rock at the
> hot sulphur baths in Dorres in the Pyrenees

Ordeals are intrinsic

So far as we can understand His methods, God ordains that we undergo doubts and trials and temptations so as to highlight, and then enhance, those aspects of our spiritual life which need to be strengthened: humility, gentleness, patience, perseverance, obedience, self-discipline, fellow-feeling and participation, and the constant watch for opportunities to serve the (often unspoken) needs of other people.

A mark of inner growth is being more patient with your hindrances,[146] the chief ones being lust, sloth, impatience, ill-will and anger, worry and restlessness, and sceptical doubt. These tendencies block our sight of the truth. In Hebrew the name Satan means 'the hinderer'.

> Whoever thinks a faultless piece to see,
> Thinks what ne'er was, nor is, nor e'er shall be.
>
> Alexander Pope, *An Essay on Criticism*

As far as possible, obstacles should be met, not with surprise or despair, but objectively and with courage (Psalm 27:14). God may be strengthening us to bear heavier burdens and face larger trials (Psalm 107:24; 1 Kings 8:12).

---

[146] 'Our virtues would be proud if our faults whipped them not' (*All's Well That Ends Well*, IV iii).

One of the criteria for maturity is the ability to tolerate ambiguity. If we fight obstacles, we may increase their size and power. Instead, we need to try to work with them and, if possible, learn from them. Indeed, blockages can lead to openings, giving us more insight into our self, and more compassion for other people.

How much of our faith is predicated on hoping for a smooth life, with all of our desires fulfilled? As Oscar Wilde wrote in *The Picture of Dorian Gray*, 'Anybody can be good in the country'; or, we could add, in the summer, or when things are going well.

A mature person accepts the givenness of loss, as well as the givenness of success, with undimmed trust in God's loving intention. If a question cannot get a definitive answer, if a conflict cannot be clearly resolved, then we shall have to learn from the conflict and, as it were, live the question.

The greater the need for growth, the more excruciating are the birth-pangs. This is true of childbirth, a baby cutting teeth, the squalls of teenage rebellion through to the mayhem of a long-awaited revolution. The pang (or distress) inherent in all forms of growth is compounded by the particular and perpetual tensions of spiritual life, caused by our contemplating and stretching towards a light and a wholeness which – in the limitations of our human condition – we can never reach or even clearly see. We should rejoice and be thankful for even the first small, short step(s) in the right direction.

Sometimes we are pulled out of a rut or humbled by being challenged and questioned: by a temptation, a shaming memory or a missed opportunity. Samuel Rutherford writes, 'Our pride must have winter weather to rot it away.'[147] An apparent setback, if we continue to listen for its meaning and purpose, may turn out to be positive and purposeful. Only in eternity

---

[147] Samuel Rutherford, *The Loveliness of Christ: Selections from the Letters of Samuel Rutherford 1600–1661* (Idaho: Community Christian Ministries, 2012) Letter CIX to Lady Boyd. Aberdeen, March 1637.

will we know the true ratio of negative to positive elements in a life event:

> My soul, sit thou a patient looker-on;
> Judge not the play before the play is done:
> Her plot hath many changes; every day
> Speaks a new scene; the last act crowns the play.

Francis Quarles, Epigram, *Respice Finem*

In winter, and sometimes also in early spring, trees look barren, plants seem bare. But soon green shoots sprout, leaves and flowers herald warmer, more colourful days. Shedding, bareness and waiting are all the integral partners of the process of life, growth, change and movement – in the fashioning of human character, as well as in nature's seasons. Spring and summer prove that growth was constant.

3. Approaching the summit

Mountaineering (Psalm 24:3–5) offers a metaphor for the third testing phase of the spiritual journey. From ancient times, and in all cultures, mountains have been symbolic of steadiness and aspiration (goal). Mountain is also a metaphor for contemplation (the journey towards God within). When you are in a place of extreme danger and isolation, you are compelled to explore your inner landscape.

The mystics tell us that the higher the stage, the more the responsibility and the more acute the tension. When a climber nears a summit, risks of a slip or a fall are greater, guides and rescue services are far away, the air is thinner and breath shorter, and all personal reserves – physical, mental and emotional – are lower. And soon they have to face the potential hazards of the descent. A climber cannot relax at their moment of triumph: people who try to reach the top of Mount Everest are more likely to be killed on the way down than on the way up. One in eight of those who reach the summit do not return alive.

The sublime beauty of a mountain is also a hostile beauty. The climber has had to brave many dangers: broken bones, frostbite, snow blindness, sunburn, altitude sickness, blizzard, ice and the danger of being buried by an avalanche or slumping seracs (ice boulders). When climbing in a hostile environment, one can veer within seconds between elation and panic. In the same way, periods of spiritual growth sometimes cause a temporary depletion of resources. Exhaustion may lead to impaired judgement.

Temptations

In the spiritual life, the major near-summit dangers include the allure of pride, complacency, self-satisfaction, spiritual jealousy, spiritual greed and assuming one has arrived, or has nearly done so. Merton warns, 'How many there must be who have smothered the first steps of contemplation by piling wood on the fire before it was well lit.'[148]

In addition watch out for hypocrisy, comparing oneself with others and their stage of growth, lack of urgency, routines and observances which have lost their life and edge, lack of constant surrender and abandonment to grace. These are enemies of spirituality, and they all need to be tracked down. Complacency stalks the aspirant: an ever-present danger often in disguise:

> There was a person who was astonished how easily
> he moved along the road of eternity: the fact is that
> he was racing along it downhill.

Franz Kafka, *The Complete Aphorisms*

---

[148] Thomas Merton, *New Seeds of Contemplation* (New York: New Directions, 2007) p.207.

i. Pride

Self-satisfied thoughts about achievement limit and stultify potential. Preening is not made safe by the fact that the goal or cause is in itself good. Spiritual growth, and all forms of self-denial and of fidelity to love in action – these are meant to be secrets between self and God and, in part, secrets even from oneself (Matthew 6:3–4):

> For the virtuous, vice is the relish of virtue.
>
> Paul Valéry, *Bad Thoughts and Not So Bad*

A virtue (because ostensibly a worthy aim) can so easily become extreme. For example, asceticism (or any form or degree of self-discipline) can become overheated, stubborn, aloof and joyless if pursued to the exclusion of balancing factors in the whole lifestyle. We need to avoid the blinkers of one-sided focus.

Proteus warns: 'as in the sweetest bud the eating canker dwells' (*The Two Gentlemen of Verona*, I i). Pride warps good qualities, making a confident person reckless, and a charismatic manipulate. Pride distorts the vision of those who are arrogant: they are so convinced of their rectitude that they can no longer see what is right and true and pure. The proud lose their balance. Beware a person 'who in strong madness dreams himself divine' (Chesterton, *Alone*).

The key to a healthy asceticism is having the right motivation. If we cannot squarely face the unconscious factors influencing our choices, we will simply transfer old habits (of competitiveness, desire to be noticed, wanting to shine, or to justify ourselves) to the spiritual sphere.

Thomas Keating tells the story of a young man from a macho culture in which outdrinking one's mates is the one sure sign of being a real man. Wanting to escape from his years of indulgence, he joins an austere religious order, the Trappists. In his first Lent, the monks can no longer maintain the bread and water diet. One by one, they have to recover in the infirmary. As the bell rings for the Paschal Vigil, he is the only monk still eating in the refectory. To his shame, he feels a familiar surge of vanity.[149]

Pride fools people into believing that they can conquer a mountain peak solely by their own efforts – without sherpas or oxygen supply. ''Tis pride, rank pride, and haughtiness of soul: I think the Romans call it stoicism' (Addison, *Cato*, I iv).

Christians are taught to fast, not to prove our endurance (to self and others), but as a form of prayer. By our relaxed self-denial, we are saying to Almighty God, 'I trust You, now and for all time. I acknowledge my total dependence on You for every breath and step.' We fast so as to restore our inner and spiritual life to its rightful place.

Hubris is usually a defence against feelings of hollowness, anxiety and low self-esteem.

> Of all the causes which conspire to blind
> Man's erring judgment, and misguide the mind
> What the weak head with strongest bias rules,
> Is *pride*, the never-failing vice of fools.
> Whatever nature has in worth denied,
> She gives in large recruits of needful pride.

Alexander Pope, *An Essay on Criticism*, II

We may become overly self-conscious, and even calculating, in spiritual life, if we keep taking the temperature of the heat of our fervour. At home, when she was young, the girl who was soon to become St Thérèse of Lisieux, was taught by her elder sister to keep a daily diary of her acts of self-denial. Later, at her Carmelite convent, the novice mistress encouraged Thérèse to continue this practice. But, helped by her gift of self-

---

[149] Thomas Keating, *Invitation to Love: The Way of Christian Contemplation* (London: Bloomsbury, 2012) p.15.

awareness, she soon abandoned it. Instead of seeing her religious life as a process of eradicating blemishes, and compiling a record of good conduct, she dedicated herself to her 'Little Way' – pleasing Jesus at all times by little acts of selflessness.[150] 'Him first, Him last, Him midst, and without end' (*Paradise Lost*, Book v). Thérèse realised that the central danger is in seeing and using spiritual experience as an end in itself, rather than as a route towards transcending.

Spiritual pride places more emphasis on human effort and energy than on God's grace and gifts. And we need to be wary of pride's subtle seductiveness, tempting us to feel smug about our capacity for love and influence and good works; for penance and self-denial and sacrifice; and for endurance of loss, sadness, suffering.

> 'Tis too much prov'd, that with devotion's visage
> And pious action, we do sugar o'er
> The Devil himself
>
> *Hamlet*, III, i

Some forms of spiritual grasping are hard to recognise, because they have traits of the authentic. For example, on the danger of false humility, St Francis de Sales observes that 'self-dispraise is no more than a tricky kind of boasting'.[151] Exaggerated or self-satisfied (self-serving) goodness can be hard to unmask. Every virtue has in it the seed of its own potential subversion, the spar that will cause its own capsize.

---

[150] In essence, the Little Way is an attitude of soul whereby we look to God with the heart of a child and, knowing our poverty but knowing too the power and merciful love of God, we live the details of our daily lives in a spirit of trust and acceptance, 'with love as our only activity'. I am grateful to Fr Vincent O'Hara OCD for sharing this definition. See St Thérèse, trans. Ronald Knox, *Autobiography of St Thérèse* (New York: P. J. Kennedy & Sons, 1958) Book 3, Manuscript B, xxxiv.

[151] St Francis de Sales, *Spiritual Maxims of St Francis de Sales* (London: Longman Green & Co, 1954) p.117.

It is wise for a spiritual aspirant to be guarded and circumspect about who, if anyone, they tell of their religious experiences – and, if they do, to be highly aware of their motives. Baron von Hügel advised his niece, Gwendolen Greene, who edited his letters, 'Be relatively silent about great things. Let them grow inside you.'[152]

> Then I saw that there was a way to hell, even from
> the gates of heaven.
>
> *The Pilgrim's Progress*, part i

In T. S. Eliot's play about St Thomas à Becket, *Murder in the Cathedral*, Thomas faces a fourth temptation: he had been expecting three. This fourth temptation was to become a martyr – not with purity of intention, but to satisfy vanity and revenge: from the other side of the grave, he would be able to shake his fist at Henry II: 'Saint and Martyr rule from the tomb', is the Tempter's barb. Becket ruminates about the danger of a potentially brave deed undergone for devious self-serving motives:

> The last temptation is the greatest treason:
> To do the right deed for the wrong reason ...
> Servant of God has chance of greater sin
> And sorrow, than the man who serves a king.
> For those who serve the greater cause *may make the cause serve them*,
> Still doing right...[153]

[152] Friedrich von Hügel. *Letters from Baron Friedrich von Hügel to a Niece* (J. M. Dent & Sons, 1928) Introduction, ix.
[153] T. S. Eliot, *Murder in the Cathedral* (London: Faber & Faber, 1974) Part I. Author's italics.

ii. Spiritual greed

Be wary of spiritual greed. High-soaring hopes about the tone of prayer life – hopes for long periods of serenity and experiences of ecstasy – can lead one to fall into a trap (Psalm 131:1–2). Unmet expectations bring disappointment. Disappointment can cause discouragement, then a sense of failure, and lack of enthusiasm for prayer:

> The fly that touches the honey cannot fly; so the soul that clings to spiritual sweetness ruins its own freedom and hinders contemplation.
>
> St John of the Cross, *Spiritual Sentences and Maxims*

'Prayer is the rejection of concepts', Evagrius Ponticus states in his *Chapters on Prayer*, 70. He advises our discarding not only false images of God, but also any concepts/expectations as to mood during prayer, and all assessing of performance – including the very yoking of prayer with performance.

> Look that nothing remains in your conscious mind but a naked intent stretching unto God, not clothed in any particular about God ... but only that He is as He is ... so that you are one with Him ... who is the Totality.[154]

Just as the basic guideline for meditation is that all feelings, all mind chatter and bodily sensations are to be met calmly, evenly and with equanimity, so also every aspect and state of personal life and of the religious quest – and especially those situations which call for determination, endurance, perseverance – are to be seen and faced in a relaxed way.

---

[154] Anonymous English monk, author of The Cloud of Unknowing, *The Book of Privy Counselling*, chapter I.

Beware of the danger of making prayer an end in itself. Many of us are preoccupied with how we feel while praying: are we at peace, with a sense of well-being, or are we plagued by disquiet and distractions? If you assume that prayer (or spiritual life as a whole) should always be filled with peace and light, you will suffer a double blow: not only the experience of desolation (short-term or prolonged) but also the hurt of dented (because unrealistic) expectations. Spiritual life is like the waves of the sea, subject to ebb and flow. The important thing is to keep swimming.

God assesses the quality of prayer by how we live: in purity of intention, gentleness of speech and manner, loving-kindness in deed, honesty and sincerity in every activity. If ever you feel dull or weary in your spiritual life, you can gain new heart from St Thérèse of Lisieux. When on retreat, just before the clothing ceremony to symbolise enclosure, she too experienced dryness of spirit. Because this trial came at such a special time, we can imagine the sadness it caused. But she was not confused or confined by her feelings, or lack of them: precisely because she did not over-identify with feelings, they did not define her, nor the priorities for her spiritual life. The experience did not shake her inmost peace. Her soul knew and trusted, and held steady. And from her soul level came this clear and affirming voice: 'All shall be for Him, all!'[155]

By contrast, you may sometimes feel serene while praying, and you may have glimpses of ecstasy. Serenity or ecstasy are to be received thankfully, but should not be sought. They may be part of the spiritual journey for some people, at some stage(s). They are not the destination:

> On consolations: Like fair weather, such pleasures do not last ... We must from time to time renounce

---

[155] St Thérèse de Lisieux, Letter to Mère Agnès de Jésus, January 1889, in *Thoughts of the Servant of God, Thérèse of the Child Jesus*, trans. an Irish Carmelite (New York: Kennedy and Sons, 1915).

these sweetnesses, tendernesses, and consolations, withdrawing our heart from them, and protesting that while we humbly accept them and love them, because God sends them, and they excite us to love Him, yet it is not these we seek, but God Himself, and His holy love; not the consolations, but the Consoler ... Be ready to say as well upon Calvary as upon Tabor: 'O Lord, it is good for me to be with Thee, whether Thou be upon the Cross, or in Thy glory.'

St Francis de Sales, *Introduction to the Devout Life*

We are called to receive spiritual highs humbly: *receive*, not rest or rely on. Ecstatic experiences are erratic. They are less important than the rhythm of faith, and our constant return to self-giving resulting in slow, steady coming to maturity over many years.

William Law is severe and unsparing about spiritual epicurism: 'A soul may be as fully fixed in selfishness through a fondness of sensual enjoyments in spiritual experiences, as by a fondness for earthly satisfactions.'[156] Virginia Woolf concurs: 'Our abstention saves us from much gust and rhetoric, much high-stepping and cloud-prancing.'[157] The Lord's light should be desired, not craved.

Expectations for the quality or tone of prayer life should be realistic and somewhat low-pitched. When saints and mystics write about how to cope with distractions when praying, they are not prescribing cures for less-favoured mortals. They are speaking from their own experience. St Teresa was beset by distractions for more than a decade. But she kept trusting – and so can we – in God's often hidden work. The hour of greatest

---

[156] William Law, *The Complete Works (17 in 1) Kindle Edition* (Amazon Digital Services, 2013).
[157] Virginia Woolf, 'Modern Fiction', in *The Common Reader*, Volume I, pp.146–155.

cost can also be (or become) the hour of greatest unsought reward:

> For nothing can be sole or whole
> That has not been rent.

W. B. Yeats, 'Crazy Jane Talks with the Bishop' in
The Winding Stair and Other Poems

Prayers

Almighty God, I entrust my past to Your mercy, the present to Your love, and the future to Your wisdom.

Lord of tender mercies, may I accept all forms of sadness or suffering with courage, remaining unruffled, relying on Your graces and trusting in eventual renewal from Your ever-healing hands, which bestow unceasing saving action.

May I see and use all annoyances, and all larger tests of my faith and fortitude, as nudges or spurs to growth – as friend, colleague, neighbour; above all, as Your loyal honoured son/daughter.

III
Safeguards: Responsiveness, Resilience and Humility

'Content thyself to be obscurely good'

Joseph Addison, Cato, IV iv

There are several qualities which support and safeguard this journey. Among them are *responsiveness, resilience* and *humility*.

1. Responsiveness

The first of these special qualities is the willingness to be led and guided by God's will, hour by hour, even moment by moment. This process is both receptive and active because, having heard, you are called on to respond.

Gather and then focus all your thoughts and emotions, your yielded-up will, so that you are only attention. As you wait for the radiance of His grace, your entire being will be ready and supple to be shaped by the divine will. When God is perceived in the centre of all people, all activities, all moments of time, then life gains new depth, new purpose – even new certainty. If only we can become alert in our listening, and ever-more watchful.

2. Resilience

Resilience (Proverbs 24:16) is vital during both minor and major testings, such as periods of delay, doubt or temptation, and may need the support of a spiritual director. Do you, as it were, let God be God, by trusting His longer perspective? The way to do this is to widen the lens of inner sight. For example, when in the midst of suffering or struggle, we can seldom and scarcely imagine how the experience of our own pain may soon warm and soften our empathy with the needs and feelings and the sorrows of other people. An end can also be a beginning, even if we do not see this at the time: 'Defeat may be victory in disguise; the lowest ebb is the turn of the tide' (Henry Wadsworth Longfellow, 'Loss and Gain').

Trust that God in His mercy will strengthen us, and compensate for what outward circumstances deny, and then give so much more: far more than we deserve or expect (Philippians 4:13).

Since perhaps the ninth century, pilgrims have walked on El Camino de Santiago, leading to the Cathedral in the city of Santiago de Compostela. The sepulchre of St James is one of the holy places of Christendom, originally sought by the faithful – in times of plague and other calamities – to beg the saint's prayers and ask for God, in His mercy, to redeem them from their failings.

Along the route, pilgrims are encouraged by signs with the word *Ultreia* (from a twelfth-century song in Latin from the *Codex Calixtinus*). It means – to give several translations – 'yet farther, still more, keep going'. For a spiritual aspirant, *Ultreia* means 'go beyond'.

Daily persistence is itself a form of heroism. Endurance of pain/loss/suffering is the supreme test of character, requiring humility as well as patience: self-pity or even the smallest traces of pride in one's ability to cope – these are enemies of humility.

Waiting patiently gives depth to our faithful surrender and strength to our trust in Him.

The final safeguard, humility, being the most important, fills the remainder of this chapter.

3. Humility

After a church service, a Scottish schoolgirl, shy and nervous, went up to Bobby Jones, the majestic American golfer. She handed him an envelope and a pen for a prized autograph. 'With pleasure, young lady. On one condition...' He paused, and she wondered what was coming next. Under a message of good wishes, Bobby Jones signed his name on the envelope. Then he searched in his jacket pockets for his copy of that morning's service sheet: 'Now will you please do the same for me?'

Protector of all the virtues

Humility has central place, and the longest chapter, in St Benedict's *Rule*, and – for good reason – humility is placed first among the Beatitudes. All the saints are convinced that sincere humility is the base, prop and protector of all the virtues. This is because humility is the daughter of purity and modesty, and humility is truth with a human brow.

> All the virtues are nothing without humility: take, for example, the Pharisees... Theirs was an external righteousness ... To possess all the virtues, except humility, is like being shipwrecked as you enter port.[158]

---

[158] Alexander Elchaninov, *The Diary of a Russian Priest* (New York: St Vladimir's Seminary Press, 1997) p.77.

At an important stage of his life, Benjamin Franklin decided to work on one virtue each week. He felt he was making excellent progress in this form of self-growth until the week devoted to humility: every time he tried to confront his public persona and examine his real inner nature, he never seemed able to shake off, and break free from, pride in how well he was doing. Just as a loving person keeps no score of the missteps of other people, so a humble person does not tally his own good actions.

The word 'humility' comes from the Latin *humus*, meaning soil or fertile ground. To be humble is to be earthed, well-grounded, to have one's 'feet on the ground'; to feel content (Philippians 4:11; 1 Timothy 6:6, 8; Hebrews 13:5), and to see God in what *is*, now. The fairest offspring of nature, a flower, has its roots in earth and manure. In the perfume of pansies and violets there hovers still the faint strange scent of earth – the under-earth in all its heavy, humid darkness. Mingling with the blue of the morning sky is the black of the potent *humus*. Else the scent would be sickly sweet.

If a person's energy does not fully flow into their feet, their relationship with the ground will be tenuous: the soles of their shoes will show that their tread does not make full contact. Metaphorically, they are a lightweight. A light contact – as for an electrical circuit – is not always enough to ensure the flow of the current. To be humble is to be grounded.

Humility is receptive and allows impinging. We can love – from our depth of being – only if we allow ourselves to be deeply affected (but not overcome) by the other person's wounds, needs and hopes.

Some people gladly bend in serving others, but are wary and unbending when given offers of kindness. They know the humility of helping, but not the humility of receiving. They are stuck in a single role: this is not a well-rounded humility. Not only are they denying themselves what is potentially nourishing; they forget that they are also denying other people the pleasure of giving:

> There is a pride in giving,
> and a pride in not receiving.

Alexander Pope, 'Pride', *Characters and Observations*

Humility is not self-inflated, not too proud to be helped, has a just view of personal worth, and delights in healthy mutual dependence.

Teamwork

Seeing one's successes as the fruit of others' efforts, of teamwork, gives humility. The first conquering of Everest – which was in May 1953, Coronation year – was the culmination of a massive and carefully planned expedition, itself the beneficiary of ten (major) previous attempts and including the deaths of many brave predecessors. Colonel (later Sir) John Hunt assembled and trained a team of ten of the world's climbers. Their support base had 350 porters and 20 sherpas.

In these times when celebrities are always on the lookout for the next photo opportunity, we may look askance at the unworldly innocence of Sir Edmund Hillary, a bee-keeper from New Zealand, and Tenzing Norgay, a Nepalese sherpa who could not read but knew Everest better than anyone else. W. F. Deedes writes of the first two people to stand on the summit of the world's highest mountain. Being low on oxygen and aware of many lurking dangers, they stayed at the top for only 15 minutes:

On reaching the top of the mountain, Hillary took photographs of Tenzing, but did not ask Tenzing to take any of him.

'It didn't occur to me. I was a bit naïve, I suppose. But it wasn't important to me.'[159]

In the journey of life and the adventure of faith, we need the support and guidance and strength of fellow pilgrims (John 15). Am I a good team player? Am I quick, am I sincere, in giving most of the credit to other people, or do I try to hog the glory after a success? A humble person is always glad when others get the credit. In his *Spiritual Conferences*, St Francis de Sales says, 'Provided God is glorified, we must not care by whom.'

Always more

According to a Nepalese saying, a mountain always has more to teach us. Unsated and unsubdued, the as-yet-unrealised spurs us on. On the earthly stage of the quest, we may reach a succession of new plateaux, but we never arrive at a final goal. We always have further to go: more to learn, more to find, more to give. The heroic self-truth of the saints makes them ever-more aware of the distance yet to be travelled to attain union with God.

From the sayings of the desert fathers, we read of Abba Pambo who, in the hour of departing this life, said to the men who stood near him, 'From the time I came to this place in the desert, and built a cell here, I do not remember eating bread that was not earned by the work of my own hands, nor do I remember saying anything for which I was sorry. And yet I go to the Lord as one who has not even made a beginning in the service of God.'[160]

[159] W. F. Deedes, *Brief Lives* (London: Macmillan, 2004).
[160] Benedicta Ward, ed., *The Sayings of the Desert Fathers* (London: Mowbrays, 1975) pp. 164–166.

Virtues and vices are of a strange nature; for the more we have, the fewer we think we have.

Alexander Pope, 'Virtue', *Characters and Observations*

If we look to God – first and last – how can we ever see our attainment with undue satisfaction? All our talents are His gifts. The ultimate doer is God Himself, speaking and acting through us. Thus true love asks nothing in return – neither gratitude, nor enhancement of reputation. The one true goal of our life and love and labour is the kingdom of God and *His* glory.

Free from ostentation

Mistakenly, we overidentify not only with what we do, but also with the way other people see us and speak about us (or how we imagine other people regard us). May all that I think and feel, say and do, be free of any motive other than to please God – asking myself, not "'What will people say?" but "'What will the angels think?'" (De Sales, *Introduction to the Devout Life*, chapter V).

The central call and claim of humility is that we speak and work and love with conviction, free of ostentation. 'The finer a diamond, the lighter should be its setting; the richer the bezel, the poorer the stone' (Chamfort, *Reflections on Life and Society*).

Humility in loyal service encourages action and love, but quiet action, quiet loving; covert penance, patience in suffering, so that only God knows the cost; hidden prayer; reserving the depth of the self for God and the beloved; meeting gain or sorrow, serene in soul (2 Thessalonians 3:3, 5), knowing who gives us strength. Let others see the fruit, but not the gardening, the preparation.

St Francis de Sales insists on interior humility as the source of modest behaviour:

I would indeed, that our words, were always as near as possible suited to our affections, that so we might follow in all things and everywhere a cordial sincerity and candour. ... We should either not use words of humility, or else use them with a sincere interior sentiment conformable to what we pronounce outwardly. Let us never cast down our eyes but when we humble our hearts; never seem to desire to be the lowest, unless we really desire it.

Introduction to the Devout Life

Humility (or self-truth) lives open to what *is*: feels warm when praised, but does not fawn or swoon at the feet of flattery (Romans 12:3);[161] learns from justified criticism, but is not unduly hurt by unfair accusation or attack. 'You can tell the character of every man when you see how he receives praise' (Seneca, *Epistles*, 52,12).

[Do not] trust your humility if you are mortified when you are not noticed.

Lavater, *Aphorisms on Man*

Founded on self-esteem

Despite the popular view, humility is not passive, indecisive or weak. In what (to some people) may seem a paradox, humility needs – is based on – strength and courage (2 Corinthians 12:9–10), self-awareness and healthy self-esteem.

In early August 1941, Sergeant James Ward, a 22-year-old New Zealander of the RAF's 75 (NZ) Squadron, was awarded the Victoria Cross. On the night of 7th July 1941, he was second pilot of a Wellington bomber returning from a raid on

---

[161] 'Love the art in yourself, and not yourself in the art' (Constantin Stanislavski, *My Life in Art* (London: Routledge, 1987).

Munster. While flying over the Zuiderzee at 13,000 feet, his plane was attacked from below by an ME 110, a two-seater bomber/night-fighter.

With a rope (from the aircraft dinghy) tied around his waist (linking him to the cockpit) he managed to climb onto the starboard wing and put out the fire. Positioned as he was (behind the engine), the slipstream from the airscrew nearly blew him off the wing. In spite of these alarms, the battered Wellington landed home safely.

Churchill, an inveterate admirer of daring exploits, invited this shy hero to Downing Street. Churchill – then in the high noon of his renown – asked many questions, but Ward, awestruck to be in the Prime Minister's office, could manage only a few words in reply.

Seeing the man's discomfort (in some ways, perhaps, more of an ordeal than the instinctive courage needed for the dousing of the fire), Churchill asked, 'Are you feeling humble and awkward to be here today, at the heart of government?'

'Yes, sir.'

'Then you can imagine how humble and awkward I feel to be in *your* presence.'[162]

Using your gifts

Humility has two sides. We are rightly cautioned – from childhood on – not to try to appear more than we naturally are. But if humility means 'not more than' (Psalm 131:1), it also means 'not less than'. Real humility does not involve grovelling. In Charles Dickens' novel *David Copperfield*, Uriah Heep was a toady: being a creep, he made people cringe. To be humble means to know yourself through and through, and this self-knowledge, with self-acceptance, gives a person stability,

---

[162] Although apparently not mentioned in this encounter, Churchill (at about the same age) had been in life-threatening situations as a war correspondent in Cuba, India and South Africa. C. Fadiman, *The Little Brown Book of Anecdotes* (London: Little Brown, 1985) p.122.

balance and confidence: not assuming, not pretending, not imposing. Flaccid self-deprecation is as inauthentic as hubris and vanity.

What should be one of our greatest fears? That in older age we have to admit our name is 'Might-have-been'. On the Day of Judgement, we shall not be asked, 'Why were you not like Moses (or St Teresa of Ávila)?', but 'Why were you not fully John (or Joan)? Why didn't you live up to your name, your true self?'

We especially find God alongside us when we are making the best of what He gives us, when we use our time judiciously, when we fully honour His gift of life, and when we dare to extend the boundary of our skills and talents.

How often – even (or especially) before we have begun – do we label a task or enterprise as impossible, far beyond our capabilities? So much depends on our thought patterns – our inner vocabulary and inner dialogue – and persistence in accepting challenges. Doubts do need to be examined and questioned, but we also need to listen for, and trust, the still, small voice that says, 'I will try. I might just be able to do it. I might even do it well.'

With the passing of time, humility increases. The more you learn, the more you realise how little you know, how much you have yet to learn. Sir Isaac Newton said of himself:

> I do not know what I may appear to the world; but to myself I seem to have been only like a boy playing on the sea-shore, and diverting myself by now and then finding a smoother pebble or a prettier shell than ordinary, while the great ocean of truth lay all undiscovered before me. [163]

---

[163] David Brewster's *Memoirs of the Life, Writings and Discoveries of Sir Isaac Newton*, Volume II (New York: J. & J. Harper, 1832) pp.300–301.

The farther you travel on the spiritual journey, ever greater seems the distance between where you are now and wholeness, or union with God: the ache for 'far-off, receding loveliness' (Neville Cardus).

Prayers

I thankfully accept all endowments. All possessions, all personal qualities, I receive and hold in trust, as the means of serving other people. I will therefore guard and hone and train and joyfully express all my resources, so that I may fulfil the reason for my existence – the prospering of Thy kingdom of love on earth.

Help me to surrender all to You, to be an active agent, a channel of Your love, faithfully doing all in Your Name, and only seeking Your approval.

May I work unceasingly, generously, in Your service; and only and always for Your greater glory. May love replace self-seeking in every cell of my body and being.

IV
Mindfulness

Praise in the common things of life,
Its goings out and in;
Praise in each duty and each deed,
However small and mean.

Horatius Bonar, 'Fill Thou my Life, O Lord my God'

The main religions of the ancient East have many names for what they call 'mindfulness', and what a Christian calls 'recollection'. The capacity for recollection hinges upon attention to the one thing necessary – the Companionship of God. Its attainment requires us to prune away all the other interests and attachments that claim our focus. St John of the Cross explains, 'This is the reason why, under the old law, the altar of sacrifice was to be hollow within. It is the will of God that the soul should be empty of all created things, so that it may become a fitting altar of His Majesty.'[164]

Whatever our cultural background, whatever our religious tradition, we can all benefit and learn from contemplating the full implications, and infinite depths, of each of the following short terms, which have such wide meaning and potential personal value:

---

[164] 'Thou shalt not make it solid, but empty and hollow in the inside.' Exodus 27:8. St John of the Cross, trans. David Lewis, *The Complete Works of St John of the Cross* (London: Longman, Roberts, Green, 1864); *Ascent of Mount Carmel*, Book I, ch V, p.22.

one-pointedness
bare attention
pure perception
relaxed awareness
simple noticing
silent witness
quiet acceptance
open, desiring only God
non-interfering focus
choiceless (unjudging) observing
spacious mind
witness mind
open mind
clear seeing
full alertness
direct and fresh experience
relaxed watchfulness/vigilance

Mindfulness means doing every activity with total clarity, and in a spirit of celebration. Thus you walk, not just to get somewhere, but for the pleasure of loose-limbed rhythmic walking – relaxed, alert, involved, the whole self coordinated, enjoying the lift and fall of every step, aware – moment by moment – of self and surroundings and companion.

One-pointed attention brings silence. And this attention, this silence, is contemplation. In the peace of silent awareness, you see life's innate oneness. At the same time, with this quality of attention, you can see all the richness and variety of detail. Meditation is not an escape from life: meditation is an embrace of the very heart and centre of all creation.

Try first in small, simple ways not to let the mind in – not to verbalise or even name. Become more aware of your self as witness. You will have the best chance of seeing widely, totally – and with fulfilment – when you are content to just *be*. In the light of pure perception, you move beyond like or dislike, and perceive God in each person and place, each encounter, each event.

How can we attain the quality, the state, of pure attention? A lucid mind is not just the result of techniques for focus and concentration, however useful. Ultimately, clarity and alertness come from and need a pure heart and a clean lifestyle, for the very fabric of a person's psyche is moulded and shaped by what they *think*.

First attempts to become more mindful may need to be deliberate, because the ever-wandering mind swings, like a young monkey, from the branch of restlessness to the branches of distraction and inattention, agitation and inquisitiveness. The mind frets and squabbles, and gives a constant (not always welcome) voiceover.

Gradually, as your mind becomes tamed and trained, and more open and flexible and compliant, the practice of mindfulness becomes natural, spontaneous and self-activating, enabling you to think, speak, and act with increasing ease and economy, born of constant awareness: observing, but not becoming attached.

In order to enjoy a contemplative, wondering approach to everyday life, we need poverty in the very widest sense – being selective about all forms of input and stimulus. Only then will we have the outer and inner space to pause and then to observe. To observe is to attend, mark, retain, praise and (implicitly) serve. A spirit of wonder is the first, finest gift for – and from – spiritual living. Wonder anoints the eyes with innocence.

Everyday sacraments

Everyday activities, from driving one's car to sweeping the floor, can be imbued with prayer, yielding not only a sense of – but a real connection with – the living presence of Almighty

God. Creator God, please show me, teach me, where to look, how to look and what to look – and live – for. May we never 'sleepwalk' during the day. May we always be ready to be surprised by what Browning called 'the sunset touch' ('Bishop Bloughram's Apology').

When we hallow our everyday routines, we glorify God by our care and attention. The spiritual life is to see the eternal in the temporal, and then to witness: to manifest the divine through activity and the way we treat the material world. Even – especially – the smallest aspects of life have their honoured place in God's handiwork.

Do we see each task as worthy in itself, and not just something we have to do (or endure) in order to make other (seemingly more rewarding) activities possible? This approach – which we observe when children are immersed in apparently trivial pursuits – is termed 'autotelic'. 'Autotelic' is derived from the Greek words *auto* (self) and *telos* (goal). Any action undertaken is regarded as self-contained and of intrinsic value. It is done, experienced and respected for itself. In this way, the commonplace is transfigured. Individual purpose merges with and is guided by the will of God.

At a school in India, the children share in the upkeep of the buildings and gardens. In a film of daily life at the school, a boy of six or seven is shown volunteering – from a range of choices – to clean the pond. With an older child giving watchful support, Jamie clears the scum from the surface of the small pond. He moves with care, works with diligence, and is clearly pleased with the result. He is not doing a 'task' or a 'chore' – both being generic terms with a negative or routine connotation – and he does not regard this work as 'dirty' or 'duty'.

Men and women alike can profit from imitating the virtuous wife lauded in Proverbs 31, and highly praised by Solomon. She is caring in the neighbourhood – 'strength and dignity are her clothing' – and she is equally diligent in the home, never neglecting her spinning-wheel (Proverbs 31:19–25).

Everyday tasks need not be seen or carried out as mere practical necessities. These activities (in and outside the home) are what I call 'everyday sacraments', begging us to see them in this way. A renaming – from 'tasks' to 'sacraments' – can help to foster a wider, more creative attitude.

Duty needs real purpose: it only comes alive for us when we start with this higher intent, an overarching spirit for the work. Begrudged duty is then transformed into joyful service of God, family, neighbour. May I see every task – even the clearing of my in-tray – as part of the co-building of Thy kingdom.

Pause

Our use of the telephone can be a useful exercise in mindfulness and patience – respecting the caller, respecting time and tempo... The phone rings. Pause and let it ring a few times. Exhale old air, then breathe in – gently, slowly, fully. Now reach for the phone, calm in mind and mood and voice. Clear awareness of the movement of breath creates a vital space before speech, and before the possible expression of emotion. In that space, that last moment of safety, you can choose whether or not to speak; you can amend, refashion, what you had originally intended to say, and also its tone.

We can use this approach before any activity. Just prior to starting, relax even subtle signs of tension in body, mind, feelings and motives. Listen for any irritation in yourself and/or about specific other people. Locate – but do not overidentify with – any negativity currently inside of you: doubts or worries, the babbling mind, inhibited or frightened emotions. Tune in to your observer side, and then allow observer and participator to unite, in a spirit of love and listening and service. Locate the still point within, and speak and behave from your centre. Pause and pray before you reply to criticism. When tempted, pause. Keep recentring yourself.

Oh, to be better (more frequent) in pausing. Above all, avoid the danger of catching sight of yourself in the midst of loving service.

Thinking often creates a barrier between us and the moment of experience. At such times, we are not intimate with this moment, this person, this landscape. Within seconds we become mired in concepts, in likes and dislikes, or the mind wanders far from what is in front of us right now. Pure love is free, generous, gratuitous (in the best sense): 'When you give alms do not let your left hand know what your right hand is doing ...' (Matthew 6:3–4).

Walking

Many people walk so fast that their feet scarcely seem to be touching the surface of the pavement. They blur the distinction between a walk and a run. Often they are eating and drinking while they walk, or using a mobile telephone, or listening to music on their headphones. They are not grounded. They are probably in flight from solitude and their need for intimacy. Preoccupied with other (often future) activities, they are missing the sights and sounds of their route: people, buildings, clouds, trees and flowers, children playing. The more, and the more deeply, you observe, the more connected you feel – *to* and *within*.

> The thought of some work will run in my head, and I am not where my body is; I am out of my senses. In my walks I would fain return to my senses. What business have I in the woods, if I am thinking of something outside of the woods?
>
> Henry David Thoreau, *Walking*, Part I, 13

Keep the head upright, and maintain an upright relationship between head, neck and spine. Notice carefully the position of your neck, the fulcrum of good posture. Observe the position of your shoulders and the swing of your arms. Be aware of each foot as it rises and falls (striking the ground with a force equal to twice your bodyweight).

Do not try to alter any habit or pattern of your way of walking. Observing yourself with full present-awareness will usually of itself give your walk balance, rhythm and symmetry. Your body wants to be in balance, with economy of movement. By observing any tension or imbalance, you encourage your body to realign and correct itself. All walking can be a walking meditation: 'A walk for walk's sake' (Paul Klee, *Pedagogical Sketchbook*). Enjoy developing your own characteristic stride, your own style of rhythmic walking, maximising ease and economy of movement.

> In those vernal seasons of the year, when the air is calm and pleasant, it were an injury and sullenness against nature not to go out, and see her riches, and partake in her rejoicing with heaven and earth.
>
> Milton, *Of Education*

Mindful eating

Mindful eating is a model for all forms of awareness in daily life, because eating is a primal experience. Almost half of Britons usually have their supper while watching television, and British families spend more time together in their car than at the kitchen (or dining room) table. Yet the meal is one of the most symbolic and precious of all potential encounters (Matthew 26:26–29).

Grace before meals reminds us that all food is God-sent (Deuteronomy 8:10), and that we are to use the energy from food to serve both Him and our companion.[165] The Masai

---

[165] Literally, a person with whom we share bread.

word for 'Eucharist' means 'food for the heart'. Meals are also symbolic of the bond between humanity and nature; of human fellowship and mutual dependence; celebration of life, and the mystery of life and death. The plucking of fruit, the harvesting of grain, the culling of vegetables, are all necessary for sustaining life.

Mealtimes (and their preparation and aftermath) offer scope for extended prayerful thought, sending a spirit of thankfulness to God for His gift of your life and for the gifts of nature and other people:

> In some way or other, the cotton-workers of Carolina, or the rice-growers of China, are connected with me; and, to a faint yet real degree, part of me. Their vibration of life reaches me, touches me, and affects me ... For we are all more or less connected, all more or less in touch: all humanity.
>
> D. H. Lawrence, 'Nobody Loves Me', in *Phoenix*

While preparing a meal, feel compassion for the many who are less fortunate. As you eat, picture the Lord as your host or guest.

We need a reverential ambience at mealtimes. At a practical level, be careful about what you eat, as to choice (and order) of dishes and their nutritional balance, and as to quantities. The Japanese island of Okinawa is home to one of the world's longest-living and healthiest people. They have a Confucius-inspired adage, *hara hachi bu*, which means 'stop eating when you are 80 per cent full'.[166] The satisfaction many of us feel after a full meal is not a sign that this quantity was needed, but that greed has disappeared – for the time being.

---

[166] Bradley J. Willcox and D. J. Willcox, *The Okinawa Diet Plan* (California: Three Rivers Press, 2005).

Enjoy each food type. Savour the flavour, the texture, the sensation, of every mouthful. While chewing, put your cutlery on the plate. Giving the saliva's enzymes time to work will improve digestion and boost energy levels. Nine thousand taste buds come to our aid when we choose and chew our food.

Eat at a measured pace so as not to override your body's mechanism, the hypothalamus, which gives you feedback about satiety: the stomach can take 20 to 30 minutes to let the brain know that one has had enough food. Listen for signals from the solar plexus (the area between the stomach and bottom of the ribcage). A long-term pattern of overriding the hypothalamus – lasting into adulthood and leading to obesity – may begin in the first weeks of life, if a baby is fed by the clock rather than on demand, because the child does not learn to listen for, express and respect felt needs – when to eat and how much.

And watch how you are eating. Do you lean forward as if to snatch or grab the food from your plate? How many times do you chew? Do you put down your fork or spoon between each mouthful?

A man from the West came to stay for a week at an Indian monastery. His lessons in living began during his first meal: an early-morning breakfast. Fruits had just been served, and already he had almost finished (or demolished) a large juicy orange.

Seeing the newcomer eat so heedlessly, the resident teacher said: 'Mr Johnson, your instruction can begin right away. You simply have no idea how to eat an orange.'

At first the visitor was dumbstruck. Eventually he mumbled: 'But, I have been eating oranges all my life. As you can see, I love them.'

The teacher grinned. 'You do not eat; you *consume*. You say that you love oranges, but do you really *enjoy* them? Now let me show you how to eat an orange; or any other food, for that matter.'

'You no sooner have one segment in your mouth, and you are ready with the next one. You are always thinking about the future, the next bite. You are never in the present; and so you never really relish what you eat.

'When a piece of food is in your mouth, keep your hands in your lap. Concentrate. Be fully where you are. Be mindful of your every movement.'

Samuel Johnson's advice was to chew food 32 times before swallowing. Perhaps Johnson was intuitive in at least half-seeing the rationale for his advice. We now know that thorough mastication not only favours digestion and the enjoying of flavours, it also ensures bioavailability: our body taking the maximum nutritional value from the food we eat.

Chewing stimulates peristalsis. Moreover, chewing mixes food with enzymes released in saliva (plus others produced in the mouth) – this is where digestion starts – potentially enabling digestion of 30 to 40 per cent of starches before food even reaches the stomach. The more liquid the food is when it leaves the mouth, the better for both digestion and nutrition.

The whole process is so well and carefully designed, if only we will cooperate. Different types of food – fats, proteins, carbohydrates – are digested in different parts of the intestinal tract. Slower eating aids the sending of messages from the saliva to cells in each part of the digestive process that they should now prepare to receive food of each specific type.

The final and clinching benefit of chewing slowly and for longer is that the food will pass through the body more quickly: food that lingers incites potentially harmful bacteria to erode the lining of the intestine. Thus the benefits of slow eating are social, aesthetic, nutritional and medical.

There are risks to eating in front of a screen. When our main focus is on TV, work, or traffic, we are apt to overeat, often without realising it. Conversely, if you eat with full attention, you are more likely to notice when you are full. No other activity gives so much scope for practising mindfulness.

Breathing

Another current trend is the rapid rate of speech: shallow breathing makes the voice come mainly from the throat, rather than from the mid-region. Any saxophonist or opera singer will tell you that deep breathing begins in the diaphragm.

Most of us use but a fraction of our lung capacity – partly because of our sedentary lifestyle, but mainly because of tension and unskilful habit, causing us, in stressful situations, to respond at far less than our feelings-potential, even allowing for the conventions of public and social life.

Just as mind and body are closely linked, so also there is a reciprocal relationship between breathing and physical states, and between breathing and emotional states. For example, in an atmosphere of love or reconciliation, the breath tends to be slow, smooth and gentle – symbolic of harmony (in oneself and in a close relationship). By contrast, grief, sadness, depression, pain or shock cause us to hold the breath. Resentment, anger, anxiety, agitation, fear or panic produce rapid, shallow staccato breathing.

The first and most apparent deficit of shallow breathing is nervous edge and lack of poise. The second, very subversive effect is for the body to wear an iron band of repression around the diaphragm. This maintains the disconnect between mind and feelings which our exam-driven, information-led society – always elbowing and out of breath – does little to help bridge. Thus many people use shallow breathing as an anaesthetic to avoid feeling their current hurt or past pains. The diaphragm is where 'letting go, letting be, allowing to become' has to begin.

If the free movement of the diaphragm is blocked, the auxiliary muscles, higher up, take over. The result is tense, shallow, chest-level breathing, which often shows that the person is trapped within the small world of the lower self. This person will not allow the breath to come and go naturally because of a subconscious fear of not taking in enough oxygen unless they are in charge. They lack basic trust.

Breathing is a metaphor for life itself, and also for letting go. Full/deep inhalation is only possible if preceded by a (preferably slow) full exhalation: all old air out, new air in. Breath is also a symbol of engagement, participation. People who have been thwarted in love or rejected outright retaliate by refusing to make a full exchange with the world. With shallow breathing (from throat and chest only) they snatch the minimum amount of air. When at last they are ready to let themselves touch and be touched by people and by life itself, they express themselves with deep sighs, tears, chuckles and even by daring to sing.

The positive results of breathing naturally include renewal, vitality, confidence, personal integration and a real sense of participation and service: a *metanoia*, with the whole person more attuned to the Divine, as a *subjectum dei*. Correct respiration facilitates all forms of inspiration (as the shared Latin root would lead us to expect).

The more one trusts God – always at work, protecting and nourishing, and always available for extra energy and insight if the venture is worthy – the more dependable this companionship feels.

The slower we breathe, the more relaxed we are in mind and in movement. But no effort is needed to alter the pace or quality of our breathing. No two breaths are the same. We simply watch how we are breathing, split second by split second. We watch short or long, rough or fine, jagged or silky, and all the graduations in between.

We also note accompanying sensations in all parts of the body, from the scalp all the way down to our toes and the soles of the feet. These sensations cover the whole range, from tension to calmness. Our close observing will by itself bring welcome change – not only to our breathing, but also to body, mind and emotional state (of which our pattern of breathing is a barometer). As in other areas of spiritual life, the small provides training for the large. By allowing repeated actions to slow themselves down naturally – breathing, walking, eating, speaking – you prepare yourself to be poised and God-centred in times of pain, struggle or challenge.

The more closely you relate to your feelings, the more rapidly you will 'hear' the arising of a sensation. If it is a negative emotion, you now have the chance – before it wells up – to *choose*: 'Do I just listen to these feelings and learn from them? Or shall I express them? If so, when, how and in what tone?' This early warning system can be applied to any mindset or pattern of behaviour, thus preventing stuckness or proliferation. The aim is always to hear or catch (and work with) the inner process as early as possible.

Our Western conditioning makes us want to be in control. But the aim here is not to try to make the breathing 'perfect', deeper, slower. Instead, we are invited to let our breathing *be* – in the same way that we are encouraged to hand back all that we have, and are, to God Himself.

Wise body use

A new journey of self-awareness is probably best begun with clearer observing of – and more work on – body use in all forms, such as posture, gesture and movement; the balance between action and rest; and the choice, amount and speed of intake of food and drink.

Listen to, and always respect, your body's inherent wisdom. Attention to the body is a prime way of reclaiming oneself, reintegrating body, mind and feelings. Body awareness thus mobilises energy, sharpens concentration, restores calm and keeps one in the present.

No branch of self-respect is more vital than esteem for the body. We have sound biblical authority for this: 'Your body is a temple of the Holy Spirit within you, which you have from God ... you were bought with a price. So glorify God in your body' (1 Corinthians 6:19, 20).

St Bernard of Clairvaux describes the attitude of a person who has surrendered more and more to God: 'the body is loved, and all the goods of the body for the sake of the soul, and the goods of the soul for the sake of God, and God for his own sake.'[167]

All health – psychological and spiritual, as well as bodily – depends on being a good steward of your own vitality: 'I appeal to you therefore, brethren, by the mercies of God, to present your bodies as a living sacrifice, holy and acceptable to God, which is your spiritual worship' (Romans 12:1). When we indulge ourselves in small matters, we build a habit of giving in to inclination on bigger occasions. Take to heart Christ's counsel: 'If any want to become my followers, let them deny themselves and take up their cross and follow me' (Matthew 16:24, NRSVA). Luke 9:23 adds that we are to do this 'daily'.

Your body is part of your life capital. It is your means of witness. The moment the body is neglected, growth and wholeness and even learning will all suffer. Attention to wise body use – clear awareness of posture, gesture, movement and action – roots us in present reality, and restores art and adventure to everyday tasks, giving daily life its full stature, its widest meaning and its ultimate spiritual purpose.

Our supreme example is the life of Christ: for Him, every moment was and is a redemptive moment. Wine, laughter, healing, bathing the feet of His disciples: for Jesus, all aspects of life were sacramental. Can we bridge the separation we tend to make between the material and the spiritual? How mindful

---

[167] St Bernard of Clairvaux, 'On Loving God' in G. R. Evans, trans., *St Bernard of Clairvaux: Selected Works* (London: Paulist Press, 1987) p.204.

are we when we mow the lawn or have a shower? *The smallest action, if done with love, is infinitely precious to the eyes of God.* Do we see duty and delight as partners?

Parents have a priceless role in fostering – especially by example – care for the body by the young. Your body is to be seen not as a means to various ends, not as just a fleshy object that helps you accomplish, but as part of your relationship with God, a return offering to Him, in thanks for the gift of life and His continuous nourishing.

How I treat and hold my body (my bearing or deportment) shows my level of respect – for my self, for the privilege of living, and for my opportunities to serve. My body is my ally, my agent in becoming an evolved person, focused on my Father.

Taming the tongue

Few parts of the body have more potential for danger as well as good, as the tongue (Psalm 52:2). It can lead us into (or be the agent of) many forms of excess through loss of control over desire and impulse: anger, lying and deceit, gossip and backbiting, gluttony and binge drinking, casual sex and infidelity. 'Loquacity storms the ear, but modesty takes the heart' (Robert South, *A Discourse Against Long and Extempore Prayers*).

How often – when we are speaking or just about to – do we remember that all our words, everything we say, and the tone and the timing and the length – the how, the when and the how long – are a form of action? Our words have far more power – and will have much more influence, positive or negative – than we will ever know or realise:

> Could mortal lip divine
> The undeveloped Freight

Of a delivered syllable,
'T would crumble at the weight.

Emily Dickinson, 'Could Mortal Lip Divine'

Emily Dickinson's vivid phrase 'undeveloped Freight' is the poet's way of warning us about words that are given and received as dense: words which the other person's psyche is forced to gulp down, like the gullet being fed with unchewed globules of unpalatable food. Therefore let us become ever-more mindful of our speech in every situation – the what, how, when and how long – and simultaneously try to imagine how the other person's conscious and unconscious will be hearing and eating and trying to digest. This will give me peace as well as the other person, because our conversation will not have a bad aftertaste in their mind and feelings, nor in mine.

We are warned that 'on the day of judgment men will render account for every careless word they utter; for by your words you will be justified, and by your words you will be condemned' (Matthew 12:36–37).

The present moment

This present moment is time's timeless junction: as well as having its own current value and importance, this moment embraces past and future, being partly formed by the past, and (by what happens now) helping to shape the future. This very moment you can choose to plant roots of future health of life, in service of 'ultimate good'.[168]

If every moment is a gift of God, waiting for us to etch it into eternity, then the only authentic response is to be fully 'in the moment', and live it with gratitude and generosity: beginning to glimpse the limitless realm while we are still in this

---

[168] Dietrich Bonhoeffer, *Ethics* (London: SCM, 1955).

life. 'He who believes has eternal life' (John 6:47). Note the present tense.

Search for every opportunity to let God work in you and through you, for the expansion of His kingdom.

In Tolstoy's tale *Three Questions*, the hermit tells the king: 'Remember this: There is only one time that is important – Now! It is the most important because it is the only time when we have any power.' And even this power may be residual, only partial. In every enterprise, vocation or journey, there is a dialectic between writing our own story and letting our story shape us.

Unless you focus on your real circumstances, you will be widening the gap between 'what I want' and 'what *is*'. Regrets about the past and fears about the future cause tension and stumbling, and are literally a diversion, unless they are faced and worked through, and lessened in impact. Only if your thoughts and feelings are up to date, and you are not in the grip of worries about what is to come, are you truly free to enjoy who or what is in front of you now.

'Present' used to convey the sense of being alert, and also of being available, as illustrated by Psalm 46:1: 'God is our refuge and strength, a very present help in trouble.' Being present frees and readies you to be a servant. The paradox is that being present makes you both weighty and light: weighty, in the sense of fullness, all parts united, harmonious, rich in humanity and enriched by others; light, in the sense of being supple and flexible, adapting – but not selling yourself short. The word 'present' comes from the Latin for 'to be near, face to face with'. The more you are present to yourself, the more you are present to other people. You will then have personal presence.

Personal presence makes you worthy of that vivid definition of a person of culture: you have more wood in the shed than in the fireplace. If you know you have resources in reserve, you have ease and confidence. Your authority is then natural, never pushy; weighty but not heavy. Authority implies originality, being in touch with your origin – or, as a religious person would say, your Origin. One's personal presence inspires other people to speak and live from their own originality. Presence is natural, uncontrived.

By being fully in this present moment, we discover or rediscover a special spiritual truth: spiritual life consists not only in seeking God (this is necessary, because our earthly search for ever-closer union is lifelong), but also in realising that, because of His perpetual presence, you can be with Him now: horizontal time (*chronos*) and vertical time (*kairos*) intersect. This moment, every moment, is touched by eternity.

Each moment is unique. Each action – however often repeated – is, in subtle and various ways, different; and has potential for new learning, new experience in the moment, while things happen.

> A rainbow and a cuckoo's song
> May never come together again.

William Henry Davies, 'A Great Time'

Living in the present moment consists in a threefold watching over body, mind and soul: by attention, respectively, to breath, thought and prayer.

Observing the rate and depth of your breathing quietens (and also makes alert) your *body*. Quelling any unnecessary thoughts or feelings about past or future keeps the *mind* pointed at the current activity, rather than flitting like a honeybee from one flower to another. The very fear of stray thoughts is itself a stray thought. And *praying* – constant adoring of God – puts all worldly preoccupations in their only true and valid perspective: the expansion of self-giving, for the everlasting glory of His kingdom.

We need to keep realigning ourselves with Christ, so as to witness all our experiences and all fidgeting of the mind from His perspective. Time is a sacred gift: if only we can remember, and keep remembering, this truth. If we experience the depth, the divinity, of time, then whatever we do – from major events to the smallest of daily tasks – we will do with care and devotion, and warmth of heart. When you are Argus-eyed to life in its fullness (Matthew 13:16), when you receive and respond to time as a grace, then time will reveal its innate fast-moving spaciousness, a quality better felt than described.

'Alertly living this present moment' is not like a drive on a fast or easy highway. The only secret is lifelong, unremitting vigilance. Restlessness and distractions of the mind together prevent us from remembering – and being all the time aware of – the possibility of our communion with God. Failures or shortcomings or omissions often stem from being forgetful, and thus heedless, of His perpetual presence and guidance.

'Only that day dawns to which we are awake' (Thoreau, *Walden*, Conclusion). Be attentive, all-awake, by looking and listening for what God is offering you, in an infinite variety of ways (Psalm 143:10). This is contemplative living. Moreover, praise (such as for the sight of a young family, or a kindness received, or a service rendered) inspires cheerfulness.

> Bonhoeffer [when he was in prison in Buchenwald]
> … was all humility and sweetness. He always seemed
> to radiate an atmosphere of happiness and joy in
> every smallest event of life.[169]

Just as the beauty of a butterfly is all the more poignant because its life span is measured only in weeks, so also each moment, because fleeting, is precious, even holy. It is the very nature of joy (or true love) to arrive suddenly, unexpectedly, as gift.

Perhaps we analyse too much – writes the Jungian analyst! In order to see cleanly, with a pure eye, and to be fully receptive to each unfolding moment, we need to go beyond

---

[169] S. Payne Best, *The Venlo Incident* (London: Hutchinson and Co., 1950) p.180.

our narrow self-image, beyond conflict, beyond the mind's tricks, beyond the artificial barrier between self and others, or self and nature.

> When we let the woods breathe their mystic voices in our ear, we see how futile it is to spend so much of our time slicing things finer and finer with the intellect when the body of the world is so fun and so warm, and longs so imperiously to be pressed to the heart.[170]

You can walk in a park, in silent awareness of creation, not seeking to partake of its glory, but being ready – open and transparent, guileless, ingenuous, childlike – in case an uninvited but welcome sight or guest chooses to reveal themselves in their own unique way. To feel, to experience, *without overtly looking for*. To be in this state is to enter the place of benediction. If we open a window, a cool breeze may or may not come into the room. Grace can arrive anywhere, and at any time, but only to a person with a still mind.

Committed artists and scientists provide examples of how to make the most of every moment, because, in some cases, they are willing to sacrifice anything in wholehearted pursuit of their vocation. But being involved needs the compensating ability to let go. This was well illustrated by an injunction of St Benedict, to the effect that, when the monastery bell rings, all monks should stop whatever they are doing.

When first we try to be more alert, we may only realise after an event or encounter what has been happening – outside, and also in heart and mind (of self and others). Given more time and practice, we can become more enrichingly in touch: more alive to the gift of each moment of experience as it unfolds, and avoid St Augustine's regret: 'Too late I loved Thee ...

---

[170] Virginia Woolf, *The Common Reader*, Volume II, pp.173–186.

Thou wert within, and I abroad ... Thou wert with me, but I was not with Thee' (*Confessions*, Book X, 27).

As we mature, and see more clearly our global interdependence, we can become more adept at in-the-moment gratitude. Conversely, one by-product of thankfulness is that it keeps our main focus on the present. Being present-orientated increases efficiency, enjoyment and contentment: we celebrate what we *have* rather than snatch for what we *want*. St Francis de Sales suggests that we should surround every activity, every experience, with an aura of thanksgiving: 'Be like a person who is opening an endless succession of gifts' (*Introduction to the Devout Life*).

Will Rogers (American actor and master of homespun wit) was once asked what he would do if he had only five days left to live. He replied, 'Just continue my present approach to life: Take one day at a time.' A fulfilled life depends not only on 'one day at a time', but also on concentrating on one activity at a time. Kierkegaard gave this title to his work on self-examination: *Purity of Heart Is to Will One Thing*. And what is the one thing necessary? To listen for and *do* the will of God at every moment, night and day.

Prayers

All through this and every day, may I constantly lift mind and soul to remembrance of You, and reach forth, in love, to everyone I meet. I yearn to gladden Your most holy heart.

Before I speak, may I weigh what I intend to say on the scales of eternal truth. Before every action, may I establish myself in love and in Your peace-giving presence, my indwelling Companion.

O God, grant me a vivid sense of Your presence, all around me and within me. May all that I think and say and do stem from – and return to – You. Grant and preserve sanctity in my soul.

V
Non-striving

He who binds to himself a joy
Doth the wingèd life destroy;
But he who kisses the joy as it flies
Lives in Eternity's sunrise.[171]

In meditation, we learn the art of non-striving, non-forcing, non-interfering and involved non-attachment: relying on – and being nurtured by – 'That patience which – in contrast to everyday life, which bids us haste – puts us in touch with all that surpasses us' (Rilke).[172]

If a tennis player goes on court for a big match with their mind full of coaching tips – placing of the feet, type of grip, angle of racket head, curve of swing, aim and placing, disguise and variety of shot – they are likely to be slow to react and robotic in mind and movement: in a word, predictable. Techniques (and tactics) need to be used flexibly, or else they lose impact. Which one now? How do I express it in *this* moment and in *this* context?

The more you consciously think while in action, the more likely you are to slip or miscue or overdo. The art is not to dwell on formulas or techniques during the event/experience –

---

[171] William Blake, 'Several Questions Answered', no.1, *MS Notebook*.
[172] Rainer Maria Rilke, trans. J. Banard Green and M. Herter. Norton, Letter to Auguste Rodin, 29 December 1908. *Letters of Rainer Maria Rilke 1892–1910* (New York: W. W. Norton & Co., 1945).

assuming that all of them have been diligently learned, practised and released.

This does not mean 'just let it happen'. It means to be aware but not self-conscious. Relax and trust your body: its innate need and wish is to move in a natural and economical way. Your body is and will be coordinated, provided your ego does not get in the way.

Every activity can be a means of learning and liberation, but only if you are not trying to attain any goal – even liberation itself! Gardening, serving tea, making pots: there is to be no conscious purpose except total awareness of each movement of the mind and the body. A right, relaxed attitude is all:

> Under such banners militant, the soul
> Seeks for no trophies, struggles for no spoils
> That may attest her prowess, blest in thoughts
> That are their own perfection and reward,
> Strong in herself and in beatitude
> That hides her, like the mighty flood of Nile…

William Wordsworth, *The Prelude*, Book IV

Love is to be allowed to flow through us: it has its own wisdom, its own purpose and direction, its own ways of expression found in the moment. We no longer plan or manufacture words or gestures or caresses, or brushstrokes: they emerge, are discovered in the moment. 'God knows. God guides my hand' (Matisse).[173]

It is the same with music: 'Man, if you have to ask what rhythm is, you ain't got it!' quipped Louis Armstrong. Rhythm arises, is present, not only from our innate musical talent but also from our whole integrated being: at one with the

---

[173] Jack Flam, ed. Henri Matisse in interview with Léon Degand, 1945, in *Matisse on Art* (California: University of California Press, 1995) pp.159–165.

composer, the music, the audience, one's instrument and one's own deepest self.

The best accomplishments – in art, in sport, in any creative enterprise (not 'endeavour') – have a spirit of play, of flow, of being in tune: 'in the zone', as tennis players say. Long preparation, sustained self-discipline and hours of patient practice bring us to the time of test – the exposure of public performance. Then – on the platform or stage of life – we gently assist the event or encounter to unfold in its own best way: *comme ça arrive*.

No forcing or contriving, no anxiety or proving, no self-vaunting, no eyeballing. We may even have a sensation of 'Look – no hands!' Later we ask ourself, 'Did *I* really do that?' What has happened here? We have allowed the Creator to make artists of us.

Letting things happen

For balance in personal and spiritual life, it is vital to know the difference between *making* and *letting* things happen. One learns how they differ, not only with the mind, but by experience – watching yourself in the moment of activity and noting how *making* is often stiff and rigid, tense and intense.

Letting is much more relaxed than *making*. Being more economical of energy – and hence truly liberating – *letting* is much more fulfilling, and can be sustained with ease for far longer. Michelangelo is reported to have said, 'I do not create sculptures. I uncover the form which was hidden in marble.' But we must not stereotype *making* as totally negative. It is our best ally when it is in a creative dynamic with *letting*.

What is your own tendency? Do you 'make' or 'let' things happen? And what is your usual ratio (or combination) between these two modes? Do you 'make' or 'take' a photograph? Some artists and photographers have spoken of the difference between 'looking for' and 'looking at'. 'Looking for' starts with preconceptions; 'looking at' is watching simply.

As soon as we notice that we are half-awake, the dream fades. If we overanalyse a fairy tale or a relationship or prayer, we lose something. The practice of mindfulness entails experiencing whatever *is*, right now – not evading, not overidentifying, and not goal-directed. This precise yet wide-ranging awareness is a form of joy. Throughout the whole of our life, we shall need to keep returning home to this point of balance. If you are meditating *for something*, then you are concocting, not truly meditating – i.e., dwelling with a heart open only to God, with a quiet mind. The innocent eye sees without expectations, concepts or analysis.

Skill in sport offers models for finding the mid-point between holding on and letting go. There is a true (and instructive) story about Bill Tilden, an American tennis player who was prominent in the 1920s. In a vital match in one of the leading tournaments, he was within a point or two of defeat. While he was serving, he said to himself, 'Heck, I've got nothing to lose. I might as well go all-out now.' Tilden won that game, that close set, and then the match.

Actionless action

How often are we so focused on ambition and expectation (and remembering how good the previous occasion was) that we miss much of the beauty of what God is already doing, and giving, now? How often are we intent on our behaviour (or performance), rather than keeping our gaze on God, surrendering control, and trusting that – in every moment – He will speak and act through us, by awakening and giving vigour to our best self?

In spiritual life, balance is all: not only balance between contemplation and action – being separate and yet involved –

but also balance in attitude, finding our own middle path between half-heartedness and excess zeal. No impatience, no self-willed forcing, no overdrive, no contrivance or forcing. More action, less activism: 'Grasp not at much, for fear thou losest all' (George Herbert, 'Sin').

In place of any tendency to grasp, let us have open, trusting hands: hands that are not flat (passive), not clenched (tense and overactive), but cupped. Cupped hands symbolise an entire self-opening. Here is an endearing and instructive story about St Kevin from the Celtic tradition (Giraldus Cambrensis, *Topographia Hibernica*, ii 28):

> He went for his usual Lent retreat to a little hut for prayer and reading and contemplation. As he knelt – with one hand stretched out through the window and lifted towards heaven – a blackbird settled on it, and laid an egg as if she had found a new nest. The saint, so moved by this act of trust, remained in all patience and gentleness until the young ones were fully hatched. He did not close nor withdraw his hand: he held it out unwearied, shaping it for the purpose.

What a parable we have here about our relationships and our attitudes: simple, receptive, open to unexpected forms of service. Gentle, patient, unwearied and adapting to the other. May I begin to contemplate and not devour. May I let God, and the needs of my neighbour, shape me.

The art is to relax, not just next Sunday, or on your summer holiday, but now in the very midst of activity: relaxation as a state of mind, emotions and body. May we become the peace we so long for:

> Calm soul of all things! make it mine
> To feel, amid the city's jar,

That there abides a peace of thine,
Man did not make, and cannot mar.

Matthew Arnold, 'Lines written in Kensington Gardens'

Inspiration and creativity

Edison, the prolific American inventor, said that 'genius is one per cent inspiration, and 99 per cent perspiration'. That one per cent includes rather a lot! Edison knew that innovation is often sparked by ideas or experiments outside daily work routines. He was dismissed from his job as a telegrapher at Western Union 'for not concentrating on his primary responsibilities, and doing too much moonlighting'. His knowledge, skills and creative methodology could have been worth millions to Western Union.

In six history-making years, 1876–1882, Edison's New Jersey workshop, Menlo Park Laboratory, was responsible – among other inventions – for the phonograph, the telephone carbon-transmitter, electric lighting and improvements to the telegraph.

Edison had a natural talent for stimulating ingenuity. His colleagues – mostly young, single men – lived in a nearby boarding house. From time to time they had what we would now call 'brainstorming sessions'. They often worked late into the night, but stopped now and then for a drink and a singsong beside an organ at one end of the main room. They were always ready to help each other with a project. It was a relatively informal, collegiate environment. Edison explained at the time, 'Hell, there ain't no rules in here. We're trying to accomplish things!'[174]

---

[174] William S. Pretzer, ed., *Working at Inventing: Thomas A. Edison and the Menlo Park Experience* (Michigan: Henry Ford Museum & Greenfield Village, 1989).

Some of the best and most famous discoveries, and those of most enduring benefit to all the human race, have come – to scientist or inventor – either in dreams, or else during unexpected times, when the seeker was not consciously focusing on the problem to be solved. Dreaming is a form of mental play, like a game of memory and image played inside the brain. With rational thought suspended, insight and new-found links can arise – often answering a question which the waking mind has been unable to resolve.

Einstein (who was reputed to sleep for 10 or 11 hours a night) said that a dream helped him to formulate his theory of relativity: he dreamt that he was speeding down a mountainside on a sled, faster and faster until starlight refracted into strange colours as he approached the speed of light.

After trying to solve the puzzle for years, the molecular structure of the benzene ring was revealed to August Kekule, the pioneer of organic chemistry, in a dream in 1865 in which a snake swallowed its tail.

Archimedes found the principles of hydrostatics while lolling in his bath. Einstein told colleagues that he got some of his best ideas while shaving. And Housman concurs: 'Experience has taught me, when I am shaving of a morning, to keep watch over my thoughts because – if a line of poetry strays into my memory – my skin bristles so that the razor ceases to act' (*The Name and Nature of Poetry*).

Descartes seldom got out of bed before 11am. During his morning musings, he made many of his greatest discoveries, including the Cartesian coordinates, which he devised while wondering how to pinpoint a fly on the ceiling of his bedroom.

Times such as these – when the mind is relaxed, hovering, receptive and responsive – give space for intuition and deep wisdom to arise. Towards the end of his life, Brahms, who laboured long over each of his scores, told friends he had decided to stop composing so that he could fully enjoy his last years. When a new work was given its première, a friend reminded Brahms of that vow not to write any more music. Brahms explained that he felt so happy at the prospect of resting that inspiration came to him unbidden.

Some of Beethoven's most inspired music was conceived while he strolled alone in woods, exploring the paths not only of Austria, but of his imagination; the frontiers of his innermost feelings; and the image-bank of his memory. He said he was 'an instrument on which the universe plays'. 'He loved to be alone with Nature. She was his only confidante', wrote the Countess Thérèse von Brunsvik. In Vienna he refused to take lodgings in a house as soon as he realised that there were no trees around it.[175]

Periods of strong concentration, sustained application, clear a path for the mind to freewheel. Thus do scientists advance and break through. Thus philosophy forms, coheres, evolves. New linking blends the newly found with historical patterns. A work of art is conceived; music is composed or heard; and poetry comes unsought:

> Of my celestial Patroness, who deigns
> Her nightly visitation unimplor'd,
> And dictates to me slumb'ring, or inspires
> Easy my unpremeditated verse.

John Milton, *Paradise Lost*, Book ix

Often insights cannot be born until inner controls and conscious application are relaxed. Thus some breakthroughs occur in the shift or transition from work to rest. Poincaré, writing about his own creative process, emphasised that rest is needed so that the unconscious has more space both to generate and to coalesce. The more open you are and the more relaxed you feel, the more the creative/enterprising parts of

---

[175] Trans. Gertrude Russell, *Recollections of Thérèse von Brunsvik* (London: Fisher Unwin, 1893) p.73.

your unconscious will deliver original ideas and solutions, or words if you are soon to speak in public. You can prepare yourself for the possibility of inspiration by being alert and awake, centred and grounded, fluid and flexible, and by daily courting of your muse, if you are artistic:

> I was all ear,
> And took in strains that might create a soul.

> John Milton, *Comus*

Because play is an experience of the transitional area between subjective and objective, creativity has a connection with play and a mood or spirit of playfulness. Richard Strauss enjoyed the card game Skat, and Stravinsky was an avid card player. Elgar was a racegoer. Mozart's masterpieces germinated when he was playing bowls or billiards, or jesting with friends. On the autograph score of his 'Twelve Duos for Basset Horns' (K.487), Mozart wrote, 'Vienna, 27 July while playing skittles'.

These reflections about inspiration give us a model for meditation: a careful blending of relaxed concentration and detached immersion.

Surrender

Ecstasy happens – or is more likely to come – when we stop striving (or lusting) for it. Our part is to prepare the way by relaxing, lightening/loosening expectations and entrusting our self to the gifts and the timing of God's grace.

The etymology of the word 'surrender' is helpful here. 'Sur' from the Latin *super* signifies 'over, above, beyond, super, highest'. 'Render' is from the late Latin *rendere* 'give back'. Thus 'to surrender' is to yield to the reign of God. When you do this, you will see people and events in a new way, from a fresh angle, and with more depth of both understanding and patience

(Proverbs 16:32). All our endeavour is to be for God, and –
with Him – for our neighbour. In pleasure and in success, we
are to thank Him; and then to kneel, praying, 'But I only desire
Thee.'[176]

Letting go entails two main aspects in your relationship with
God: entrusting the whole of your earthly life to Him, and, in
specific terms, yielding all control and daily direction to the
Almighty. Letting go is not a static mode, a passive state. On
the contrary, it means constant alertness to the divine
omnipresence, in the faith that He will make clear to us the
precise manifestation of our witness and vocation. Our God is
sovereign: in His holy wisdom and foresight He knows what
He wishes us to learn, and how and when and where.

We grow not only by what we add but – a prior act – by the
accretions we cut away – the cul-de-sac desires and activities;
the stuck habits of thought, speech and behaviour. These are
limpets onto the self. Every so often eliminate the superfluous
(or stultifying) from your life: an object, an unattainable desire,
a stifling attitude, an ardent attachment, an ensnaring activity.
Pruning is an essential part of fruitfulness. We cut away in
order to prepare for something better.

In Western society, meditation is countercultural:

Western society	Meditation
verbal	silent
mind	heart and soul
thought	pure awareness
doing	being
outer	inner
expecting	desiring only God
impatient	persevering
quick fix	lifelong journey

---

[176] The last two sentences of this paragraph are based on a letter from Rome,
23rd December 1920, by Dom. John Chapman, *Spiritual Letters* (London: Sheed
& Ward, 1935) pp. 96, 97.

tangible	elusive
control	let go
success or failure	non-competitive
goal-centred	being fully where you are
hunting	yielding
wanting	waiting
what I do	what God does

Meditation is to align yourself with Him, instead of identifying with the pseudo-self, often based on an idealised self-image. This creative movement allows God's peace and strength to work and flow through you. Surrender a needless and endless self-struggle, and expand to the dimension of grace, the Spirit's graceful flow.

In the West especially, we are preoccupied with 'how to' questions: how to win a contract; how to dress; how to make love; even how to smile. Alongside my learning of the really essential skills, I need to allow His Spirit to infuse and permeate my whole being: to sound throughout (*personare*) all I say and do.

This willing form of abandonment to God is an active, not a passive, mode: an act of trust born of complete confidence in Him. In August 1897 – weak and exhausted, and with only a few more weeks to live – St Thérèse wrote to her spiritual brother, Maurice Bellière, who was about to go to Algiers to enter the novitiate of the White Fathers: 'How sweet it is to abandon oneself into His arms without fears or desires.'[177] 'He is greater than all His works' (Sirach 43:28). 'Seek in His praises all thy joy.'[178] 'If our love were but more simple.'[179]

---

[177] St Thérèse de Lisieux, trans. F. J. Sheed, *Collected Letters of St Thérèse of Lisieux* (London: Sheed & Ward, 1949) p. 324.
[178] From Ernst Arndt's hymn 'I Know in Whom I Put My Trust'.
[179] From F. W. Faber's hymn 'There's a Wideness in God's Mercy'.

Alignment

Spiritual life begins and ends in staying in line. When a person is aligned, even the elements respond to his prayers, as a story about St John of the Cross reveals. By way of background, John had endured extreme childhood poverty, bereavement, imprisonment, physical and emotional abuse, rejection, humiliation, sickness, exclusion and calumny at the hands of his own religious community, all of which served to conform him in a remarkable way to his crucified Saviour.

When a stubble fire threatened to engulf his monastery, the danger was so great that the friars were proposing to evacuate. St John told them to wait. He stationed half his confrères before the tabernacle, to beseech the Lord's help in prayer, and he sent the other half to fight the fire. He himself knelt in prayer at the hedge which separated the field from the monastery. The flames hovered ominously over his head, and then retreated. John emerged with a few beads of sweat on his forehead, and asked his brothers, with 'a laughing face which stole your heart away' (to quote fellow friar P. Francisco de San Hilarión), if they were tired. When the brothers opened the church doors to let out the smoke, a hare took refuge in the folds of the holy friar's habit.[180]

When you are centred, deliverance can come right where you are. Years awaited, to release inner and outer tension is to reveal the joy of freedom. To align our whole self to God's every wish will bring us ever-closer to His throne and abode. With poised attention, rest calmly in God's hands (Matthew 11:28). Pray that your whole being may be turned to Him, tuned to Him, so that you may come to know the regal constancy of His living Love – so alive to our every need and movement, and so life-giving.

---

[180] Crisógono de Jesús, *The Life of St John of the Cross* (London: Longmans, 1958) pp.283-4.

Detachment

Thoreau said that we are made rich not only by what we have, but also by what we let go. He also observed that, as we simplify our lifestyle, the laws of the universe seem simpler. This is because we and our values are in accord with them.

> No person ever gave up so much that he could not find something else to let go. Few people, knowing what this means, can stand it long, [and yet] it is a just requital, a just exchange. To the extent that you eliminate self from your activities, God comes into them – but not more and no less. Begin with that, and let it cost you your uttermost. In this way, and no other, is true peace to be found.
>
> Eckhart, 'Of Denial', *The Talks of Instruction*

It is only safe to heap up treasures in and for the kingdom of heaven, which begins here on Earth. Rousseau's advice is to play the paring-down game of Robinson Crusoe. Examine each desire: is it a real need? 'The more he cast away, the more he had' (John Bunyan, Shepherd Boy's Song, *The Pilgrim's Progress*, part ii).

The way of non-attachment can be learned and expressed by the way you see and use material things, and even the way you touch and handle these gifts from God. Here is a simple self-audit:

- Knowing that the more you possess, the more there is to maintain and guard, do you enjoy all the benefits of your society, while dodging the equally many traps?

- How well do you distinguish between genuine need and self-willed want?

- Where is your main focus? Where is your lasting treasure (Matthew 6:19–21)?

- Do you use all things with an attitude of non-possessiveness, with love and care, modesty and moderation?

- Do you treat the material world as serving your spiritual life as well as your practical life: as an aid to your ultimate fulfilment in God only, and as prompting you to love the Giver more than His gifts?

It is less a question of what you have, nor even how much and how many, but of your mind's tendency, your disposition. Use all you touch for the glory of God (1 Corinthians 10:31) who made everything. May we enjoy material things under the governance of the Spirit.

If we are greedy, we miss the grace of being grateful. If gratitude is absent, nothing provides fulfilment. A society and a people eager for instant gratification become trapped in a web of ever-proliferating unmet desires. Melancholy in the midst of abundance. As de Sales observed, 'Doves sated find cherries bitter' (*Introduction*).

Like all that is precious – in human life and in the material world – we need to give our personal endowment the utmost protection. The desert fathers – to honour their experience of God's friendship – spoke of *apatheia* – all their facilities, aptitudes and desires held in balance before Him and for Him. *Apatheia* does not here mean 'apathy'; it describes a wise and healthy detachment, an avoidance of negative or destructive feelings, a freedom from all that might torment one's self or chafe one's stability.

Gradually, we can learn the art of being occupied without becoming preoccupied, committed and relatively detached at the same time. Patience and perseverance yield more than sudden but short-lived bursts of fervour. Spiritual growth is akin to much of life throughout nature: coming slowly to maturity. Does a professional jockey keep tugging on the reins, or does he guide his horse with a steady hand, free and flexible? *Travailler moins, produire plus.*

In India there is a method of catching monkeys (to keep as pets) which can teach us about the process – and even mortal danger – of an unhealthy degree of attachment. Coconut husks are affixed to stumps. Inside each husk is a nut, or a small handful of nuts. A monkey is attracted to the bait – goodies put around the outside of the husk. He reaches inside to seize the prized nut. When doing this, he makes a fist, and so he cannot take his hand out of the husk. His captor advances and takes hold of him. If only the monkey had been wise and flexible enough to let go of the nut, he could have scampered away. After all, he is in a jungle: there is no lack of food.

What produces overattachment? Delusion, greed, fear, rigidity, loneliness and lack of alertness. Clear, honest observing – in the moment of desire – is the first stage of letting go of attachments, either partly or completely.

The way of non-attachment needs to be clearly seen, accurately named and formulated: not as a withdrawal but, rather, as a maintaining of creative distance. What does 'creative distance' mean? Involved, committed, deeply related in love, and participating fully (1 Timothy 6:18) in all the life of family and friendships, of work and community, but with important provisos: not driven, nor driving when relating to others; not possessed nor possessive; not manipulating nor crowding; not harried nor hurried. Creative detachment is not sought for its own sake. The purpose is to cultivate an attitude of least interference with the natural flow – of life and of each individual.

Striving and surrender are not compatible. If you are overeager to achieve something, notice the force of your intention. Watch your faster breathing and feel your tenser muscles. This clear observing, this quality of attention, can take you to a state of relaxed awareness. God Himself is at the heart of this readiness.

There is a vast difference between ego-led desire and desire that is offered up to the Almighty. Ego-led desire can be narrow, cramped and grasping – as hard as a tightly clenched fist. We therefore need to ponder widely, 'What do I hope for? What is God's wish? If there is disparity between my desire and God's will, how can I close this gap?'

When we crave, we often overestimate the value and possible benefits of what (or who) we long for. In overall attitude, non-attachment is discreet; moderate in all things, especially in appetite (Colossians 3:5); careful when responding to impulses.

An attitude of non-possessiveness means respecting the autonomy of other people: not dominating, not patronising, not cultivating an unhealthy dependence; and, unlike Polonius, not 'grappling friends to thy soul with hoops of steel' (*Hamlet* I, iii). Love, even love, can run (or stumble) into a mire of excess, such as by being overprotective.

Possessiveness is always counterproductive – for oneself, for the other person and for the relationship. It is the ultimate repellent.

A mutual and spacious giving of the freedom to *be* is the best atmosphere for love to flourish. Lasting love needs several forms of mutual respect, such as for each other's character, vulnerable side and autonomy. Love enables: love gives a climate, an environment, an ambience, which frees the other person to be himself (and to be more than he realised he could ever be) – in strength, in vulnerability, in good or in testing times, needing no pretence, no falseness, no forcing:

> We need in love to practise only this: letting each other go. For holding on comes easily: we do not need to learn it.

> Rilke, 'Requiem for a Friend'

When we know, deep down, that we are truly loved and accepted – seen and respected, valued and enjoyed, for who we really intrinsically are – we have an unparalleled ease and security. We do not have to try to please each other. Our constant expressions of thanks and appreciation do not set a standard, do not create pressure. I know I am loved because of all that I am: not in spite of vulnerability and limitations, but in some measure because of them.

The desire for wholeness is a quest for what we already have. What we long for is what we innately are – children of God (Romans 8:16).

It is God's prayer, not 'my' prayer

In both active prayer and in 'infused or passive prayer', it is God who initiates our desire, invigorates our will and invites our love (1 John 4:19). As the theologian von Hügel reminds us, God is 'secretly inciting what He openly crowns' (Matthew 6:3–4).

Because God is the All-in-all, we can say the words of St Augustine: 'Thou art the Love wherewith my heart loves Thee.' This is a personally felt echo of 1 John 4:19: 'We love, because he first loved us.'

Evelyn Underhill, in her 1922 treatise *The Degrees of Prayer*, suggests that the best atmosphere for the soul's progress is 'the unspoilt, trustful, unsophisticated apprehension of a little child'. Never strive towards a form or phase of prayer, or seek to attain a state or stage of the religious journey, for which you are not yet ready (Isaiah 28:16). Let go of self-conscious devotional efforts: less perspiration, more inspiration.

We have to prepare the soil for the receiving of God's strength and grace, allowing His Spirit to work in us and through us (i.e., within the heart and then in our outer life). Our responsibility is perpetual self-offering – for God and souls.

By the discipline of silence, we grow ever-more sensitive to the Eternal, listening to Him, becoming amenable and alert in our responses to His every wish. Prayer life needs quiet attention to God: the freeing of inner space, so that, in the deepest recesses of our soul, God can meet us, Heart to heart. Preparations for prayer – as to place, time and posture – facilitate this attitude of openness: a readiness for God to do the rest – to pray in you, with you and through you.

Detached from self-will, and not in search of gain or reward, nor looking for joy and rapture, come to your prayer time with a clean (and thus serene) faith, a willing spirit, a peaceful heart, and as silent a mind as you are then capable of. Exult in sitting peacefully, give all loving attention to God, and enjoy being in the presence of His grandeur, with awe and wonder. From such devoted attention is born a sacred silence, far more eloquent to your soul than even the most pious words.

In this spirit of abandonment to God's abundance, and His good pleasure, you cease posing questions, such as where you may be on the Jacob's ladder of prayer and spirituality. Simply be at one with God, and enter into a bond, a loving union – deep, personal and intimate – with your God, and be content to remain there for as long as God wishes.

Many aspirants think more about their seeking for God – which is at best sporadic – than of the constancy of His coming to them (1 John 4:10): indeed, His being with them now. Much strain will be eased from this search if you remember and rejoice in God's coming to you – sometimes in vivid events, but also daily in quiet (but nonetheless symbolic) ways which plead never to be taken for granted. The secret of non-striving is to focus on – and abide in – the givenness of God.

Don't judge prayer time

In the practice of prayer or meditation, we should be wary of judging success according to feelings. Indeed, it might be wise not to measure or try to judge success at all. A hard, testing experience of prayer – dry, dull, dark, with no evident consolations, such as when we do not feel in a suitable mood to pray, or when besieged by distracting thoughts, or if a vulnerable part of the psyche has been opened up – may in the long term be as fruitful, if not more so, as prayer times which are relaxed, fluent, joyful and filled with calm.

One helpful way to avoid judging success or failure in prayer is not to label experience – during it or afterwards. If you say to yourself that the prayer time was bad, or not good enough, you may set up a negative pattern in your prayer life: a cycle of doubt, fear, despair, defeat.

Conversely, if you say you have had a good experience, you may build ambitions for the next time, and these ambitions may not be fulfilled. This, too, as in the previous example, leads to disappointment. In either case, energy and attention are leaking from the present. 'The most intolerable pain is produced by trying to prolong [or repeat] the keenest pleasure' (Shaw, Beauty and Happiness, Art and Riches, *Maxims for Revolutionists*). All experience labelling, using positive or negative words, is usually detrimental.

St Teresa suggests that some people aim for high-toned exquisite experience: the aesthetics are rated more highly than the union. The road and route are deified more than the King Himself. St John of the Cross gave five signs that a nun – despite being convinced she was having visions – was in a state of delusion:[181]

---

[181] St John of the Cross,. trans. David Lewis, 'Letters' in *The Complete Works*, Volume II (London: Longman Green, 1864).

- too much desire to experience and enjoy visions;
- too much self-assurance;
- determination to persuade others that she has a special gift;
- these 'visions' do not increase her humility;
- her words and her descriptions do not sound like the language of truth.

The via media: not seeking perfection

We need to try, persist and endure, but not overdo. Reach forth but avoid overstretch. 'A man may so overdo it in looking too far ahead, that he may stumble the more for it' (George Savile, 'Of Caution and Suspicion', *Miscellaneous Thoughts and Reflections*).

St Francis de Sales cautions against vainglory and overambition:

> The enemy often suggests a great desire of things that are absent, and which will never happen to us, so that he may divert our mind from present objects, from which, trivial as they are, we might obtain great profit.

> *Introduction to the Devout Life*

Because the search for perfection never ends, strain, tension and frustration inevitably get in the way of clear focus and awareness and, in turn, there is wastage of time, as well as of physical and emotional energy. Take, as an analogy, a violinist tuning his instrument: if he tries to achieve perfection, and seeks exactly the right degree of tautness of string, he usually sets a fraction too far.

Take but degree away, untune that string,
And, hark, what discord follows!

Troilus and Cressida, I iii

Before you start any activity, note – in your attitude and body – the difference between breathless, hot-blooded intention and calm intention. Then – instead of becoming entangled in an unceasing web of perfection-searching, endless because never satisfied – you will find flowing freedom, and develop a rich and enriching humanity: with high standards, but not hectoring self or others. Let us be satisfied – adapting the words of Theodore Roosevelt – to say, 'I do the best I can, where I am, with all that you – O Lord – give me.'

Treat your body in the same way. Too much austerity and asceticism is destructive and self-defeating; too much pleasure impedes healthy personal growth. Seek balance in every aspect of your life, including your spiritual search. If we try to create a personal Utopia, we may find that – perhaps long unaware – we have slowly built a prison around us and those we love.

In order to encapsulate the art of non-striving in a one-liner, we shall have to rely on the words of St Paul (Romans 10:20), quoting Isaiah:

'I have been found by those who did not seek me;
I have shown myself to those who did not ask for me.'

Prayers

Renouncing all self-preoccupation, I yield to You the whole of my self and all aspects of my life: desires and petitions, affections, all interests and actions, every corner of my being and doing, for I believe that curbing self-will can help teach me eternal truths, and allow You to direct my every thought and step.

You are my strength. I rely on Your steadying, all-sustaining power, always accompanying me. I rest all my hope in Your grace.

May I make today and every day a perpetual song of praise and thanksgiving, in ever-closer harmony with Your holy will.

VI
Ingredients of Spiritual Life

Leave no unguarded place,
No weakness of the soul;
Take every virtue, every grace,
And fortify the whole.

Charles Wesley, hymn, 'Soldiers of Christ, Arise'

Detail and method may vary from era to era, but the ingredients of spiritual life are similar in our time, to those in the hard but exhilarating days of the desert fathers. This similarity need not surprise us: it is no coincidence, no quirk of history. Continuity in the basics of spiritual life is a testament to their enduring worth.

What are the spiritual practices? In addition to manual or domestic work, and forms of service to others, there are eight main areas: (1) acts of regular or periodic self-denial; (2) acts of penance; (3) recreation; (4) recollection and other forms of prayer; (5) growth in virtue; (6) self-examination; (7) communal worship; and (8) reflective reading of Sacred Scripture and other inspiring books about spiritual life. The first six of these areas are explored below, and (8) *lectio divina* is considered in chapter III of Part 3.

Acts of self-denial

In spiritual life, there can be no scope or latitude without discipline, and no discipline without daily denial (discriminating in its extent and intensity).

This outer denial or muting of eyes, tongue, hands, impulse – is best formed, and best maintained, by attitude – strength of conviction more than force of will, as Shaw confirms when writing about major temptations: 'Virtue consists, not [so much] in abstaining from use, but in not desiring it.'[182] The holding back is relaxed, not tense. Outer poise reflects inner mastery.

We need most vigilance when we think we have gained self-mastery in a particular area. In reality there is always more work to do: 'Like a path in autumn: soon after it has been swept clear, it is once more covered with dry leaves' (Kafka, *The Complete Aphorisms*, 15).

If we seek clear focus and recollection during prayer time, then at all other times we will need to be constantly watchful over how we use the mind and senses. The way we are in daily life helps prayer times, and prayer helps daily life.

Watchfulness does not imply rigidity. There is a vast difference between being straight and upright (Psalm 15:2; 84:11), and being stiff. A disciplined mind (Proverbs 16:32), like a disciplined body, is alert and graceful. St Bernard of Clairvaux said, 'To surrender to God with love is to yield back to Him what is already His' (*On Loving God*). Thus we fast – if we do! – in order to increase our respect for all of God's daily gifts – to us, to humanity and to the natural world.

Discipline can be clenched, rigid and escapist; or discipline can be *kind*. It can be uplifting or fraught: 'Neither jovial nor magnanimous, centred in a self which – in spite of its tremor of receptivity – seldom embraces or creates what is outside itself

---

[182] George Bernard Shaw, 'Virtues and Vices', Maxims for Revolutionists in *Man and Superman* (London: Constable, 1947).

and beyond' (Virginia Woolf, *Modern Fiction*). Where is your blend of discipline in this spectrum? Are you well rounded in your whole approach to the Way?

Ascetics can fall into excess: 'When an intensely loyal but narrow mind is grasped by the feeling of fanaticism (loyalty taken to a convulsive extreme) … It idealises the devotion itself.' William James goes on to observe that when ascetics restrain themselves because of fear (whether self-imposed or from an externally enforced regime), they tend to become tight and stunted. Their growth into fuller humanity is constricted. The dangers are dire and potentially pathological. They include sanctimony, parsimony, naivety, self-absorption, scrupulosity, prudery, masochism and being short-tempered.[183]

Self-discipline, like chastity, is saved and redeemed from becoming self-absorbed, an end in itself, when seen and lived in context – as part of an Other-centred vocation. Those who are on the path need to stay spiritually agile. And they do well to keep in mind the numerous wider forms of self-denial – such as patience, not succumbing to self-pity after a setback, keeping silence, bearing with the faults of others, or being kind to someone you find unappealing.

Techniques and devotions are fine if they are not idolised, not seen as primary or as ends in themselves. Trust your instincts and the purity of your intentions. God looks with deep-searching eyes at intention, orientation and direction. Tone and timbre are vital. If the person and their motives are balanced, the tone of their customs and their life will be creative, not obsessive; expansive, not restrictive.[184] They blend

---

[183] William James, *The Varieties of Religious Experience* (London: Longmans, Green & Co., 1902) Lectures XIV and XV. 'The true medicine to cure us of pride, is to keep down and thwart touchiness of mind', St Philip Neri, Fr Faber, ed., *If God be With Us: Maxims of St Philip Neri* (Leominster: Gracewing, 1994) p.42.

[184] 'The minute attention to propriety stops the growth of virtue', Mary Wollstonecraft, letter to her younger sister Everina, 4th March 1787, in J. Todd, ed., *The Collected Letters of Mary Wollstonecraft* (Columbia: Columbia University Press, 2004).

high standards with compassion – towards self and others. True self-discipline shows the fruit of its work, but does not broadcast: does not boast about the daily tending and gardening.

Richard Avedon, an American fashion and portrait photographer, took one of his first photographs at the age of nine when he was taken to a concert given by Rachmaninov. Afterwards the young boy waited by the stage door with a Brownie box camera. By coincidence, the composer lived in the same apartment building as Avedon's grandparents. He later recalled listening to the great musician practising at the piano, hour after hour: 'Maybe that is where I learned about discipline; what is so compelling about any craft; and what is beautiful about rigour.'[185]

The sophisticated are often envious of the guileless. Simplicity is a form of genius. Direct, straight and single-minded – in their sincerity and in all the colours of their humanity – the unlettered are often closer to God than the intellectual surrounded by turgid tomes, or the stiff-necked (self-admiring) ascetic cramped (and made crabby) by his ungracious sacrifices![186]

> In these deep solitudes and awful cells,
> Where heavenly pensive contemplation dwells,
> And ever-musing melancholy reigns.
>
> Alexander Pope, 'Eloisa to Abelard'

I do not picture many of the saints – certainly not St Francis of Assisi – as aloof in their piety, or of furrowed brow. Their motto is: charity with cheerfulness (Matthew 6:16). If the first attribute of a saint is devotion to God and neighbour, the

---

[185] *Current Biography Yearbook, 1973* (New York: H. H. Wilson & Co., 1976) p.23.
[186] 'A man whose blood is very snow-broth; one who never feels the wanton stings and motions of the sense' (*Measure for Measure*, I iv).

second is surely joy. The labours of our earthly life prepare us for the joys of the life to come.

On the twin subjects of intensity and frequency of practice, St Francis de Sales advises, 'A continual and moderate sobriety is preferable to violent abstinences practised by fits and alternated with great relaxations.' Restraint is to be exercised wherever the craving is greatest, in holding back from the object to which you feel most bound. He continues,

> Reform should begin in and with all the desires of our heart (Joel 2:12) because our actions mirror the quality and disposition of our heart … It is more efficacious to cleanse and purify our heart than to mortify the flesh.

Introduction to the Devout Life

More than any other aspect of spiritual life, mortification needs a relaxed attitude and a gentle tone. Mortification is meant to be a secret between you and God (and your spiritual director, if you have one) – without pride, without advertisement (Matthew 6).[187] Indeed, to parade (or overdo) self-denial is rapidly to imprison and poison it – for self and others.

Shakespeare tells us – and ascetics in particular – about the need for balance: 'What revels are in hand? Is there no play, to ease the anguish of a torturing hour?' (*A Midsummer Night's Dream*, V i).

Acts of penance

The season of Lent is, at root, not about self-punishment or endurance but rather a redefining of life lived from the heart. Nor are the observances of Lent designed to free the soul from

---

[187] 'Praising their own lean and sallow abstinence' (Milton, *Comus*).

the body: fasting is not a way to forget or denigrate the body, but a reminder to render due care, and also to celebrate the complex wonder of what God has bequeathed to you.

Penitence is not only a backward-looking remorse. It has two sides or aspects. The Lenten series of small deaths is, first, a turning aside from what is petty or unworthy; anything that smothers and stifles the joys of a sincere follower.

Lent is also a looking forward – after being tested – to freedom and newness of life. Indeed, the name of this season comes from old English for the lengthening of daylight hours, as winter gives way to spring. Discipline leads to freedom. Moreover, discipline itself needs a spirit of freedom: the labour does not feed the ego; there is no gloating on the personal cost, the rising at 4am for the first office of the day:

> For as in bodies, thus in souls, we find
> What wants in blood and spirits, swell'd with wind;
> Pride, where wit fails, steps in to our defence,
> And fills up the mighty void of sense!

Alexander Pope, *An Essay on Criticism*

Like love, a healthy (and therefore authentic) self-denial 'is not puffed up … seeketh not her own' (1 Corinthians 13:4, 5, KJV), and shuns the mirror of self-regard. Moreover – again to adopt the Pauline description of love – true self-denial is kind.

Just as the various forms of sacrifice have their positive side – being derived from the Latin 'make holy' – so also penitence is meant to be positive and forward-looking. Penitence begins with honest evaluation of past and present, and points to a new and wholehearted resolution for the future. If there is no penitence, there can be no progress.

The hallmark of genuine self-denial (in contrast to the preening, self-satisfied variety that is proud and self-righteous) and of all forms of sacrifice, large or small, is that their tone and ultimate motive are life-affirming – not repression, but

313

evolution. Acts of self-denial are creative when the instinct for life is at their heart and centre. The aim is to be freed from the bondage of a self-serving life: to be free for God and for widespread service in His name. *To Him alone is the glory and the reputation*. To discipline the body is not just to deny: the aim is to *affirm* – to foster and manifest your body's potential for excellence, as a sanctuary of God.

Contrition and renunciation, repentance and reparations: all are first steps only. God does not wish us to be obstinate or self-righteous in our asceticism. To grow to their full and God-intended bloom, penances need light and warmth, and a wide horizon. The purpose of penance is release, not restriction; humble goodness, not flawless performance.

> Perfection is a barrier. One puts perfection between oneself and others. Between oneself and one's self.[188]

Just as we should be specific in prayer, praise and thanksgiving, so also we should give details when repenting – perhaps choosing one item of regret each week, not overloading our remorse. Being specific highlights unskilful behaviour, increases learning and makes us more alert in future to avoid stuck reactive patterns. In sacramental confession we encounter God's mercy. As well as offering assurance of release from the burden of guilt and sin, it supplies supernatural grace to help us do better in the future. We leave the confessional lighter, with a clean slate, for we have a God who not only forgives the sins of a true penitent; He forgets (Ezekiel 18:22).

Repentance (*metanoia*) can entail a resetting of mind and heart, will and focus. St Augustine spoke of repentance as leading to transformation. Picture the way disordered iron filings form a pattern – often an aesthetically pleasing one –

---

[188] Paul Valéry, trans. S. Gilbert, *Complete Works of Paul Valéry, Volume 14: Analects* (Princeton: Princeton University Press, 2015) p.20.

when a magnet is placed near them. When we open our whole self to God's touch and design, we allow Him – if He so wishes – to rearrange and coordinate the strands of our life and our being: our values and aims, our energy and use of time, our motives, our destination – and a new vision of the way to it. In his book *The Cost of Discipleship*, Bonhoeffer writes about 'costly grace': it is costly because God invites us to forsake everything for love of Him. Perhaps the amount of grace that God grants is in proportion to our gratitude and our cooperation – our glad and active acceptance, our full use of every gift and skill from His hand.

Recreation

As we grow in maturity, we become more self-aware. This means we do more frequent self-listening – and deeper heeding of what emerges from attending to body, mind, emotions and soul. Above all, we keep examining intentions and actions: Are we being true to our integrity? We thus continue to realign with our true self.

This realigning, this inspecting and cleaning of the dark places of mind and memory and motives, is necessary if we are to grow (Psalm 51:6). It is serious, earnest work – and often painful. For this reason, those trying to lead a spiritual life need their Sabbath: one day in the week when spiritual routines and practices are to some extent relaxed, as well as being a day when we rest from work.

When you are in an art gallery, it is only by standing back that you can see a painting as a whole, and fully admire the result of detailed brushwork, colour, contour, use of space and of light and shade. Proper perspective is all. So also in contemplative living: vocation needs vacation.

The more creative the life, the greater the need for alone time. Encounter – especially in any form of caring or healing – is one of the highest (and most complex and exacting) forms of creativity. Thus people in the caring professions have an extra need for aloneness, but they are the very ones who find it hardest to find (or make) time for solitude – partly because of the needs of the people they see each day and work with, and partly because some of us overidentify with the helper role. We speak of 'touching base' with friends or family: do we allow enough time to touch base with our self? Time to reflect, assimilate, integrate, savour and plan; time also just to *be*.

An anecdote about one of the desert fathers, Abbot Antony (St Antony the Great), tells how he was relaxing and conversing with some monks. A game hunter saw them, and expressed both surprise and disapproval. Abbot Anthony said, 'Put an arrow to your bow, and shoot the arrow.' This the hunter did. 'Now shoot another,' said the elder, smiling. 'And another, and another.'

The hunter protested, 'If I bend the bow all the time, it will break.'

Anthony replied, 'So it is with the work for God. If we pushed ourselves beyond our natural limits, we brethren would collapse. It is thus vital, from time to time, to relax our efforts.'[189] Recreation is one of the best ways to recreate the self.

Recollection

Do you truly seek union with God? Then keep recollected (Psalm 20:7–8). Recollection is far more than recalling the mind to God the ever-present. Recollection is also a mobilising of all faculties and resources, readying the body and centring the heart in Him; or – seen differently – sensing Him in the heart's centre.

---

[189] Ward, ed., *Sayings of the Desert Fathers*, p.3.

You need not look either here or there. He is no
farther away than the door of your heart. He stands
there, lingering, waiting for us to be ready: to open
the door and let Him in.[190]

Recollection is akin to the poise and vigilance of athlete or
musician, in the potentially tense moments before action: the
sprinter, with feet in the starting blocks and fingers pointed at
the line; a pianist, as they bring their hands from their lap to
hover above the keyboard, for a few seconds of inner
dedication.

The purpose of prayer is to remind ourself that God lives
within us and reigns around us. God-consciousness, like all our
faculties, responds to training. And thus constant brief
aspirations towards God – glances of confident love, lifting
heart and mind to Him – foster our relation with the Eternal.
These frequent self-openings to God colour all we do, and
purify all we are. The longer and more loyally we persevere in
spiritual searching, the more surely do we cease to separate our
practical life from our prayer life, for we shall see that all of life
points beyond itself.

In addition to gazing on God at spontaneous moments of
the day, brief prayer and recollection can be time-led or event-
led, or both. Time-led remembrance of Him can, for example,
be hourly or half-hourly.

For event-led recollection, bow to God, inwardly or
outwardly or both, when you get up and at bedtime, before you
start and after you finish all forms of work, before and after
you meet people, on leaving and returning home (Psalm 121:8),
and before and after meals. And also pray during all activities,
doing everything with clear mindfulness, noticing posture and
movement and each stage of each action, minor as well as
major:

---

[190] Meister Eckhart, trans. Claud Field, *Meister Eckhart's Sermons* (London:
Allenson, 1909), Sermon on Luke 2:42.

> We must work quietly, calmly and lovingly before
> God, beseeching Him to accept our labours.[191]

Remember to pray during transitions and turning points of your day. Prayer can turn even the short delays and waiting of daily life into positive, fruitful events – time for repose and communion, calming oneself and other people nearby. For example, you can pray while halted at traffic lights, washing up, or while standing in a shop or supermarket queue.

Just as in a classical concerto every bar of passage work has its own purpose and dignity, so also every minute of transition time has potential (and perhaps unforeseen) value. Far from resenting having to wait, we can thank God for creating this unexpected space – time for more communing with Him; time also to prepare for our next act of love and service. Tolstoy said that the handling of transitions is one of the most vital gifts for a writer of fiction. This is true also for daily life, as well as for major life changes.

When reason has taken you as far as it can – in your understanding of God, and His arrivals in daily life – let your spiritual instincts take over. Then, with grace, you may be able to see faint outlines of His veiled epiphanies. 'Then will He sometimes send a beam of spiritual light, piercing this cloud of unknowing that is betwixt thee and Him' (*The Cloud of Unknowing*, chapter xxvi).

We can only ever begin to know what and who we truly love. Love is the purest and most direct form in which reality is shown to us: 'So, let us say … Since we love, we know enough' (Robert Browning, 'A Pillar at Sebzevar').

---

[191] Brother Lawrence, *The Practice of the Presence of God*, Maxims: Necessary Practices for Attaining the Spiritual Life, n. 3.

Arrow prayers

The form of prayer discussed below – which combines self-examination, self-awareness and a self-offering – uses single words or short phrases: for use as frequent affirmations and as a way of inspiring – and keeping one's focus on – higher values.

Throughout day and night, offer fond glances to God, frequent and ardent (The Song of Solomon 4:9; 2 Corinthians 4:18):

> Prayer is a short dart of longing love.
>
> *The Cloud of Unknowing*, vi

> The easiest means of practicing vocal prayer consists in uttering fervent expressions of affection. ... They are in order at all times and in all places, at work, at meals, at recreation, at home or away from home. They may take the form of acts of desire, surrender, love, oblation, or self-denial; they may be acts of petition, thanksgiving, humility, confidence and the like.
>
> St Alphonsus Liguouri, *The School of Christian Perfection*

These prayers – spontaneous, time-led, event-led – may be short (Matthew 6:7), but, if felt and expressed by the whole person, you will gradually come to see God as the ever-present Reality, your Creator, your support and Sustainer, and your Comforter in whom you can always find refuge and strength: 'Sufficient is Thine arm alone, And our defence is sure' (Watts, 'O God, our help in ages past').

You can retain something from the day's *lectio divina*, use prayers of your own devising, or choose a prayer hallowed by long tradition. Some possibilities include:

- St Francis of Assisi's prayer – 'My God, my All'; or 'My God, I love you';

- 'O Lord make haste to help me' (recommended by John Cassian);

- 'Jesus' or 'Yeshua';

- 'Come Holy Spirit';

- 'Abba, Father';

- St Faustina's prayer – 'Jesus, I trust in you';

- 'Lord Jesus Christ, Son of God, have mercy on me' (the Jesus Prayer, favoured in the Orthodox Church);

- 'Thy will be done';

- Fr Don Dolindo Ruotolo's prayer – 'Oh Jesus, I surrender myself to You; take care of everything'; or

- 'I give You thanks for all things'.

The author of *The Cloud of Unknowing* (chapter 37) recommends a short word like 'Love', or 'God' or 'Help'. These affirmations and invocations are to be made with awe, mindful that God's name is an aspect of His holy nature and character. Prayer is to the soul what bloodflow is to the body. Repeat them, never in a routine or mechanical way, but from the whole of you. Absorb them into your heart and mind. Let them reach the very depths of your being. Speak them inwardly and they will speak back to you all through the day's changing circumstances, colouring them (i.e., both the prayers and the circumstances) with ever-new meaning and purpose. Prayers are to be lived.

Their use helps to unite aspiration with action. These short prayers will gradually mould – to their godly pattern – your body and mind and soul. Because the words are so few and so simple, they help us to soar beyond language into the mystery of silence. At the heart of silence is the presence of God Himself.

The adoring gaze, the spontaneous loving glances (articulated throughout Psalm 68), remind us of His holy presence, keeping us open, attuned, sensitive to God's touch, and responsive:

> One single grateful thought, raised to Heaven, is a perfect prayer.

> Lessing, *Minna von Barnhelm*, ii, 7

The Cloud of Unknowing suggests letting your chosen word or phrase resound, in mind and heart and soul. One aid for this is to alternate short, simple aspirations with pauses of integrating silence.

No transformation will take place unless aspiration is heart-led – warm, committed and *felt*. John Bunyan said, 'It is better to have a heart breathing few words than many words without a heart.'

> Words are like leaves; and where most abound,
> Much fruit of sense beneath is rarely found.

> Alexander Pope, *An Essay on Criticism*

The choosing of a short prayer for the day kindles desire (Psalm 73:25). It will inspire you to want to love: for God's glory only, by offering to Him your use of each moment. Bound together with the Company of Heaven, the more you pray, the more you will want to pray – until praying becomes as constant (and life-giving) as breathing.

A positive momentum will be created. Morale – spiritual and psychological – will improve. An undertone of prayer will impel and permeate every action, lifting each into the climate and atmosphere of the holy (Psalm 73:28).

Short prayers become engraved in the deepest recesses of one's being, and slowly yield some of their secret treasure – provided you live these prayers, faithfully and consistently. The benefits of prayer far outnumber the total number of days or hours during which you pray. Among the rewards and encouragements of repeating a specially chosen brief prayer, while in the midst of action, are to:

God
Recall us to the atmosphere of Eternity
Keep faith vibrant
Refocus aspirations
Increase the desire to praise
Ensure a steady commitment
Renew a sense of surrender
Remind us of our dependence: our need to receive, before we can convey
Bolster the stability of devotion
Rededicate our energy, and all our faculties

Self
Help us maintain our true direction
Preserve calmness
Maintain perseverance and endurance
Make firm the Godward disposition of body, will, heart and soul

Others
Show solidarity with the needs of our neighbour
Purify motives
Ready us to do God's will, and only His will
Colour all aspects of our daily life, so that we see unity in variety
Reaffirm our self-consecration to God, who made us to be His loving servants

In all methods of prayer, 'little and often' is better than 'much but seldom'. The simpler the prayer style, the easier it will be to bring the spirit of prayer into daily life. One action is far more beneficial than 1,000 pious wishes. Speak (or sing) your fervent aspirations. Above all, begin.

Growth in virtue

If you wish to discover God's way, then, as part of your morning devotions, choose (and all day cherish) one or several of Christ's qualities. Meditate often on His mercy and love, His purity, His forgiveness and goodness. During the day, remember your chosen perfection as your model and example, so as to be and behave as the Almighty would wish. This is what Wordsworth termed 'meditated action' – to be contemplative during because contemplative before.[192]

An alternative to contemplating the goodness of God or His constancy (2 Timothy 2:13; Hebrews 13:8) is to choose a virtue you wish to strengthen or sustain. The seven virtues comprise the three Christian virtues (faith, hope and charity: 1 Corinthians 13:13) and Plato's four cardinal (or natural) virtues: justice, prudence, temperance and fortitude.

Alternatively, you could choose one of the nine fruits of the Spirit (Galatians 5:22–23): love, joy, peace, patience/long-suffering, gentleness, goodness, faith, meekness, self-control. De- Sales adds purity, discretion in speech, humility, mortification of the heart, simplicity/poverty, obedience, thoughtfulness for others, forbearance, diligence, modesty and perseverance. If you are conscious of a particular weakness, choose to work on the contrary virtue, for 'the chains of habit

---

[192] 'Discourse of the Wanderer', and 'An Evening Visit by the Lake' in William Wordsworth, Ed. Sally Bushell, James A. Bulter, *et. al. The Excursion* (Ithaca: Cornell University Press, 2007) Book IX, Argument.

are often too small to be felt until they are too strong for us to break' (D. L. Moody).

No virtue stands alone: each helps to protect all the other virtues, and each is brought ever nearer to perfection by the other virtues. Dwell on the chosen virtue during your morning prayer time. Taste it, in the heart, as the mystics advise. Give it time to penetrate. Trust that, by frequent and loving returns, the virtue will become deeply assimilated. Resolve to develop and apply it as often as you can, all through the day. It will stir (or disturb) you, and will thus do its work deep within. Respond to the grace of the moment.

In an unforced way, recall – and continue to name – the virtue during times of transition (Luke 22:41); periods of leisure; during spells of special need or affliction; and whenever the virtue-thought spontaneously arises (Romans 12:12).

> Love virtue, she alone is free,
> She can teach ye how to climb.

John Milton, *Comus*

By translating virtues and religious themes into action, they become an integral part of you and your conduct, expressions of your personality, having made the descent from the voice to the mind, and then from the mind to the heart. The aim – after contemplation and experience of living the chosen value or virtue – is fully to identify with its nature, its tone, and its enduring meaning: with the aid of grace, to become the virtue.

Virtue (*kalós*) is vitality (akin to the Greek work for manliness, *andreía*) allied to – and generated by – noble purpose. Spiritually motivated virtuous action makes a person *aretés*, a bearer of high values and purpose.

Choose as your model and ideal, your day-by-day inspiration, those good and often saintly people whom you know or have known, or heard of, or read about, who shine as exemplars of living, loving prayer.

Psalms 5:3 and 119:147 remind us that the first thought of the day belongs to God. In your morning prayers, determine to cherish all aspects of life and to keep listening to God, letting Him be your guardian and guide on every step of the day's journey – in loving dependence and in loving communion (Psalm 25:5). Pray that every event will be blessed by Him. Resolve to cope in a benign and mellow way with delays, difficulties, interruptions.

> Forecast what business, what conversation, what opportunities, you are likely to meet with to serve God; what temptations may befall you to offend Him, either by anger, by vanity, or any other irregularity; and prepare yourself with a firm resolution to make the best use of those means which may offer themselves to you to serve God and advance in devotion; ... And it is not enough to make this resolution; you must also prepare the means of putting it into execution.
>
> St Francis de Sales, *Introduction to the Devout Life*

Having identified areas of personal growth to be specially watched during the day – pray about them, one by one. For example, you could hope to win over by gentleness someone who has slighted you. Love is the queen of virtues, commanding all the activity of a free being. It is valid to pray that love may be our centre of gravity but, of ourselves, we are not able to give unconditional love. At best we can be a channel of God's infinite reservoir of warmth and affection (1 Corinthians 15:10; Philippians 2:13). Unconditional love flows forth from a soul aligned and united with the infinite source.

Self-examination

In your evening devotions, consider how often you have remembered and practised the virtue or theme you have chosen for the day. In your enquiry, be specific about times and occasions. Ask yourself what progress you feel you have made to incorporate the virtue and make it an integral part of your daily life.

Review events or encounters which you could have handled better, and from which you can now learn, and about which you can make resolutions. But beware the danger of religious indigestion. It is far more helpful to work on one or two lapses, in depth and in detail, than to multiply your contrition items, and thus overload your willing conscience (Ecclesiastes 5:2; Matthew 6:7).

Seek forgiveness for those times during the day when you did not (or did not fully) respond to His love, and the opportunities He has provided. Ask God to fortify you, and to help you do better tomorrow. Thank Him for both daily and special blessings, item by item. And reflect on any new insight about the wisdom of God's timing.

In your reflections, you may find links joining what had at first seemed unrelated. And you may now discern many more incidents which reveal God's helping hand. Look forward to a new day, and any noteworthy events you are likely to be involved in. Greet also the chance to turn today's mishaps into tomorrow's learning.

Be content to make progress with one virtue at a time, because improvement in one aspect of life influences the others. Thus spiritual growth becomes cumulative. In the end, all virtues coalesce into the supreme virtue of love.

Be patient with your personal growth and the progress of your spiritual life. Build your temple of prayer little by little, brick by brick. Do not overload yourself. He who tries to snatch all, drops all. A regular examination of conscience fashions from our good intentions, a sturdy piety (Romans 12:2; Psalm 139:23–24).

In addition to a daily examination of conscience, it can be helpful to periodically reflect upon the byways and paths you have walked upon so far. Here are some questions we can ask ourselves:

- Do I take good care of my body?

- How well do I balance work with rest, recreation and leisure?

- My pleasures – are they truly enriching?

- Am I moderate in use of money?

- Material things – am I thankful for them while I am using them?

- Do I crave or hoard? Or do I view all possessions in a spirit of stewardship?

- Are there any ways in which I can simplify my lifestyle?

- How do I cope with life's uncertainties?

- How resilient am I when confronting delay, criticism, setbacks?

- Do I treat every problem as a challenge?

- Am I sincere and reliable towards other people? Do I seek unity? Do I accept differences – of opinion, values, personality and background?

- What is the tone of my communicating with others? Am I ever defensive or manipulative? Do I sometimes have a hidden agenda, or am I open and straightforward?

- Where is my time focus? Nostalgic (or angst-ridden) about the past? Overly concerned about the future, rather than making prudent provision? Do I usually focus on the present?

- Can I be more creative in my use of time? How can I allow more time and space in my life for the things that really matter?

- Do I constantly review my priorities?

- What inclinations sway my heart? What desires threaten to possess me?

- Is my tempo calm – whenever I move, walk, work, eat, speak?

- Is there a gap between concept and commitment, devotions and deeds? If so, how wide is it, and can I bridge it?[193]

Or you could use the Beatitudes (Matthew 5:3–12) as your framework for self-enquiry:

- How free am I from pride or vanity?

- Do I allow myself to feel loss, sorrow and grief?

- Am I modest?

- Do I thirst for truth, and hunger for justice?

- Am I at all times forgiving?

- Is my whole being (body, mind, heart and soul) concentrated on (and consecrated to) closer union with God? How pure is my heart?

- Where and when, and with whom, can I be a peacemaker?

- Am I willing to accept criticism for a course of action (or a cause) I believe in?

---

[193] 'Giving yourself your word to do something ought to be as sacred as giving your word to others', André Gide, trans. Justin O'Brien, *Journals 1889–1913*, Volume I (Chicago: University of Illinois Press, 2000), 8th February 1907, p.107.

Any of these areas of personal life can be material for prayer. If so, the reflections could end with a pledge to unite your will to the movements of grace. Prayer is true prayer only if it ends with new determination for a more loving future.

Flexibility

If we aspire to be living witnesses to His ever-unfolding eternal truth, we must not become too enamoured of any one notion, any one rhythm or approach or way of perceiving. Instead of copying other people's ways and patterns, however worthy, we can enjoy making and remaking our own designs for the good life.

Each individual – in accordance with capacity and temperament – needs to find the best and most apt proportioning of time for spiritual exercises. Having found a suitable combination, we need to keep a flexible approach – as to frequency, duration, times of day, intensity and methods. The six safeguards of spiritual life are simplicity, sincerity, openness, experiment, stability/continuity and balance. These protect 'the patient bulbs of my hopes' (D. H. Lawrence, 'Discipline').

Every day we need to refind our centre and our balance, with a simplicity that becomes progressively more profound and graceful. A change in needs or health or outer circumstances, or being at a different age or stage of growth, may cause us to alter content, the method or rhythm, the combination or the amount. This flexibility will help keep spiritual practices live, dynamic and meaningful. These activities should never become ends in themselves. They are meant to be geared and offered for their ultimate purpose: rendering glory to God. The goal of all disciplines, all forms of religious practice, is not 'to escape from' but 'to become free for'.

Then go beyond methods and techniques, in pure receptivity to God's action: love transcends (and educates) technique. The value of prayer depends not so much on the form we choose, nor on the words we use – long or short, formal or informal, articulate expression or sighs of longing. What matters is the depth of our faith and the warmth of our fervour.

At one stage of her journey, St Teresa wanted to emulate the rigorous penances of Catherine of Cardona. When Teresa's confessor forbade her to do so, she was tempted to disobey until God said to her, 'My daughter, your way is good and safe. I value your obedience more than an imitation of her penance.' This is no generic ranking: it is a reminder that we must each be true to our own route.

Religious practices are not meant for regimentation but for freedom in our witness and the blossoming of our journey to the Godhead. Our capacity for taking infinite paths needs to be relaxed; open to imagination, inspiration and variety. A Greek myth tells how Bellerophon – hero of Corinth and slayer of the monster Chimera – was one day riding the winged horse Pegasus, symbol of inspiration. By an act of folly, betrayal or swank he fell to the ground, and limped through life ever after. On any creative path, balance is all.

Our life purpose and destiny is to work but never force, always to accept, and conform to, God's wishes, and to let Him work through us, in divine–human cooperation and partnership, participating – in all possible ways – in spreading His holy Word, and helping to incarnate God's kingdom. Be ever grateful for God's never-failing reliability and consistency (Lamentations 3:23). Rejoice in His dependability (James 1:17), 'a prop to our infirmity' (Wordsworth, *The Prelude*, Book II).

Give centrality in your life to prayer. From prayer, everything else flows. This is the authentic way to sustain your integrity, and the only way to maintain real discipleship. For just as you have need and hope of God (Lamentations 3:24), so He has hopes for you.

Prayers

May I keep faithful to the plan and order of each day, without any fussiness or rigidity, and be flexible, at every moment, to the promptings that come from Your holy perspective.

I resolve to veil austerities behind a discreet, self-effacing manner: may I show real tenderness for the delicacy of other souls; and, at all times, acceptance, forgiveness, generosity. May my disciplines thus remain safe and secure, because prudent and secret – being for You, and known only by You.

Grant, O God, that I may be modest of appetite (in all forms), and prudent in use of all the faculties You give me.

My Shield, my Stronghold, You have brought me safely to the light of a new day, and a new beginning. I consecrate myself afresh to You, Lord, Indwelling and Transcendent. By Your grace, may I keep mind and heart stayed on You.

VII
The Day

O Lord, who hast brought me from the sleep of last
night
Unto the joyous light of this new day,
Be Thou ever bringing me from the first gleams of
this day
Unto the guiding light of eternal life.

Celtic prayer

A book could be written about the value of getting up an hour earlier than usual, to greet 'the innocent brightness of a newborn Day' (Wordsworth, 'Ode on the Intimations of Immortality'). A survey of great composers showed that a majority were at their most creative just before or just after breakfast. Our day can be determined by how we use its first hour. Depending on personal needs, this hour can provide:

- a communing with God by prayer, meditation and reflection;

- time to limber up;

- a deepening of your stability and concentration by watching your breath;

- a preview of the coming day's events: seeing them in their true perspective so that energy (physical, intellectual and emotional) is saved for what is really important;

- a reminder of reserve strengths, which may be needed for challenges, expected or unexpected;

- time to get centred/balanced/coordinated and well paced for the rest of the day, so that, as often as possible, I listen, speak and behave from my best self.

It is a major boost for morale – throughout the day – to have used the first hour or two so productively. But this time is not only preparatory: it is precious, and to be prized, in and for itself: 'Oh that we had spent but one day in this world thoroughly well!' (Thomas à Kempis, *The Imitation of Christ*).

Each day is given to us by God – if we listen for the message of its uniqueness – with a special shape and colouring, and is filled with opportunities – some of which will never recur. Every hour is precious: 'This is the day which the Lord has made; let us rejoice and be glad in it' (Psalm 118:24).

Our sharpened awareness of each day's possibilities, and our own potential for missing out – neglecting, not seeing, or seeing but not taking action on what we see – can increase our sense of responsibility to greet and co-design each day in harmony and partnership with God (1 Corinthians 3:9). How we spend our days is how we spend our life.

> You should be a good economist of your moments.[194]

If you consecrate the whole of your life to God – each day, each hour, each moment – then all your activities converge into a holy simplicity. All the variety and multiplicity of life become unified, and – if it be God's wish – you will have deeper union with Him.

Each person, each event, each moment (whether joyful or painful), offers potential for learning and for spiritual growth.

---

[194] Lord Chesterfield, *Letters to His Son*, Letter CLXXXVII, 20th July 1749.

Above all, we need to trust in His ultimate plan and purpose for our life: 'Whatever God wills is most consoling, whether it is comfort or discomfort' (Eckhart, 'About the Will', *The Talks of Instruction*).

Routine

The desert fathers (from St Antony of Egypt onwards) did manual work every day except Sunday. On visits, St Athanasius (Antony's first biographer) usually found him contentedly weaving mats or baskets. Living the life of a renunciate, Anthony's day also included very early rising, pastoral interviews with other monks, reading sacred texts, and many hours on his knees in prayer.

Daily routines and observances can help us to keep our eyes on God and our service of Him. People in religious orders know the value of regularity and rhythm in their day. We can also learn from various professions about the importance of personal rituals. For example, many surgeons prepare for a major operation by being on automatic pilot in the early morning: they eat the same breakfast, put on the same clothes and drive to the hospital by their favourite route. They adopt these customs not usually because they are superstitious, but because it helps them to maintain clarity of attention: all their energy, all their concentration, is needed in the operating theatre. They will be ready to improvise, often at moments of crisis.

Adhering to a relatively structured day saves the mind from having to make many minor decisions and gives freedom to listen for the will and voice of God. But regularity need not mean repetitiveness (of attitude and/or action): like an artist or a musician, you can improvise, as the moment and the circumstances indicate. If every day has a threefold blend – continuity, spontaneity and rhythm – then God's living presence will be your guide, your ground base. The Way is very simple: each day walk, pray, eat, sleep, carry out your duties, read sacred Scripture. Do these things with full attention. Your opportunities for awakening are everywhere.

The imperative is to make the most of each day, each hour. Every day can be a summary of life, lived with the same vigour as if it were one's last. This means hoping, but not expecting; longing for, but also willing to let go; concentrating on the present, and leaving results and the future to God.

If I hold on to a desire too tightly, I am not fully allowing God to put His hand on the situation. My clutching feels like a solo effort accompanied by fear. God longs for it to be collaborative.

Grounding the day in prayer

The ultimate devotion is prayer woven into the fabric of daily life. Most people who seek to serve God through their work and relationships will build a framework of prayer to start and end each day. The first and the last word of the day belong to Him. If you want to become a loyal servant of God, be more prayer-full – from the very first moments after you wake up. Immediately, lift your heart and mind to Him. As soon as you wake up, remind yourself that God is present with you (now and always), and rejoice. Not only remind yourself, feel and experience His presence. Now be present to Him (Psalm 73:23, 28), and resolve to maintain communion.

Express to God your complete confidence and your hope (Psalm 71; Hebrews 6:18–19). Entrust yourself, consecrate yourself and your day to Him, your strength. All that you do will gain in depth (Matthew 13:8), energy and stillness. Offer everything to Him – all hopes and hurts, all coming events (the known and the unforeseen). Pray that you will stay in contact with Him. Thank your Maker for another day to love Him and serve Him. Finally, yield each of these prayers to God's sovereign action.

Many people find it both helpful and natural to begin and end their time of devotion with praise, the prayer of humble adoration. Here is an inspiring prayer by St Ignatius that is especially suitable for morning devotions:

> Fill us, we pray Thee, with Thy light and life that we may show forth Thy wondrous glory. Grant that Thy love may so fill our life that we may count nothing too small to do for Thee, and nothing too big to bear.

Having begun your devotions – using words and/or images, if you wish – enter the prayer of quiet: simple watching, and watching simply (Habakkuk 2:1, 3), with loving attentiveness. To pray is to kneel in dependence (Hebrews 4:9, 10).

At the end of your morning prayer make core resolves for the coming day, such as to maintain purity of heart, and a vivid sense of God's companionship. And pray that all your actions will be done in union with Him, in the service of His kingdom of love. The doer is God Himself (Isaiah 26:12). He produces our capacity for action, and inspires us to use our talents with and for love.

Midday is a brief rest on the day's journey, giving an opportunity to listen, no longer to the sounds of the world but to the sound of silence, and to find time to be alone with God (Psalm 55:17; Daniel 6:10). Having shut the doors of home and prayer room (or office), close also, as far as possible, the inner door – against unruliness and turmoil (Matthew 6:6). We do well to remember that the body's stillness is an ally of inner stillness.

Review/renew your good intentions, and pray for the strength to accomplish all your resolutions. Thank Him for the grace and privilege of your vocation. As well as strengthening your bond with God and sharing with Him the silence of eternity, noon-time prayers are ideal for intercession, and for sanctifying time, especially those periods of the day which you normally waste, or regard as unprofitable. Then you will not be slave to the passing show, but receive each moment from the hand of God – each moment to be spent giving Him glory.

As important as regular and more formal prayer times is the praying in between, when contemplation merges into loving service: the Word inspires – *becomes* – the doing of the Word (James 1:22).

> Remember God's presence as often as you can during the day … Sensing His eyes upon you – filled with incomparable love – pray: 'O God, why do I not look for you in the way that you are always looking on me? Why, when you think always of me, do I think so seldom of you? O my soul, my true home is in Him; but where am I most of the time?' … They who love God can never cease to think on Him, sigh for Him, aspire to Him, and speak to Him; and would, if it were possible, engrave the sacred name of Jesus on the breasts of all mankind. To this all things invite them, as there is no creature that does not declare to them the praises of their beloved.

St Francis de Sales, *Introduction to the Devout Life*

Tune all of yourself – body and mind, heart and soul – to God's wavelength. How are you to do this? Accept everything He presents to you. And in return, offer Him your whole day and night. Thank Him for His goodness (Psalm 26:6–7). Praise Him for all His gifts, and for specific gifts. Praise God for Himself. We grow by giving. Set aside half an hour to make the following meditation suggested by St Ignatius:

> I will ponder with great affection how much the Lord our God has done for me, and how much He has given me; and, finally, how much … the same

Lord desires to give of Himself to me, according to His divine decrees.

Then I shall reflect upon myself, and consider according to all reason and justice, what I ought to offer back to the Divine Majesty – that is, all I possess, and myself with it. Thus, as one who is moved by great feeling, I shall make this offering of myself.

St Ignatius, *Spiritual Exercises*

Interweave your life with constant conversation with God: intimate dialogue, yet with no diminution of respect and homage for His divinity. Indeed, God made us for this intimacy with Him. Nothing delights Him more. Tell God of your hopes and plans, your fears and wounds (Psalm 27:5), your joys – whatever is on your mind or in your emotional life.

All through the day, stay aware of God, ever at your side, walking with you – to protect, calm, guide and inspire. While you are in the very midst of all activities, remind yourself that you are always united to the Almighty. You are His child; God is your Creator and Sustainer. Praise Him for this, your highest good.

> Do as the little children do; little children who, with one hand hold fast to their father, and with the other gather strawberries or blackberries along the hedges; do you, while gathering and managing the goods of this world with one hand, with the other always hold fast the hand of your heavenly Father, turning to Him from time to time to see if your actions or occupations are pleasing to Him; but take heed, above all things, that you never let go His hand, thinking to gather more; for should He let you go, you will not be able to take another step without falling. ... Thus will God work with you, in you, and

for you, and your labour shall be followed by consolation.

St Francis de Sales, *Introduction to the Devout Life*

If you are God-centred, then your part in this divine–human dialogue is threefold: to *wait*, to *hear* and then to *respond*. 'Speak, Lord, for your servant is listening' (1 Samuel 3:9, NIV UK). Allow this daily conversation to become friendship. How marvellous that this is what our Sovereign Majesty is also most hoping for.

Now, and at each moment, God is available and ever-present in the very core and centre of your soul. In addition, He is always wishing to speak to you, via all the events and circumstances of everyday life. Your role is to match God's presence by being present to Him, in loving remembrance (1 Thessalonians 5:18). Earthly life is our preparation and proving ground for life in eternity.

In your evening devotions, thank God for the untold number of benefits He gives, and for any special graces you have received. Raise heart and mind to God – as you did when you woke up, and as you have been trying to do from then until now. Reoffer to Him all the work and happenings of the day. Then ask yourself:

- In what ways, and by which people, has God been calling me?

- Have I been watchful and sensitive: to Him, to myself, to others?

- How have I responded? Consider any neglect: of people, of duty or of responsibility, and above all, any faltering of attention to Him. Recall events which you could have handled better, with more tact.

- Have I allowed God to reach me, touch me, guide me?

- Have I hallowed both time and His holy name?

- Am I increasing in love?

Gaze on God with the eye of the soul, and then conclude with a brief prayer: Please grant me a peaceful night. I entrust my body and soul, all my relatives and friends, to the care of Your providence. Accompany your drift into sleep with a prayer word or phrase, or aspiration, taking St Teresa of Ávila's advice: 'as you ready yourself for sleep, see yourself as releasing your mind and body into the arms of God'.

> When the soft dews of kindly sleep
> My wearied eyelids gently steep,
> Be my last thought, how sweet to rest
> For ever on my Saviour's breast.
>
> John Keble, hymn, 'Sun of My Soul, Thou Saviour Dear'

How grand is the place of honour we should accord to prayer – every day of our life, and all day. In the triad model, your prayer to *God* is adoration and thanksgiving; prayer for *self-healing* is (in part) confession and a plea for absolution, and His forgiveness; prayer for *others* is placing their needs in the arms of the God of mercy.

Prayers

May I value the divine importance of this day, seeing it as an integral part or portion of my whole life – specially designed and fashioned by You, and therefore irreplaceable.

In love and obedience, and with action matching aspiration, I offer unto You the results of all that I shall do this day. May it

*please You to grant me more strength, hour by hour, to
cultivate a spirit of consecration in all I think and say and do,
dedicating each moment of my life to You.*

*In all things – major and seemingly minor – may I correspond
to Your graces, and fulfil Your hopes for me this day, mindful
that some of its offerings and opportunities may never recur.*

OTHERS

I
Chastity

*And for His dwelling and His throne
Chooseth the pure in heart.*

John Keble, hymn, 'Blest are the Pure in Heart'

Reverence for the other – an I:Thou relationship – entails chastity: in the sense not necessarily of celibacy (a form of self-denial, to which a few are called), but of *guarding the gift of self for marriage* and the *sanctifying of affection*. In specific terms, this means care and balance in food, drink, sex, sleep, rest (Mark 6:31), exercise and recreation, and a chaste use of each of the senses – especially discretion over what we see, for sight is the most influential of the senses (Luke 11:34), and potentially the most wayward. Hence Rousseau in *Émile* says we should restrain the impetuosity of the eye, for what we see inscribes itself deeply on the psyche.

In a seminal Chicago symposium, René Spitz reported on his and his Denver colleagues' observations that it is the gift of vision that first serves to integrate messages received from the other senses.[195] As Joan Erikson puts it: 'We begin life with our relatedness to the eyes [and relatedness via the eyes] ... It is with the eyes that concern and love are communicated, and also anger. Growing maturity does not alter this eye-relatedness

---

[195] See Maria W. Piers, ed., *Play and Development: A Symposium* (New York: W. W. Norton & Co., 1972).

for, all through life, our social intercourse is eye-focused: the eye blesses or curses.'[196] It expresses what we would never dare put into words: 'Love's tongue is in the eyes' (Phineas Fletcher, *Piscatory Eclogues*, V, xiii).

The way I use my senses, and the way I treat my body, speaks of, reveals, or exposes how I regard my whole self. You protect yourself – and respect others – by ensuring that what you eat and drink, and what you see and hear and communicate, are all wholesome and balanced.

Chastity is for all, not only for the celibate (Matthew 5:8). Chastity – for someone single – means abstaining from sex, and the marginal field leading to it. It means respecting boundaries, and guarding purity of heart. Within a committed relationship, chastity means having a pure eye and a betrothed heart – seeing marriage as God's finest possible gift, elevated and also earthed: the daily, hourly living of one's awed vision, in a spirit of delight and thanksgiving.

A religious attitude to life only shuns experience that is enjoyed for its own sake. Chaste action ensures a right and healthy use of God-given powers: for union and for love. A chaste person does not see the loved one lustfully, does not glut or gorge on the sensual. Of course, this does not preclude desire: it hallows arousal rather than denying it. Sex, seen as sacred, is the consummation of oneness. Chaste living is the protector, the trustee, of intimacy. Chastity gives perspective, thus preventing (or rescuing) love from the hovering danger of becoming indulgent, enclosed. Chastity is fullness of life and the fulfilment of love. Chastity weds discretion and direction to passion.

Ultimately, it is for the self-truth of each of us to find a personal vision and version of what it means to be chaste. As we mature spiritually, this self-truth – as it applies to emotional

---

[196] Joan Erikson, 'Eye to Eye' in Gyorgy Kepes, ed., *The Man-Made Object* (New York: George Braziller, 1966).

health, any issue of ethics, and any aspect of conduct – will become more and more clear.

Chastity involves watchfulness: of impulse (in thoughts, feelings and behaviour), speech, sincerity of motive, and manner and tone of action. Like every true form of chastity, this careful observing, in the moment, is all for positive purpose: more knowledge of God and His ways, ever-closer union, more faithful witness and expression of Love, and choosing healthy outlets for our affections. Chastity has the potential to influence and benefit our whole conduct of life. Self-mastery is the first and finest of all victories.

You work on the self in order to transcend your self. Healthy chastity is loving/forgiving, not punitive; elevating, not compressing (or repressing). This is because true chastity (like true charity) comes from the heart, and returns to the (now warmer) heart.

Chastity ensures sound values, and reasonable expectations of life and of other people. Chastity is not intended to be negative, nor an end in itself. A chaste approach to life clears a path for joy, true freedom, and delight in the beauty of holiness (Psalm 29:2). St Francis de Sales writes, 'A person who knows best how to control his natural inclinations is more open to spiritual inspirations.' Every morning, pray that God will create a clean heart within you (Psalm 51:10).

Just as self-discipline is rescued from pride and narrowness by rooting its heart and purpose in love, so also with chastity. Chastity – not as negation but affirmation; not avoidance but Presence. Thomas Aquinas defined celibacy as 'creating inner space to listen to the Almighty'. How, and how often, we respond to this challenge – each day reserving periods for quiet and contemplation, avoiding overactivity, being modest in the need for possessions, and not cluttering the mind with the ephemeral – will set the tone of our vocation and the purity of our witness.

Chastity foresees the likely or possible consequences of words and actions. Love preserves apt emotional distance – in relationships and towards life as a whole. Right distancing needs a delicate balance: detached involvement, renunciate participation, finding the Eternal amid the ephemeral. 'Let your own discretion be your tutor ... that you o'erstep not the modesty of nature' (*Hamlet*, III ii).

> Ah! when we muse upon the weight of years
> That cover these grey tombs, how petty seem
> The little things we dream –
> The tissue of our loves and hopes and fears
> That wraps us round and stifles us, till we
> Hear not the slow chords of the rolling spheres,
> The Eternal Music that God makes, nor see
> How on the shadow of the night appears
> The pale Dawn of the glory that shall be.

> Rupert Brooke, 'The Pyramids', VI

Chastity for love's glory – indeed, any action dedicated to love – points beyond itself, maintains an atmosphere of awe, and lifts self, companion and the relationship to the care of the All-transcending. Chastity is the trustee and guarantor of the sanctity and sacrament of marriage: 'At the close of life you will be examined as to your love' (St John of the Cross, *Spiritual Sentences and Maxims*).

Prayers

Today is new, unique. Help me come to each hour of this day as one who sees and acts anew. May You wipe clean my body, my mind and my heart, so as to prepare a pure sanctuary for Your indwelling.

May I do all things with purity of heart, solely for love of You.

Knowing how one spark can make a flame of love, may I reveal the Reality of the Presence to every person I meet. May You be known and loved through my words, my example, my attitude, my whole being.

II
A Creative Relationship

How do I love thee? Let me count the ways.
I love thee to the depth and breadth and height
My soul can reach ...
For the ends of being and ideal grace.

I love thee to the level of every day's
Most quiet need, by sun and candlelight.
I love thee freely, as men strive for right;
I love thee purely, as they turn from praise. ...
I love thee with the breath,
Smiles, tears, of all my life ...

Elizabeth Barrett Browning, *Sonnet XLIII*, From the
Portuguese

Similarity and difference

In the consulting room, I am often asked, 'What makes a lasting relationship? A union based on many similarities, or a union of opposites?' The dialogue that follows usually modulates from an either/or question to a both/and answer. In other words, a rich and lasting relationship needs a combination of similarities and contrasts.

Many studies suggest that fulfilled couples tend to be similar across certain key areas: shared values and aspirations; a similar way of seeing and enjoying life; and parity of social class, education and intelligence. In addition, and most importantly, love is likely to thrive if the inevitable opposites – such as of opinions or some interests or temperament – are seen by both individuals not as a threat, because different, but as vital to a rich relationship!

Tolstoy – and I paraphrase – wrote that two of the main features and forces for personal growth and raised consciousness are contrast – and even contradiction. Those of you who now lock horns with your teenagers – or have in the past – will surely agree that children grow by contradiction. Their rebellions are often ways of finding their own voice. Best of all is if parents also learn and mature during and after what is often, or usually, a painful process for everyone.

There can be no true unity unless we embrace diversity. This formula is true at all levels. It means saying 'hi' to all parts of my self; it means loving my partner, not only when we are alike but also when we differ, and – so vital in these times – it means offering a hand of friendship to all members of our neighbourhood and of other nations.

> The driven ship
> May run aground because the helmsman's thought
> Lacked forces to balance opposites.[197]

Those lines are both a warning and an opportunity. The more often and the more deeply we work and really engage with our opposites – in our own self and in our core relationship – the more creative we become. Opposites give life and colour: they widen the range of our humanity. Would we enjoy play if we never had to work? Would we have such an incentive to live full-out if there were no death? If there were no darkness, would we yearn for light? God is our Creator: opposites are clearly a vital part of this design. The question is, do we treat them as such?

---

[197] Source unknown. Quoted in Chapter 34 of George Eliot's *Middlemarch.*

The art of relationship is to identify significant contrasts between the two of you, and to see these differences not as alien but as opportunities to learn and grow. Thus we see that polarity ensures and boosts individuality. Here is a two-line poem I wrote:

> Thanks to you,
> I am more me.

If the love is robust as well as tender, then the union differentiates. In true intimacy I do not lose myself in the other; rather I find myself with and alongside her. If these opposites and contrasts are seen as complementary, as part of a rich whole – rich because diverse – then the tension of differences will be a creative tension (perhaps 'tautness' is the better word). And if possible, it should ideally be a relaxed tautness, founded on balance, poise and mutual ease. Repose without pose!

Ease

> Into their inmost bower,
> Handed they went; and eased the putting off
> These troublesome disguises which we wear.
> Strait side by side were laid.

> John Milton, *Paradise Lost*, Book iv

Among the joys of true love is a feeling of home regained. Our loved one is 'our wandering home' (Chesterton, 'Bay Combe'). Wherever we are, we are together, and in permanent union. In Augustine's lovely words about his deceased friend, we are 'one soul, two bodies'. Now and into eternal life.[198]

In a partnership of true devotion, one person's silence meets the other's silent centre, witnessed by Silence itself.

---

[198] St Augustine, *Confessions*, 4, 6, 11.

I would describe one of those moments, when the
senses are exactly tuned by the rising tenderness of
the heart and according reason entices you to live in
the present moment, regardless of the past or future
– it is not rapture: it is sublime tranquillity. I have felt
it in your arms.[199]

The foundations, the prime features, for a good, lasting
relationship are ease, trust and security. In this safe space we
can each be our natural self, give voice to our deepest thoughts,
express a full range of emotions, and enjoy the comfort of
wholehearted acceptance.

I see this seamless progression: Ease + Comfort + Safety
leads to Relaxation and Openness, which together lead to
FREEDOM: the freedom to be, and to become my
full/true/natural/best self; the scope to release and express the
total range of my (until now half-hidden) humanity.

The next (and glorious) stage is that I offer to my beloved
all that she has liberated – and is still liberating – in me. Hence
we have a perfect circle in which love is recycled: my wife is the
first recipient of what she – and her God-connection – elicits
from me. This is true love's ecology.

As when his virtues shining upon others,
Heat them and they retort that heat again
To the first giver.

Troilus and Cressida, III iii

Mary Wollstonecraft, Letter to William Godwin, 4th October 1796 in J. Todd,
ed., *The Collected Letters of Mary Wollstonecraft* (Columbia: Columbia University
Press, 2004).

Divine paradigm

In a well-loved verse, John Newton celebrates some of the attributes, the many roles, of God the Son in our life:

> Jesus! my Shepherd, Husband, Friend,
> My Prophet, Priest, and King
> My Lord, my Life, my Way, my End,
> Accept the praise I bring.

> Hymn, 'How Sweet the Name of Jesus Sounds'

God's love for us is the model for our own love of people:

- He is always available, always present;
- He is totally in and alongside us when we cry and when we laugh;
- He walks and speaks at our pace;
- the All-Merciful knows our every flaw and scar;
- His warmth does not confine;
- His concern does not constrict;
- He is our strength yet He empowers;
- He inspires our prayers;
- He designs our life but He gives us responsibility for use of our body, our money, our time, our freedom.

God teaches us how to be close to a friend, a partner, a child, and yet be always watchful of emotional distance. But only God can be 'all things to all men': we should not dare to try. We can aspire to wholeness, but only He is perfect. We will never be able to meet or represent all our loved one's needs, nor should we try. A truly confident person is also a realist. He knows his limitations as well as his strong points. He stretches but does not misjudge or overreach.[200]

Solid foundations

Real love keeps on growing richer. What happens to infatuation? Quick to heat up, quick to cool down. What happens to a love that is too narrowly based – just on a highly charged sex life, or just on a cosy financial security? These relationships tend, sooner or later, to implode or fade out. Love needs a number of roots – deep and strong roots – not just one or two.

From my analytic practice and from my reflections about relationships, I have identified 19 features of a robust partnership. These – let's say most of them – are the necessary roots for love to endure:

- both partners have a healthy self-esteem;
- trust, which is based on openness, straightforwardness and honesty;
- loyalty;
- clean and open communication;
- respect;
- physical attraction;
- shared interests and values;
- attentiveness;
- caring for the health and well-being of the whole (other) person – starting with care for one's self;
- understanding and acceptance;

---

[200] Editor's note: The same is true from the feminine perspective.

- patience and forgiveness;
- mature ways of resolving problems;
- compromise;
- gratitude and appreciation;
- affirmation and encouragement;
- humour;
- respecting each other's space and solitude (inner and outer);
- both partners feel able to show vulnerability;
- scope for individual, as well as relational, growth.

If the relationship has these good foundations – another term I use is 'pillars' – then the love bond will grow. A person may say to his partner, 'My love for you is so strong today. I could not love you more than I do now.' Then, the next day, their love has expanded and deepened yet again. Why is this? Proverbs 11:24: 'One man gives freely, yet grows all the richer; another withholds what he should give, and only suffers want.' The more we give, the more we are able to give, and the more we want to give.

Each person is like a twig, and each couple is a branch on the tree of life. The tree is a metaphor for the kingdom: it is eternal, and it has been made for continuing expansion. God's infinity is the guarantee of our ongoing growth in love and service, as individuals and in relationship:

> This love that seeming great beyond the power
> Of growth, yet seemeth ever more to grow.

Samuel Taylor Coleridge, 'To Asra'

The more fully and joyfully I inhabit my self – with accurate self-esteem, alert self-awareness and consistent self-respect –

the more I cherish my partner in her uniqueness, her originality.

My love for her flows from the living spring of my humble fullness. Then – if the bond has a spirit of true oneness – the sense of self of each partner is elevated. Healthy self-esteem is a precondition for close relationship: it gives me confidence, it enables me to commit myself, to be wholehearted in my loving.

Sustaining your relationship

Starting a relationship is easier than sustaining one. How is love to be preserved, and kept new and rich and safe? The spaciousness of God offers range and protection to all human relationships: the security of God gives the couple their certain freedom. This sacred setting is love's safeguard: of all His gifts to us, love needs the most care and watchfulness (inner and outer).

Human love – and also human–divine love – involves four vital factors: noticing (and cherishing) the qualities of one's friend; contemplating these qualities, and seeking to emulate them, or be inspired by them – i.e., responding to love with one's own growth; maintaining frequent contact; and doing things together, with shared aims and values.

In the highest form of this bond, flesh is reigned over by spirit. The couple enjoy their freedom, within an indissoluble unity of two destinies.

Our daily, hourly recognition of the other as 'Thou' – to use the philosopher Martin Buber's term – makes sharing richer/fuller and also longer lasting. In shared joy at the eternal presence of the divine Thou, we say 'thou' to our partner with ever-more fondness and recognition of Him, within and between. The two lovers are messengers to each other, from the divine plenitude (of unfathomable depth), providing more than enough for a lifetime of exploring:

Today I give my soul,
This naked essence, drop of eternity: and I am giving
more than when I breathe out life with kisses, or
flow away with tears.

(Source unknown)

One of my all-time best friends was the late Arthur Bray, whom I knew as a returned Methodist missionary. On the morning of the golden wedding anniversary of Arthur and Muriel, I asked him, 'Mr Bray, what is the secret of a happy marriage?'

He replied without hesitation, 'Every day Muriel and I are still learning about each other.'

Constantly praising God, constantly thanking each other: these keep a relationship rejuvenated. Fidelity to our partner is one main way of being faithful to the Almighty. "Tis true, O heaven, were man but constant, he were perfect,' says Proteus in *The Two Gentlemen of Verona* (V iv). To celebrate our beloved daily is also, and ultimately, to praise and celebrate our Father. Human harmony is a gift, a grace, from God: it is a reflection of the divine music, the heavenly orchestra.

Here are six features which can help to keep a relationship new and lively and warmly dynamic:

- loyalty, both within and outside the home;

- expressing gratitude;

- daily new learning about each other;

- gracious acceptance of each other's individuality;

- shared praying at ever-greater depth, and with increasing freedom and openness;

- shared goals and values.

To be secure, a bond of love needs a uniting, overarching third element – the apex of the triangle: a child or children, joint service to a charity or any worthy cause, and/or devotion to God Himself. Only such a broad setting provides safeguard from the traps of domination, possessiveness, sex without love, or love of idol (Deuteronomy 8:19), or of ideal rather than the real person, who has limitations as well as strength, deep needs as well as the capacity to give. Only such a dimension gives stability for mutual self-sacrifice, and a constant readiness to adjust; for facing tensions, and for learning and growing despite – or animated by – differences of desire and temperament.

An all-enveloping joint witness gives, to human partnership, vitality and patience, depth of meaning, direction, and will to endure, and it preserves love in its innate gracefulness – given, unspoiled, with peace amid passion.

To a large extent, we are ruled by the way we perceive: a problem can be seen as a stimulus for learning. Envy can be considered a form of flattery. We can enjoy what we have instead of lusting for what we desire. We can seek to understand, rather than rush to judge or condemn. We can concentrate on our partner's gifts and graces, rather than on gaps and resistance to change. Above all, we can work on our own gaps and resistance to change.

As often as possible, we can choose kindness in place of the compulsion to be right. Instead of being preoccupied with the need to be understood, or to be loved, seek first to understand, to be the first to reach out, the first to ask for reconciliation.

Soulmate

No one (in any language?) has written with more beauty and poetic feel than Shelley about the universal poignant longing for a soulmate:

What is love? Ask him who lives, what is life? Ask him who adores, what is God? ... [Love] is that powerful attraction towards all that we conceive, or fear, or hope beyond ourselves, when we find within our own thoughts the chasm of an insufficient void, and seek to awaken in all things that are, a community with what we experience within ourselves. If we reason, we would be understood; if we imagine, we would that the airy children of our brain were born anew within another's; if we feel, we would that another's nerves should vibrate to our own, that the beams of their eyes should kindle at once and mix and melt into our own, that lips of motionless ice should not reply to lips quivering and burning with the heart's best blood. This is Love.

Percy Bysshe Shelley, 'On Love'

In the early stages of a relationship, as well as getting to know the other person, we share in her delighting in learning about us. This is one of the glories of love (and not only early on) – the renewal, the rediscovery of the self, as seen through the eyes of the loved one. An appreciative, affirming and observant partner has an acute sense of the essence of the other. This brings a reowning of the self, with a new angle of vision and from a firmer base. Her eye and her voice recall me to my original self:

> There are two births; the one when light
> First strikes the new awaken'd sense;
> The other when two souls unite,
> And we must count our life from thence:
> When you lov'd me, and I lov'd you,
> Then both of us were born anew.

William Cartright, 'To Chloe'

Coleridge here highlights a paradox of true love – the partners become ever-more one and also ever-more two. Our ability to love depends on our prior ability to stand alone, to be a person in our own right, as Rilke writes:

> Love consists in this: that two solitudes protect and border and greet each other. ... Love ... is a sublime opportunity for the individual to mature, to grow, to become a world in himself for another's sake: it is a great exacting claim upon him, a call that chooses him and summons him to a distant goal.[201]

In a deeply loving relationship, 'heart speaks to heart'. Affection heightens our insight at the same time as it gives richness to the many ways of expressing love. Thus we can say, 'I love, therefore I see far more deeply. From my heart (or Thou), I see your heart, your Thou.'

Finding and cherishing the Thou in the other person coincides with, facilitates, expansion into one's own fullness of being – for both partners, potentially.[202] Such a truly transforming relationship is only possible on a soil of trust; and in a sustaining climate of ease, honesty, openness, and shared aims and values.[203]

---

[201] Rainer Maria Rilke, trans. M.D. Herter Norton, *Letters to a Young Poet* (London: WW Norton & Co, 1934) Rome, 14th May 1904.

[202] Martin Buber, *I and Thou* (Edinburgh: T&T Clark, 1959).

[203] We must not be Panglossian about personal growth within a relationship. It can pose downside and even danger. 'You know that I love you just as you are now, darling' can be a coded way of saying, 'Don't you dare progress too much further, either at work or in your inner life, because you might then outgrow and outshine me.' This script is all the more subversive because of its overtly benign guise of loving acceptance of the other. In fact it is fear and insecurity masked as being gracious and big-hearted.

Spaciousness

When two lovers' hearts are warm with devotion, when a partnership is flourishing and well founded – this is never the work or product of the ego. Each has become an instrument of grace through which the All plays love melodies.

Fear and insecurity make demands: by trying to win, they miss the mark. True love is pure energy – a gift of purity. If you crave or press, it runs away. The lower (or narrow) self, in its insecurity, wants to stay within its own self-imposed walls. Your soul-nature is revealed by how you love. Love cannot thrive (or even live) in an air of compulsion. You cannot force a flower to spread its fragrance: scent is heaven-sent.

Greedy or insincere love can be 'flung Lucifer-like from Heaven to Hell'. True graced love can 'soar from earth to ecstasies unwist'.[204] Love is an attuning to the Love which has existed always. For this reason, true love is not depleting: it is restoring to both the lover and the beloved.

The (inevitably) less-than-perfect human being now in my arms is more wonderful, and far more lovable, than my most vivid daydream of an ideal woman and partner. And it is from this mutual cherishing that we each evolve daily nearer to God's unique design. I love my wife not only as she is, but with eyes that see her as she can be – and, with grace, will be. Growth – hers, mine, ours – is the aim and the criterion.

We are now open to be profoundly affected by each other. In this constant reciprocal seeing and longing and touching, two beings become one unit. And yet – if this mutual dependence is healthy (because of the relative strength of self-worth in each partner) and if there is no attempt by either person to merge, to lose one's self in the other – the uniqueness of each is elicited and enhanced: in the presence of

---

[204] Both lines are from Rupert Brooke's sonnet of January 1910, 'I Said I Splendidly Loved You'.

the beloved, I excel.[205] She is a person – *the* person – to learn from and learn with; a partner to live for.

This mutual enrichment, in an ever-closer relationship, is respectful still of distance. Indeed it is vital, for health of relationship, to care for and nurture the space between you and your partner. It is from this creative, living, loving distance that one can see – through a clear (or clearer) lens – self, partner, the love-bond, and all your individual and shared hopes, fears, longings, expectations and needs for healing. The first guideline for any form or level of relationship is to respect autonomy – especially as to freedom of choice, natural tempo, and personal opinions and values.

From this spirit of freedom, the two partners become more articulate to each other – able to speak both more richly and more precisely than with anyone else. With my loved one, I find my voice – in the very widest sense. My voice is the symbol, the expression of my whole evolving self.

There are three parallel (and mutually reinforcing) journeys of personal and spiritual growth: of person A, of person B, and of their partnership. Each journey, each movement higher and deeper, protects and nurtures the other two. And crucially, each person retains their own integrity, their own unique blend of foible, glory and aspiration.

Projections

How do we deal with our less elevated motives in a relationship? We may never be able to stop our projecting, such as on to beauty of face, and/or figure:

> How near to good is what is fair!
> Which we no sooner see,

---

[205] Cf Henri Cartier-Bresson: 'Two complementary colours placed side by side emphasise both; but mixed together they annihilate each other', *The Decisive Moment* (Göttingen: Steidl, 2014).

But with the lines and outward air,
Our senses taken be.

Ben Jonson, 'Love Freed from Ignorance and Folly'

Virginia Woolf writes about the typical figure of Elizabethan love poetry: 'That great ideal, built up by a score of eloquent pens, still burns bright in our eyes. Her body was of alabaster, her legs of ivory; her hair was golden wire and her teeth pearls from the Orient. Music was in her voice and stateliness in her walk.'[206]

The best we can do is to watch – and thus moderate – our projecting: by comparing hope with the reality of experience, and by constantly observing during encounter this (often wild) flight of our imagination.

I saw a woman there –
The line of neck and cheek and chin,
The darkness of her hair,
The form of one I did not know
Sitting in my chair. ...

I made a step to her; and saw
That there was no one there.

It was some trick of the firelight
That made me see her there.
It was a chance of shade and light ...

All night I could not sleep.

Rupert Brooke, 'Home'

---

[206] Virginia Woolf, 'Donne after Three Centuries', in *The Common Reader*, Volume II. pp.24–40.

What a burden we place on the other when we project. In psychoanalysis, projection means 'perceiving a mental image as objective reality'. Hence specific (and often partly unconscious) impulses, wishes and aspects of the self (such as one's shadow side) are imagined as located in someone else, or in an institution, a racial or cultural group, or even a whole nation. I much more easily see another person's emotional scars than see and admit to – and own and work with – my own.

Keep your delight just short of outright on-your-knees wonder. Gaze with joy upon her face.[207] Delight in her profile, bone structure, dimples and form, but look also within and enjoy the whole vibrant person:

> 'Tis not a lip, or eye, we beauty call,
> But the joint force and full result of all.

Alexander Pope, *An Essay on Criticism*

When you are on the journey of love – especially the first miles – never drive past an amber light. Before your beguiled eyes glaze over, listen to memories and patterns of your own childhood (and hers); assess the track record of relationships; quickly begin to read the character and see how it has been formed.

This poem by Keats – about a lover's heady projections – will always be a relevant warning to any future generation:

> And what is love? It is a doll dressed up
> For idleness to cosset, nurse, and dandle;
> A thing of soft misnomers, so divine
> That silly youth doth think to make itself
> Divine by loving, and so goes on
> Yawning and doting a whole summer long,

---

[207] Samuel Johnson opines 'What ills from beauty spring' (*Vanity of Human Wishes*). And in his poem 'To a Young Beauty', Yeats reminds us of beauty's curse: 'I know what wages beauty gives, how hard a life her servant lives'.

Till Miss's comb is made a pearl tiara,
And common Wellingtons turn Romeo boots;

Till Cleopatra lives at Number Seven,
And Antony resides in Brunswick Square.

John Keats, 'And what is love? It is a doll dressed up'

A healthy view of love begins with the recognition, and the acceptance, that no one person can ever meet all of our needs and longings, both conscious and unconscious. This recognition shields love from its foes: narrowness, clinging, disappointment, possessiveness, exclusivity, a *folie à deux*. No emotion is more likely to wound or kill a relationship than the revenge of – often mainly unconscious – unmet childhood needs or half-remembered hurts.

To use another person for one's own (often short-term) ends is not only abuse, it is a form of theft. It is treating the person as an 'it' as opposed to seeing him or her as an individual. Dreamy expectations about love – or any aspect of life – will usually end up where they began – as dreams: 'a false creation proceeding from the heat-oppressed brain' (*Macbeth*, II i).

The more self-aware we are, and the more nuanced our view of both our loved one and the relationship, the more objectively we can separate the ideal from the real. 'Season your admiration for a while' (*Hamlet*, I ii). The health and longevity of a relationship depend on both partners constantly distinguishing between hope and reality. Two main benefits ensue.

First, the more reality-based a relationship is (and reality-based need not imply earth-bound!), the more likely it is that both partners will see disagreement or conflict as spurs to growth: for each individual and also for their relationship.

The second main benefit of clear-sightedness about a relationship can be a continuing revelation: this is the move from nympholepsy to the enjoying of a real and naturally charming presence. One of the joys of true devotion is to discover that one's partner is far more lovable, and to be cherished, than all the pink-cloud visions conjured up by imagination and fantasy.

The remembered beauties of a love-bond include (often hesitant) tenderness and the caring for mutual vulnerability. A consoling (or forgiving) smile, a comforting caress, giving (and being given) deep, sincere attention – these signs of kindness are among the most delightful gifts (some expected, some unexpected) which relationship – and life itself – can offer us.

In human love, as in mystical life, we cherish and respect what we can never fully understand: 'If, as I have, you also do / Virtue attired in woman see' (Donne, *The Undertaking*). Indeed, this never fully revealed mystery is a substantial part of the attraction of man in the eyes of woman, and woman for the man: a harmonising of contrasts.

Every person – not only our beloved – has a special charm, a unique charism: 'Dear, and yet dearer for her mystery' (Shelley, 'Hymn to Intellectual Beauty'). Some of the personality we can in time read and understand; some of the character we can trace and map – at least in outline and in pencil. But this X factor, this *je ne sais quoi*, resists – and rightly defies – burrowing attempts to describe, define or analyse:

> Cupid, that lover weakly strikes,
> Who can express what 'tis he likes.

Sir Charles Sedley, 'To Cloris'

A poignant and recurring regret among lovers is that they cannot articulate (in any form or phrase) the size and depth of their affection; but this sadness, this inevitable shortfall, is a spur to be ever-more inventive in love – by word, glance, gesture, gratitude, affirmation, attention and surprise, so as to 'free us from the weight of the unexpressed'.[208]

> Dost thou remember now
> How our eyes met; and all things changed?
>
> Rupert Brooke, 'In January'

True love – by staying in tune with Love's infinite resource – is always deeper, wider, higher and richer than we shall ever know or discover.

Healing one another's wounds

The heart and the foundation of the religious vocation is to be a channel of God's love. Love that is unjudging, uncalculating, unfailing, assiduous. Love that is constant, upheld by His purity and stillness. Love helps us to look behind the veil of appearances, seeing into the deep (and sometimes dark) spaces of self and other, receiving – into our joint strength – the wounding in our hearts.

We are never fully real to another person until – at a time that is mutually right, and for a duration and depth of intensity that are apt – we open up and offer our woundedness to be cleaned and stitched (and thus muted or healed) in the embrace of true affection:

> Between the small hands folded in her lap
> Surely a shamed head may bow down at length,
> And find forgiveness where the shadows stir
> About her lips, and wisdom in her strength,
> Peace in her peace. Come to her, come to her!
>
> Rupert Brooke, 'Unfortunate'

---

[208] Virginia Woolf, 'Notes on an Elizabethan Play', in *The Common Reader*, Volume I, pp.48–58.

In God's mercy and gift, difficulty or even tragedy can bring out the best in us. In adversity we can develop new qualities. True love gives strength. Love enlarges self and others: 'My beloved changes, and startles me into change' (D. H. Lawrence).[209]

Love cherishes the other person for himself: as he is, not as you might wish him to be. And not primarily for what he does or gives. Such is the meaning of sincerity and appreciation. Value your beloved for who she *is* before – and more often than – thanking her for all that she does for you. Admiration before need. Affirm wholeness before expressing want – if indeed, because of her insight, you even need to ask.

Without compassion (in the very widest sense of what Erich Fromm called 'undemanding alongsideness') we cannot come near to an understanding of another person. This compassionate involvement is not primarily about *doing;* rather, it is *a being with the full being* of the other.

The person I cherish is a unique combination of glory and vulnerability. This vulnerability is part of the glory of the beloved if my sole motive is to honour. I honour when I am centred, open and innocent (i.e., benign; never harming).

Using and controlling others

If I fail to see – and revere – God in a person, I do not see or value them as they really are, in their fullness. Genuine human love is not an affection we concoct or contrive.[210] A will-to-power can lead from self-aggrandisement to destruction of self

---

[209] D. H. Lawrence, 'Morality and the Novel', *The Calendar of Modern Letters,* Volume II, No. 10 (London: 1925).

[210] 'The affectation of sanctity is a blotch on the face of piety' (Johann Caspar Lavater, *Aphorisms on Man* (London: J. Johnson, 1874) p.71 n. 190.

and other, and of relationship. The cause, says Buber, is 'a dazzlingly clothed impotence'.[211]

A Don Juan or a sadist – as focused on the male role in sex, and his own needs and performance – is often compensating for a weakened sense of masculinity (in the widest sense). Emotionally, he is still a child – a child in an adult's body who uses bodies (his own and that of others) to find himself, to bolster a limp identity, to flatter a brittle sense of self.

A predatory wish to control or manipulate is often a defence – an unconscious attempt to avoid suffering, especially loss, rejection and isolation.

> Ruin hath taught me thus to ruminate
> That Time will come and take my love away.
> This thought is as a death, which cannot choose
> But weep to have that which it fears to lose.

Shakespeare, 'Sonnet LXIV'

The subliminal rationale is, 'I will use you: all of you – just for the time being – but I will not give myself to you.' But because this skews the power in the pseudo-relationship – the controller, sooner or later, provokes a whole range of new hurts, to self and other(s). Neurotic or twisted behaviour unconsciously invites what is most feared. Until the original hurt is faced and worked through, one is condemned to repeat stuck and negative patterns. The psyche usually prefers the familiar, even if dark, hence the widespread resistance to change.

In psychology we use the term 'death fear' – or more explicitly 'death-of-the-self fear' – to describe the dread of becoming totally absorbed by one's partner, swallowed up by the relationship ('You look good enough to eat'). There is a

---

[211] Martin Buber, ed. N. N. Glatzer, *The Way of Response: Martin Buber: Selections from His Writings* (New York: Schocken Books, 1966) p.169.

primal fear beneath the conscious script: 'If we get too close, too intimate, I will lose my independence.'

If we are close to God, and working towards wholeness, our touch (physical and metaphorical) will be warm and reliable. In a fundamental way, the hands are extensions of the heart – the deep feeling-faculty in the core of one's body and being. When we listen, we attend with heart as well as with head. In moments of intimacy, we learn each other's truth. Touch helps us to know, and to love more by ever-deeper existential knowing. When expressed as sincere affection and unselfish desire, touch is the embodiment (literally and in metaphor) of divine love.

> Your adoring hands
> Touch his so intimately that each understands,
> I know, most hidden things…

> Rupert Brooke, 'Jealousy'

Seeking the new is one way; seeing the new is the other. First-time seeing comes from a radical inner change – of angle and openness. Then newness is revealed in the familiar as well as in the first-time ever. To see (or judge) one's partner through the eyes of the past deprives us of seeing change and growth in the daily dynamic of creative relating. True devotion gives clear, clean sight and delicacy of feeling:

> But I, being poor, have only my dreams;
> I have spread my dreams under your feet;
> Tread softly because you tread on my dreams.

> W. B. Yeats 'He Wishes for the Cloths of Heaven' in
> The Wind Among the Reeds

God and my 'immortal beloved' are my life. 'My peak of joy is to see you happy.' Moreover, true love is reliable and daily new. It 'needs not June for beauty's heightening' (Matthew Arnold, *Thyrsis*).

Many people are craving cosmetic curves and 'caress me now' skin tone. Can personal appeal be bought over the counter or from a surgeon's knife? True beauty is the natural expression of an illumined soul: the graphic German expression is *eine grosse Ausstrahlung,* a flowing forth of radiance.

When we make an idol of a person, we are possessed by them. Freedom is surrendered in the objectifying of another person for the satisfaction of ego-based needs. To avoid this danger we need to meet each other prayerfully prepared, but without planning, without reckoning, without prescription. Each partner is then simply dependent and simply free at the same time: enhanced – not limited – by the other.

Wait!

What does it mean to be in a state of not expecting, and why is this attitude infinitely precious to self and other? Pure awareness is alert, receptive to what *is*, and glad for whatever is given. The aim is to hope or desire while also being ready to let go: to yield to His (and her) wisdom in a spirit of love, trust and full/ungrudging acceptance. He who expects, seeks; he who is expectant, waits; waits for God (and the beloved) to reply in His (and her) own way and time.

The unsought love-moment comes to us, trembling – exposed, unshielded, artless – needing the assurance of safety before full expression can be given. This gesture of beauty is often granted to us by a glance or a 'small' loving attention. Its subtle fragrance – perhaps only brief – will linger far longer in our bank of memories than all the heady wonders that our imagination conjures up or our vanity hunts for.

What I want is balanced by what you want, and crucially by what our relationship, and this encounter, is ready for. Love as 'getting' gives way to love as listening, receiving, being offered.

We are wise if we do not impose, force or manipulate timing in any relationship of love: 'Her adoration was not your demand' (Wordsworth, 'Saints').

Pressure – even subtle pressure – is the antithesis of true devotion. 'I will come to you when I will', the bold nightingale tells the emperor in Hans Andersen's fairy tale. Affection from the beloved needs emotional space in order to bestow its own poetry, its own gift of the living moment: the two lovers and time itself lit and lifted up by grace.

We do not choose or decide the right moment: we listen, we watch for it (without assuming), we respond in our fullness. A marriage proposal, for example, has to be not too early and not too late: to be premature is as clumsy as to procrastinate.

Our listening has to be acute and sensitive, respectful of the other person's pace and feel for the best time – yielding to the dynamic of circumstance and the wisdom of conjunction – or confluence, the moment of flowing together. The relationship itself has its own wisdom as to timing. Timing should feel – to both partners – comfortable, inevitable and longed for.

The divine in the human

Healthy love yields to the Spirit, Who is the purifier of our intention, word, gesture and direction. All forms of intimacy find their crown and wholeness – and safety – when based on intimacy with the divine. By celebrating the presence of God in their midst, lovers know that He is source and guide and sustainer of their affection. Mature love for each other gains fulfilment within the wider divine/human embrace. See and savour the divine: in the face, the gaze of the eyes, in the soul of the beloved, and in God's gift of the bond of friendship. Thus Hugo, on true love: 'Feel sacred Being throb within the human-being loved…'

You, who pass away and fade,
Beyond the days, beyond the skies, I sought for you,
Upon the everlasting will's eternal shores ...
Down into the lowest depths I sought,
Beneath the beating of your heart,
Below the wellspring of your vows,
Into that solemn centre wherein your life to Life is
tied,
Into the quivering depths of the unchanging,

Into the throbbing mystery of God's creation!
– It is your soul I love.

(Source unknown)

My beloved is my human agent of growth into fullness of being. With the person I adore above all others, I extend my assumed boundaries. Her presence – and even the fond memory of her, when we have to be apart – is my joy, strength, hope and meaning. She elicits the light and shade of my humanity and the full range of my manhood – from the tender to the bold.

A foretaste of heaven

When we are pure channels of divine love, we partake of the infinity of God: 'Eternity was in our lips and eyes, bliss in our brows bent' (*Antony and Cleopatra*, I iii). A blessed couple can experience not only a continuing increase of devotion – 'as more of heaven in each they see'[212] – and a heightened sense of God's presence in the home, but also a glimpse of their eternal life together.

True love can give us a sense of the timeless – a desire to create or compose harmony now, and a high hope for the

---

[212] John Keble, 'New Every Morning is the Love'.

eternal embrace: 'Imparadised in one another's arms' (*Paradise Lost*, Book iv). There is a lovely and almost scriptural passage in *The Little Mermaid* where Hans Andersen writes about true love as reassuring both partners that the soul is immortal, and that the two-as-one will live for ever. St Francis de Sales confirms this in his *Introduction*: 'Love that is spiritually inspired lasts for ever.' With grace the two of us will:

> Spend in pure converse our eternal day;
> Think each in each, immediately wise;
> Learn all we lacked before; hear, know, and say
> What this tumultuous body now denies;
> And feel, who have laid our groping hands away;
> And see, no longer blinded by our eyes.

Rupert Brooke, Sonnet: 'Not With Vain Tears'

True love speaks to us of the goodness of the Giver. The two lovers cannot think that God would fashion all the richness of rare devotion intending it to last only for a few decades. St Paul tells us that the visible is designed to help us long for the infinite. Human love is a foretaste of the life to come:

> And we are sure
> That beauty is a thing beyond the grave,
> That perfect, bright experience never falls
> To nothingness, and time will dim the moon
> Sooner than our full consummation here,
> In this odd life, will tarnish or pass away.

D. H. Lawrence, 'Moonrise' in *Look! We Have Come Through!*

Prayers

Thank You, O God, for all You are giving us to give each other. May I always help to liberate and encourage my partner's personal and professional growth. May I come to every encounter with a calm spirit and a sense of the sacred.

Dear Lord, You are the perfect partner. You are always by my side, when I laugh and when I weep.
So I do not have to look far to learn what it means to love and be loved:
You are showing me right now.
You are teaching me, training me, even now while I am praying to You, longing to be worthy of Your embrace.
You watch over me, day and night. You understand me:
You know if my intentions are self-seeking or pure.
You know if the outer appearance is a true expression of the inner person.
You encourage me to give of my best at all times.
You rejoice when I hope and aspire: when I long to grow to be a better, more faithful servant of Your kingdom.
To love means to give voice to four qualities: caring, understanding, affirming and encouraging, and being alongside – in joy or sorrow, in doubt or in strength.
May I be accepting of others, even as You accept the whole of me, Your child who longs to know Your will, and respond to Your every wish.
While I have been praying for myself, I have been beseeching You on behalf of the one I adore.
May my whole life give glory to You; and may it sing of Your goodness.

III
Others

And where there is no love,
Put love and you will find love.

St John of the Cross[213]

Spiritualising the life of the world

All of our encounters, and all of our friendships, derive their
full meaning, their richness, from our relationship with God.
Even if unpromising at first glance, every person, place and
activity gives opportunity for worship. The religious vocation –
rooted and grounded in a continuous awareness of His
presence – is to assist in the spiritualising of the life of the
world (Matthew 7:20–21; 1 John 3:18).

When you love and serve other people, you are at the same
time loving and serving God. As St Bonaventure observed,
'One becomes holy by doing ordinary things well, and by being
constantly faithful in small things.'

A saint (from the latin *sanctus*, 'holy') shares as fully as is
humanly possible in the life of Christ. For a saint is a person of
flesh and blood, failures and sufferings, and yet one who
experiences the constant undercurrent of God-filled joy.

---

[213] St John of the Cross, Letter to M María de la Encarnación, 6th July 1591, in
Collected Works, p.760.

A person of balance does not spend all their time 'communing with the skies' (Milton, *Il Penseroso*). Spiritual life is not confined to lofty paths, specific (or remote) settings, nor to particular professions. Every saint has a unique charism, a special gift of grace. Perhaps we can all remind ourselves that God has given (and is giving) each of us a combination of talents which He longs for us to enjoy and express, for our own fulfilment and in His service.

Every saintly person is *sui generis*, God-made from a once-only mould, but they tend to share some similarities:

- loyalty in obeying God's will;

- balance and a blend of action and quietness;

- simplicity;

- they are wide-seeing, involved yet detached;

- no hint or smirk of self-parading; and

- joy in loving.

Saints are humanity spiritualised. They are representatives of us all, depicting the variety of human nature, and the height and range of our aspiration. By their life and witness 'we are made more than ever aware of the inexhaustible richness of human sensibility'.[214]

Saintliness is not confined to the official saints whom the Church honours by name. Saintly people can be found wherever we may be. Are we on the lookout for them? 'To buried merit raise the tardy bust' (Samuel Johnson, *Vanity of Human Wishes*). In the New Testament, the word 'saint' originally described every baptised Christian. Not until the second century, with the cult and veneration of the martyrs, did the Catholic Church reserve the accolade 'saint' for those

---

[214] Virginia Woolf, 'Notes on an Elizabethan Play' in *Common Reader*, Volume I, p.54.

heroes and heroines of the faith who, at death, were believed to have immediately entered the household of heaven.

Saints reflect some aspects of God's nature. In their life, secular and sacred are united. They stand on a golden rung, at the conjunction of time and the Timeless. To the saints, prayer is not only an activity of the mind, nor only their heart's favourite occupation. Prayer, for them, is an expression of their whole life (Ephesians 5:19). 'A soul is the more dependent on grace, the higher the perfection to which it aspires' (Brother Lawrence, *The Practice of the Presence of God*, 4th conversation).

To really love our neighbour there are four stages: (1) immersing oneself in silence; (2) receiving God's love; (3) doing everything under the tutelage of gentleness; leading to (4) spontaneous expressions of human love.

1. Immersing oneself in silence

The saints teach us that human bonding grows, and is nourished, not only by creative encounter, but also, and especially, by the riches of silence, and all the resources, the restoration work, of peopled solitude. Why does solitude deepen friendship and enhance unity? Because solitude reminds us of – and rejoins us to – a oneness of spirit prior to our first meeting.

Wait for the inner silence to be uncovered, to come by itself – in its own time, and for as long or short as God chooses. Silence will relax and integrate body and mind and soul. Silence will ready you to receive (Psalm 62:1; Micah 7:7). Absorbed in Him, in adoring love, bask in the light and radiance of God, in a communion more eloquent than words.

2. Receiving God's love

We are always united with Him. Our recurring problem is that we forget this; our attention flickers (Genesis 28:16), and we do not always listen. The whole quest and enterprise of sanctity is directed towards a transformation: from a theoretical acceptance that God is always present, to a deep conviction of His continuous presence within and alongside (Revelation 3:20, 22), He who inspires and then ennobles all the stirrings of our soul.

3. Gentleness as tutor

God's gentleness towards you can inspire you to be more gentle and forgiving towards yourself, and therefore with others: not trying to control life or manipulate people,[215] but *allowing to be*;[216] not forcing, which causes inner and outer conflict, but staying confident in hope and trust; guarding against impatience; enjoying a sense of effortless flow; not striving (2 Timothy 2:24), craving, clinging or grasping. 'Let your gentleness be evident to all. The Lord is near' (Philippians 4:5, NIV UK).

One of the most inspiring evenings on my own journey of faith was when Metropolitan Anthony, an Archbishoop in the Russian Orthodox Church, came to a young adults group at Westminster Central Hall in May 1973. He was in the middle of an erudite exposition about icons when a reporter came into the room, unannounced, and asked the Archbishop if he could take some photographs. 'How will the great man respond?' we all wondered. He paused in mid-paragraph, got up right away to welcome the young man, posed naturally for a series of

---

215 The wish (or compulsion) to control is very often related to a fear of being controlled, usually derived from a past or ongoing struggle for dominance between child and parent(s).

216 Our ability *to be* (and to rest in the present), in contrast to doing, is a current cultural problem as well as a personal one. It is learned (or not) by one's mother's own capacity *to be*, especially when breastfeeding. Was she calm, quiet and relaxed in the experience? Did she see these times as not only giving milk but for giving emotional nurture? A state of being means a minimum of output or input, both modes in a mood of maximum relaxation. From such a capacity our alongsideness will be calmer and more fruitful.

pictures, thanked him warmly for his care and professionalism, and then resumed his discourse.

Anthony was the epitome of calm and courtesy. He gave no hint of irritation, nor of interruption. He was totally himself, superbly centred and 'in the moment'. The heart of this man was valiant. His inner and outer eye was on God. He shone with the divine presence.

Keep asking yourself, 'What would be the kindest initiative? Which words, which actions, would be the most human, the most loving, response?' We cannot separate God and neighbour: every act of service is love rendered to God Himself. As Bonhoeffer observes in *Life Together*, 'Our attitude toward our brother reflects our relationship with God.' He continues, 'I must meet my brother only as the person he already is in God's eyes.'

Nature can tutor us in sensitivity towards each other:

> Who would not lightly violate the grace
> The lowliest flower possesses in its place;
> Nor shorten the sweet life, too fugitive,
> Which nothing less than Infinite Power could give.

William Wordsworth, 'Humanity'

The scent or perfume of a flower depends on its blossoming. And this blossoming comes when the bud opens up to the warmth and light of the sun. In our friendships (of whatever level), this image translates into respecting the other person's tempo: they will give if and when, and what and how, they want (and are ready) to give. Then the relationship is allowed to expand according to its own innate rhythm and resources. The calmer (and more spacious) the pace, the deeper and more sustained the personal unfolding: this formula applies to each individual encounter and also to the relationship as a whole. Let love (and not my ego) lead.

4. Spontaneous acts of love

Life is for love: not only, of course, love in theory and in sweet words, but love in (often costly) action. Love is like a stream: if love stops flowing, it stagnates, silts, dries up. By contrast, Proverbs 11:25 assures us that 'one who waters will himself be watered'. You can only save your soul by spending yourself.

True love always aspires to enlarge its activity. Every action becomes worship when done with love, in a spirit of service – not as a series of one-off perfunctory tasks, but each having oneness of aim, unattached to results, and yielding outcomes to God. A gesture of kindness may at the time seem relatively small, but memory has a way of creating its own order of importance:

> Many of the really significant times of high emotion feature relatively small, basic actions … With what is the close friend or wife of a dying man occupied? Preserving quiet in the bedroom, carrying out the doctor's instructions, taking the temperature, applying compresses … A small physical action acquires enormous meaning and emotion.

> Constantin Stanislavski, *My Life in Art*

We may sometimes wonder how vital, or not, our own contribution is to the collective work of helping to build God's kingdom on earth. Carlyle offers reassurance: 'All work is as seed sown; it grows and spreads, and sows itself anew' (*On Boswell's Life of Jonson*). We may be relatively obscure in the eyes of the world but – in God's sight – we can be glorious in our obscurity. In a choir, every voice contributes to the whole.

Mother Teresa of Calcutta saw herself 'as a small pencil in God's hands, together writing love letters to the world'. She said, 'We ourselves feel that what we are doing is just a drop in the ocean. But if the drop was not in the ocean, I think the ocean would be less because of the missing drop.'[217]

By the seemingly small things and events of daily life, God teaches us higher truths. As we see in physics time and again, tiny actions can have huge consequences. This is the essence of 'the butterfly effect', a term coined by Ed Lorenz, a meteorologist at the Massachusetts Institute of Technology. He observed that the complexity of the Earth's weather system – with its untold number of interactions and feedback loops – meant that a sequence of relatively small effects could accumulate to produce significant weather events. In his much-quoted phrase, 'The flap of a butterfly's wings in Brazil can help to cause a tornado in Texas.'[218]

So too, our small acts of kindness have consequences we will not know of this side of heaven. By loving, we affirm the eternal value of everything we touch and everyone we meet:

> A man was walking on a beach at dawn when he saw a young woman who was picking up starfish – stranded by the retreating tide – and throwing them back into the sea, one by one.
>
> He went up to her and asked why she was doing this. The young woman replied that the starfish would die if left exposed to the morning sun.
>
> 'But this beach goes on for miles, and there are thousands of starfish. You will not be able to save them all. How can your help, your efforts, make any real difference?'

[217] Mother Teresa of Calcutta, *A Gift for God* (London: Collins, 1975) p.43.
[218] The term was first recorded from Lorenz's address at the annual meeting of the American Association for the Advancement of Science, on 29th December 1979. John Milton observes, 'It was from the rind of one apple tasted, that the knowledge of good and evil, as twins cleaving together, leaped forth into the world' (*Areopagitica*).

The woman looked at the starfish in her hand, and then threw it to the safety of the sea. 'To that one, it makes a difference.'[219]

The art of living spiritually is to see time as part of eternity (Genesis 28:12); and – in a loving self-donation, and as a means of glorifying God and attaining union with Him – to link together all of Time's duties and days on Eternity's golden thread.

Attitude and motivation

An action has value, not only because of its content or magnitude, but more especially because of the attitude and spirit in which it is done. Thus no activity is minor or trivial (Matthew 19:30) to the person who – at the heart and core of everyday life – acknowledges, and inwardly bows to, the eternal dimension. What matters to God is not only the things we do, but how and why we do them. When done with a pure heart, every action is a love-offering, done for God's honour and glory.

Our love and service are only freely given if we drop any hint of reward, or human payback, any hope of garland, even in the life to come. Such is love's burden and love's privilege. Like charm, love – in its spontaneity – is free of calculation (Matthew 6:1–4).

> Love seeketh not itself to please,
> Nor for itself hath any care;

---

[219] Alternate versions of this fable are attributed to Dan Hisle and Loren Eiseley, but it is probably much older.

But for another gives its ease,
And builds a Heaven in Hell's despair.

William Blake 'The Clod and the Pebble', *Songs of Experience*

Actions are not to be done for notice or praise or being thanked but, rather, for God's kingdom, in a spirit of worship. Most of the best acts of service are discreet, in tone and motive:

> Think not that pleasing God consists especially in performing numerous good works; but, rather, in doing them with an upright will, and without attachment, or craving for human esteem.

St John of the Cross, *Spiritual Sentences and Maxims*

> Our passions are most like to floods and streams;
> The shallow murmur, but the deep are dumb.

Sir Walter Raleigh, *Sir Walter Raleigh to the Queen*

To be spiritual is to be sincere. The Latin root conveys the sense of 'clean and untainted; pure and spotless; real, genuine, whole'. To be spiritually sincere is to be so focused on God's work that one is *sans souci* – concerned but not careworn, devoted and thus not distracted. There is no gap between how I appear – what I say and how I say it – and how I really, deeply am.

> The beauty that is borne here in the face
> The bearer knows not, but commends itself
> To others' eyes: nor doth the eye itself,
> (That most pure spirit of sense,) behold itself.

Troilus and Cressida, III iii

Empathy

When we approach another person and dare to expose our suffering or shame, what we seek is a person willing to be alongside and face the pain, and offer reassurance that there is meaning. This entails listening to both the spoken and the silent voice: a question or concern not yet (or not fully) formulated; or formulated but not yet expressed and shared.[220]

This relaxed focus, this alert and gentle concentration on the deepest needs of the other, encourages the other person to express hopes, fears, anguish in a way that feels new and original. One of the main roles for the listener is to foster an atmosphere of dialogue which is open, healing and accepting:

> Teach me to feel another's woe,
> To hide the fault I see;
> That mercy I to others show,
> That mercy show to me.

> Alexander Pope, 'The Universal Prayer'

To be fully attentive, fully present, to another person – to their uniqueness – is a manifestation of respect and generosity. Few experiences are more healing than to be in the company of someone who attends, accepts and understands, with their whole self engaged and vigilant in creative encounter. Words that do not come from interior silence can obstruct true encounter.

The more self-confident I feel and am, the more space I have (in mind, emotions and spirit) to listen to the other person with deep attention. The range and clarity of this attention generates warmth, understanding and empathy. We

---

[220] For further thoughts on 'Listening' see Robin's book, *Heart-to-Heart Listening*, scheduled for release in 2017.

can be like a sympathetic string: it is not directly bowed or plucked but its vibration enriches the tone.

In Thai, the word 'understand' implies 'to enter the heart'. To understand is so much more than an activity of the mind: it means to stand under/with/or alongside in solidarity. It means heartfelt empathy – seeing as they see, feeling as they feel.

In *Psychological Types*, Jung likens empathy to an observer yielding himself to a work of art. To appreciate – a painting or a person – is a high form of creativity. An artist relates to the landscape they are painting: they become intensely absorbed. They are in a state of heightened awareness, raised consciousness. To *feel with* and *for* another person and allow oneself to be impacted is a gift of high value.

When you are relaxed, you give other people the time and the space to be themselves. With your mind unalloyed and still, your very presence can bring stillness to every encounter. And you will be able to instil calm, even to a troubled atmosphere.

Who is my neighbour?

God calls us to love the less lovable into lovableness as an expression of our love of Him (Matthew 5:43–47): 'Forbear to judge, for we are sinners all' (*Henry VI*, Part 2, III iii). May we see every person – whom we meet or happen to pass by on the pavement – in the totality of their humanity: in turn, vain or modest; selfish or unselfish; foolish or wise; now doubting, now hoping; seeking and losing and finding. How like myself!

> For the dear God who loveth us,
> He made and loveth all.

> Coleridge, *The Rime of the Ancient Mariner*, part VII, stanza 23

Christian writers of old advocated 'the prayer of loving attention', also known as 'the prayer of simple gaze'. At the same time, God is gazing on us in everyone we meet – everyone. People lead me to God, and God sends me back to people. May I see His face and hands in everyone I meet today.

'Love your neighbour as yourself' is at the heart of the Old Testament as well as the New. But we have here another message, an equally important precept. 'Love your neighbour' appears once in the Old Testament; 'Love the stranger' 37 times. Leviticus 19:34 is explicit: 'The stranger who sojourns with you shall be to you as the native among you, and you shall love him as yourself ...' As the borders of nations become looser and more porous, travel, migration and the movement of people is rapidly increasing. This is both a challenge and a chance: to serve the God of all by serving all because they are His and mine.

How we relate to others has a very real, though often invisible impact. Six degrees of separation – a concept introduced by Hungarian writer Karinthy Frigyes – is the hypothesis that anyone can be connected to any other person in the world through a chain of relatives and acquaintances, with no more than five intermediaries (on average, according to some researchers). The number of acquaintances grows exponentially with the number of links in the chain. It has been calculated that anyone now alive is related to anyone, anywhere in the world, by no more than 30 to 32 generations removed – i.e., about 900 to 1,050 years.[221]

It is harder to dehumanise people if you know a lot about them. The global economy, the internet and global reporting, wars, terrorism and the refugee crisis, as well as climate change, mean that we know more about – and feel more concern for – those who are geographically, ethnically or culturally remote from us – because our future is bound up with theirs.

---

[221] Albert-László Barabási, *Linked: How Everything is Connected to Everything Else and What It Means for Business, Science, and Everyday Life* (New York: Plume, 2003).

God yearns for us to see His face now – not in spite of the variety and vagaries of human nature (our own as well as that of other people), but because of the full range of their humanity. Soul-to-soul meeting finds mutuality beneath surface differences. A right relationship with God fosters a right relationship with people, for you see Him in them, and cherish them for His sake.

You must do much more than just tolerate other people. Accept every person just as God accepts you – i.e., without reserve. The person you are with now – whether attractive or unappealing – is created in God's image. In prayer, we find our shared humanity – beyond differences of personality, looks, job, age, gender, education, family background, nationality or culture. 'Do not focus on the *this* and *that* in your fellow humans, and you will see God' (St Augustine, *On the Trinity*, Book VIII).

Our neighbourhood is a spiritual place specially chosen for us by the Almighty. Each tiny task, every daily duty, is to be done to the best of our ability, with love, with reverence: so conformed to the will of God that we desire only what He wants – in His way, in His sequence and at His tempo.

This is where God has, for now, placed you. These are the people, the congenial but also the less attractive, alongside whom He is training you. By collaborating with them now – in this setting, in these very circumstances, and with these opportunities and responsibilities – you will at the same time come ever closer to the reason He has created us: communion with Him. Eventually we may have 'a mysterious awakening to the fact that where we actually are is where we belong'.[222] This is the move from resignation to recognition.

In every story – in every event, encounter and experience – there is a meaning and a message. However long it takes, however stern the enquiry, we need to learn all the possible

---

[222] Thomas Merton, 'The Cell' in *Contemplation in a World of Action* (Notre Dame: University of Notre Dame Press, 1999).

lessons. Much of our discontent (or perplexity) in life comes from our resentment that reality – especially the stubbornness of some people and some circumstances – does not *and may never* fit with our notion or image of how we think it should be.

When you hear words, or see behaviour, from another person which you regard as unskilful, ask yourself if you do the same, and also if you are doing anything – perhaps unconsciously – to provoke what you find awkward and jarring. May I learn to stop my usually vain attempts to make lucid and comfortable what is intrinsically opaque and obdurate. St Macarius Monastery is in a part of the Egyptian desert called Shihet by the Copts. This means 'the place of the weighing of the soul'. It could be that wherever God is currently placing us is for the weighing, testing and expressing of our soul.

We may need to accept what (or who) resists change. Keep alert, opportunist in responding to all the (sometimes unexpected) calls for service – a smile, a deep-listening ear, a healing touch; being fully alongside with the whole of one's self. How many of these potential pastoral moments have I already missed so far today?

Take, as a superb example, St Thérèse, one of the most appealing and approachable of the saints. There was one nun in whose company she never felt comfortable. And yet, after Thérèse died so tragically young, this nun said she was sure Thérèse loved her more than she had loved anyone else in the convent.

How truly, how faithfully, she obeyed and lived up to the two core biblical injunctions: always willing to turn the other cheek, and always ready to walk the extra mile. Her central prayer was to be inflamed with God's immense love, so as to cherish other people. Her sole desire was to please God (John 8:29) in all possible ways, and thus find joy in Him.

Reliability

We should not be compartmental or selective in our relationship to God and His people. It would be unfaithful to follow Him on summer days but not on cold winter nights; to praise Him only when we are feeling well; to speak about Him, but not to follow through with love in action, generous and dependable. What profit my words of compassion, what value my protestations of support, unless I match what I say with what I do?

> The purpose of man is action, not thought – though
> it were the noblest.
>
> Carlyle, *Sartor Resartus*, Book II

Love and trust are founded – or founder – on the rock of reliability: this is the mother and father of relationship. May we prefer to be, not just to seem, good. George Herbert raised being dependable to the level of a virtue:

> Who is the honest man?
> He that doth still and strongly good pursue,
> To God, his neighbour, and himself most true:
> Whom neither force nor fawning can
> Unpinne, or wrench from giving their due.
>
> Whose honestie is not
> So loose or easie, that a ruffling winde
> Can blow away, or glittering look it blinde:
> Who rides his sure and even trot,
> While the world now rides by, now lags behinde.
>
> Who, when great trials come,
> Nor seeks, nor shunnes them; but doth calmly stay,
> Till be the thing and the example weigh:
> All being brought into a summe,
> What place or person calls for, he doth pay.

Whom none can work or wooe
To use in any thing a trick or sleight;
For above all things he abhorres deceit;
His words and works and fashion too
All of a piece, and all are cleare and straight.

Who never melts or thaws
At close tentations [sic]: when the day is done,
His goodnesse sets not, but in dark can runne:
The sunne to others writeth laws,
And is their vertue; Vertue is his Sunne.

Who, when he is to treat
With sick folks, women, those whom passions sway,
Allows for that, and keeps his constant way:
Whom other's faults do not defeat;
But though men fail him, yet his part doth play.

Whom nothing can procure,
When the wide world runnes bias from his will,
To writhe his limbes, and share, not mend the ill.
This is the Mark-man, safe and sure,
Who still is right, and prayes to be so still.

Constancie

Overflowing prayer

Prayer preserves an air of awe (Psalm 145:3) and delighted wonder: before the beauty of God's love, and His sovereignty, His centrality, in your life. God's love is 'new every morning' (John Keble). Is your love new every morning?

> One cannot remain in love unless perpetually one
> falls in love anew.
>
> F. H. Bradley, *Aphorisms*

Jan van Ruysbroeck, a Flemish mystic of the fourteenth century, described the complete life as that in which 'we dwell in work and contemplation, side by side, and we are perfectly in both of them at the same time'. Brother Lawrence perfectly exemplifies this attitude:

> In the noise and clutter of my kitchen, while several persons are at the same time calling for different things, I possess God in as great tranquillity as if I were on my knees at the Blessed Sacrament.[223]

If the tranquillity you feel when you are alone is not also experienced in the churn of daily life, then it is a one-dimensional form of tranquillity; not warm, healthy repose, but quiescence. Peacefulness is only authentic if it is prodigally shared.

Prayer – before, with and after any encounter or activity – will put you, and keep you, in closest union with your Source. The active part of spiritual life (Matthew 5:16; 7:16; 1 John 3:18) is an overflowing of inner plenitude (Matthew 6:33). St Philip Neri has given us his practical wisdom about the 'overflowing':

> To leave our prayer when we are called to do some act of charity for our neighbour, is not really a quitting of prayer, but leaving Christ for Christ, that is depriving ourselves of spiritual sweetness in order to gain souls.[224]

Our neighbour is the test, the proving ground, of our fidelity.

---

[223] Brother Lawrence, *The Practice of the Presence of God*, (London: Epworth Press, undated), end of fourth conversation.
[224] Father F. W . Faber, ed., *If God be With Us: The Maxims of St Philip Neri* (Leominster: Gracewing, 1994) p.21.

As often as possible, throughout the day, pause before you start doing things. Recentre yourself. Remind yourself that God is here with you, and thank Him. Experience His presence. This is prayer of *attention*. Then consult God. Make sure that He wants you to do this – at this time and in this way. Ask yourself and Him, 'Will this activity please Thee?' This is prayer of *intention*. While you are in the midst of action, say to God from the depth of your heart, 'I am doing this for love of Thee. Please help me to give of my best.' This is prayer of both *affection* and *commitment*.

Stop from time to time so as to refresh and intensify your consecration, by a reoffering of your present work or encounter. Pause, close your eyes for a moment, and withdraw into the very core of your self. Then pray, 'For Thee, my God. All is for Thee.' You will thus sanctify your action, and remind yourself that what you are doing is in the presence of the Almighty.

Even filing and personal admin can be seen and done as part of our readiness to serve, and giving our self freely to others. An attitude of care and devotion (and, when with people, being considerate) – these are the extras that make the ordinary extraordinary. When someone complained to St Catherine of Siena of being preoccupied by temporal occupations, she responded, 'You are the one who makes them merely temporal.' Her guidance was that the 'everyday' should be seen and experienced as sacramental – when seen with the eyes of faith.

At first, you may be trying this new angle of vision, although so simple and so natural, in a rather conscious and deliberate way. But trust that – by joining attention, intention, affection and commitment – this way of praying-while-working will become ingrained. Then the prayer of conversation merges with the prayer of action, resulting in life as prayer:

Remember then, Philothea, to make occasional retreats into the solitude of your heart, whilst outwardly engaged in business or conversation. This mental solitude cannot be prevented by the multitude of those who are about you, for they are not about your heart but about your body: so your heart may remain alone, in the presence of God alone. This was the exercise of King David amidst his many occupations, as he testifies by a thousand passages in his Psalms, as when he says, 'O Lord, as for me, I am always with Thee.' 'I have set God always before me.' 'Unto Thee I lift up mine eyes, O Thou that dwellest in the heavens.' 'My eyes are ever looking unto the Lord.'

St Francis de Sales, *Introduction to the Devout Life*

Recollected outreach

You have been seeking union in prayer. Now *live* the prayer, *live* the union. The journey inwards gives new heart and clarity for all our outward forays in His service. 'Trust those activities which foster awareness of God' (Eckhart, *Fragments*).

We are what and how we pray. We are also made and moulded by when and how often we pray. The word 'contemplation' comes from the Latin *con templum*, implying that we should always be praying because we have an inner citadel: *we are always 'with temple'*. Brother Lawrence counsels:

> We may make a chapel of our heart, whereto to escape from time to time, to talk with Him, quietly, humbly and lovingly.[225]

---

[225] Brother Lawrence, trans. Donald Attwater, *The Practice of the Presence of God* (London: Burns & Oates, 1977) fourth Letter, p.68.

The core aims of spiritual life are twofold: to bring the world, and our activities in it, under the clarity of the Light, around us and within (Psalm 119:124–125); and (like the patient repetition of your prayerword after a lapse of concentration) to keep returning to the sense of His presence – both inside and outside the self – so that this awareness, this quality of attention, becomes deeper, longer, steadier.

When we begin, the practice of recollection alternates with focus on (or preoccupation with) outer life, and we shall have to be patient with our lapses, our wanderings of mind. 'Grace is given to a sincere aim' (Eckhart, *Fragments*). Sanctity is what we allow – clear a space for – God to do in us.

When every day is devoted to God, anchored in Him (Hebrews 6:19), then daily life is alive with sacred symbolism and significance. Desk, work, food, field and face: each conveys – if only we can be open, receptive and responsive – the majesty and mystery of God. How adroitly He – who is both within and beyond – blends the holy with the homely. 'It is my practice to make all circumstances serve the spiritual good' (St Gregory Nazianzen – attributed).

Like the oscillation of a pendulum, the wider the swing towards God in prayer, the braver – and more unselfish – will be our service of love to His people. The more often you pray, and the deeper your prayers are, the more you will sense God's accompanying (Acts 17:27–28), at all times, and in all places. This is what Origen means when he says, 'The Christian life is a prayer'. It is prayer which sanctifies our relationships. To seek and see God everywhere – in every person, every encounter, every event – is the essence of contemplation in action:

> When this birth really happens, no creature can hinder you: all point you to God and to this birth …
> See only God in all.

Eckhart, Sermon, *The Eternal Birth*

Because of God's presence, every circumstance in life has not only the potential but the power to bring you into the stillness of His peace, as you edge ever-closer to correspondence with His will and His design for you (Psalm 73:24). All on and of this earth, each aspect of our daily life, points beyond itself to the Reality in our very midst – unchanging, unceasing, all-sustaining.

When you are in harmony with God, and enjoy restful yet eager union, you establish a disposition of soul (Ephesians 3:17). This prayerful inclining and ingraining (Psalm 25:5) becomes the foundation of all action, and can vivify every moment of your life, as you delight in the privilege of participating in God's saving action (Matthew 5:16).

St Basil (*Long Rules*, 37) encourages prayer while at work or when engaged in everyday activities:

> For prayer and psalmody, every hour is suitable. While our hands are busy with their tasks, we may praise God: sometimes with the tongue, or, if not, with the heart ... Thus, in the midst of our work, we can fulfil the duty of prayer, giving thanks to Him, who has granted strength to our hands for performing our tasks, and cleverness to the mind for acquiring knowledge ... Thus we gain a recollected attitude, when in every action we seek from God the success of our labours, and satisfy our debt of gratitude to Him ... and when we keep in the forefront of the mind the aim of pleasing Him.

When we stop taking for granted the events and basic materials of daily life – shelter, food, water, sunlight, and the infinitely complex workings of body and mind – much learning and deep understanding arise, while we are engaged in so-called 'commonplace, everyday life'.

Teach me, my God and King,

In all things thee to see;
And what I do in anything,
To do it as for thee!

George Herbert, 'The Elixir'

Wherever we are, God has placed us here, and with these people – family, friends and colleagues. Whatever we are called by Him to do (and this includes waiting) – however trivial it may seem to our limited sight – can be offered (to God and our neighbour) with a sense of dignity, worth and privilege. It is all part of the full life, for we are fellow-workers under God, co-creators of His kingdom (1 Corinthians 3:9; 2 Corinthians 5:20; 6:1).

The people we meet – all of them – are given for help on our way to Him, sometimes for a benefit we cannot at first foresee. And they seek us, find us and are given to us – long or briefly – for our participation (or companionship) on their way.

Everyone we touch (in whatever way), we leave our imprint with. Hence our responsibility, for their sake and for our own peace and redemption, to be sensitive and self-aware – watchful of our tone, our every word and gesture.

Unconditional love

When St Paul wrote about praying without ceasing (1 Thessalonians 5:17), he was not viewing prayer only, or even primarily, in terms of words: because the prime language, the speech of the soul, is love. And when we are loving, we are at the same time praying. Love seems, and rightly so, to come from a different area of life, when compared with some of the rest of life's experiences. Love rises above (is not unduly influenced by) the way other people view us or behave towards us: 'Love is love's reward' (Dryden, *Palamon and Arcite*, II).

Only by loving can we know something of God (1 John 4:7). What is the supreme wish of God, who is Love Eternal and who has granted us life? The gift of self, entire and wholehearted: both to Him, and in our self-giving to one another. In order to be truly free, be a willing captive of love.

To love is to be ever on the lookout for all that is true and good and beautiful, and 'of good report' (Philippians 4:8, KJV). To love is to be thankful to Almighty God for His abundance, most of all for Himself. To love is – everywhere, at all times, in all people – to see and listen for the gifts of God, the generosity of God. Love is fearless and uncompromising, yet always kind.

Love gives laser-like insight: only the loved is richly known. True love is founded on knowing the real person. This deepening of understanding (and appreciation) cannot develop and gather pace until I have withdrawn my main projections and idealisations. How much does 'I love you' mean until I have really begun to learn, discover the unexpected, deeply care, and anticipate needs and wishes? Be prompt to love, and at ease in being loved. True love is always ready to take the initiative: 'He doubly benefits the needy who gives quickly' (Publilius Syrus, Maxim 6).

Love which conforms to God's standard, love purged of self-seeking, is sacrificial (1 Corinthians 13:4–7). 'Sacrifice' takes a positive colouring and purpose from its origin, being compounded of two Latin words, meaning 'make holy'. Real love is tested and proved, deepens and grows by this self-offering. Just as a candle melts in the process of giving light, so we can be ardent in our giving way to the needs and wishes of others. 'Certainly virtue is like precious odors, most fragrant when they are incensed or crushed' (Francis Bacon, 'Of Adversity').

God loves to the point of folly. John 3:16 tells us 'For God so loved the world that he gave his only Son, that whoever believes in him should not perish but have eternal life.'

Servants of God need to be willing – and at all times ready – to be stretched, if it is His will, to the point of sacrifice. They thereby join themselves to God's own suffering in the life of humanity.

In this enlarging, we shall find new and unexpected capacities in us, and the strength to fulfil them (Ephesians 3:16–20). When He called the reluctant Jeremiah and the self-righteous Paul, God showed that He is not daunted by hesitations or limitations. If He is not daunted, why should we be, we who are ever empowered by Him (Philippians 4:13)? By loving, we understand, accept and forgive. Love is bred in an atmosphere of trust, when – in your openness and your vulnerability – you feel safe to risk and reveal all. From the nakedness of mutual vulnerability, new life is born.

Life is a training ground, designed for us to learn the art of love. In this lifelong school, we are daily examined on five basic questions, all of them about love:

- Am I open to God's love of me?

- How can I be more deserving of His goodness?

- How ready am I, in my relationships, to know and be known, to love and be loved?

- Do I look below the surface, in search of what is lovable in other people?

- How patient am I with those who are less congenial?

A person who follows the will and ways of God has faith that no human being, no encounter, no activity or enterprise, no impasse (however daunting at first sight), can resist the power or warmth of love. For this reason, their hope shines undimmed, against all odds (Romans 8:38–39).

To all your activity and experience, love gives unity, meaning and purpose. The more, and the more radically, you love God and your neighbour, the more you move towards your full potential, and rise in stature to your God-desired self, humane because richly human (Ephesians 4:32).

> Love helps us taste, here below, the sweetness of His friendship; which unites us to Him, and transforms us into Him in an ineffable manner.

Jean-Nicolas Grou, *Meditations on the Love of God*

Love integrates. Love is like a fountain, springing from the Source and returning to Him with a notion (or taste) of everlasting life, even during our time on Earth.

Human love is an expression, a manifestation, of God's love – empowering, enlightening and transcending. We can only give to each other because of *His* givenness. We can embrace because He is all-embracing. In the joint adventure of faith, our love has a chance to last, because we relate in the context of a Love which is everlasting. *He loves best who prays the most – and the deepest.* Conversely, the more often, and the more widely, you love, the more you desire to pray and to praise.

God wishes us to enlarge the boundaries of our love – in an ever-widening circle – by loving with a heart indwelt by Him, and by loving people as coming to us from Him. Cardinal John Henry Newman expands on this theme:

> How absurd it is when writers ... talk magnificently about loving the whole human race ... The real love of man must depend on practice, and therefore, must begin by exercising itself on our friends around us, otherwise it will have no existence. By trying to love our relations and friends, by submitting to their wishes, though contrary to our own, by bearing with their infirmities, by overcoming their occasional waywardness by kindness, by dwelling on their excellences, ... thus it is that we form in our hearts that root of charity, which, though small at first,

may, like the mustard seed, at last even overshadow the earth.[226]

Love is tolerant (2 Thessalonians 1:3) of difference: of personality and character, education and background. Love not only tolerates differences; God invites us to put our entire self at the service of other people, cherishing them, not in spite of, but because of, their otherness. 'To know God at all is to love Him in everyone' (Eckhart, *Fragments*).

How and in what tones does love speak? 'Consider the lilies, how they grow; they neither toil nor spin' (Luke 12:27). Love is simple, straight, open, unassuming, uncalculating and with no guile. It is offered to us by God as a free gift. How He longs for us, in turn, to serve and smile as naturally as a bird sings or a flower blooms:

> All will spy in thy face
> A blushing womanly discovering grace.

John Donne, 'On His Mistress' in *Elegies*, no.16

Love starts from the Almighty, and is to be offered back to Him. Therefore love tends towards its very source and succour, its guardian and its guide. Can we – to adapt St Paul – *remember* without ceasing? To be thankful is to remember, and to love is to remember (Deuteronomy 8:18). This is our daily, moment-by-moment challenge.

In a couplet from his hymn, 'New Every Morning' (see Lamentations 3:23), John Keble gives us a summary and synthesis of spiritual life:

> If on our daily course our mind
> Be set to hallow all we find ...

---

[226] John Henry Newman, Sermon 5: Love of Relations and Friends. *Parochial and Plain Sermons, Volume II*, 55.

In these lines can be found a prayer – a prayer for constant use. It consists of two words: 'Hallow all.'

Every moment has the potential to be welcomed, celebrated, for vocation, witness and service. When shall we hear the long-awaited harmony? When we embrace all – the divine, the human, and the divine within the human – with our uttermost: a total response and dedication of the whole person to the whole of life. True to the moment, true to my best self, true to the spirit of love.

May you *live* all the days of your life.[227]

Prayers

May I glorify You by respecting the individuality, and innate dignity, of other people: not just tolerating – but rejoicing in and learning from – any form of difference. May I thus treat others the way You treat me.

May I be a warmly approachable person for my neighbour, in a spirit of love and service, strong and constant and reliable. How dare I aspire to be more loving unless I improve all aspects of reliability?

May I never do less than I promise – and often more.

May my love – for You and my neighbour – each day grow deeper and wider. May I enjoy Your presence, and at all times render thanksgiving.

---

[227] Jonathan Swift, *Polite Conversation*, Dialogue II, 154.

Select bibliography

Hymns: Ancient and Modern (London: William Clowes & Sons, 1972).

Spiritual Classics[228]

Aquinas, St Thomas, ed. Timothy McDermott, *Summa Theologiae: A Concise Translation* (Texas: Christian Classics, 1989).

Augustine, St, *Confessions* in *The Complete Ante-Nicene & Nicene and Post-Nicene Church Fathers Collection,* 3 Series, 37 Volumes (Catholic Way Publishing, Kindle edition, 2014).

Ávila, St Teresa of, trans. David Lewis, *The Life of St Teresa of Jesus* (London: Thomas Baker, 1904).

Ávila, St Teresa of, trans. A Discalced Carmelite, *The Interior Castle* (London: Sands & Co., 1945).

Ávila, St Teresa of, trans. E. Allison Peers, *The Way of Perfection* (London: Sheed & Ward, 1946).

Bloom, Anthony, *School for Prayer* (London: Darton, Longman & Todd, 1970).

---

[228] With the exception of the works of Bloom, Valamo, Ward and Bonhoeffer, all the titles mentioned in the spiritual classics section (not necessarily the versions here listed), and all the poetry can be found on the internet – if one is content with an early translation. Useful sites are Project Gutenberg (www.gutenberg.org), Christian Ethereal Classics (www.ccel.org) and Internet Archive (https://archive.org/). Texts to which Robin returned frequently are marked with an asterisk.

Bloom, Anthony, *Living Prayer* (London: Darton, Longman Todd, 1965).

Bonhoeffer, Dietrich, *Letters and Papers from Prison* (London: SCM Press, 1953).*

Chapman, John, *Spiritual Letters* (London: Sheed & Ward, 1935).

Chariton of Valamo, Igumen, trans. E. Kadloubovsky and E. M. Palmer, *The Art of Prayer: An Orthodox Anthology* (London: Faber & Faber, 1966).

De Caussade, Jean P, *Self-Abandonement to Divine Providence* (Illinois: Tan Books, 1959).

De Sales, St Francis, *Introduction to the Devout Life* (London: Longman, Green & Co., 1891).*

De Sales, St Francis, *St Francis de Sales in his Letters* (London: Sands & Co., 1954).

John of the Cross, St, trans. David Lewis, *Spiritual Sentences and Maxims* (London: Longman Green, 1864).

John of the Cross, St, trans. Kieran Kavanaugh and Otilio Rodgriguez, *The Collected Works of St John of the Cross* (Washington: ICS, 1998).

Julian of Norwich, *Revelations of Divine Love* (London: Penguin, 1998).

Lawrence, Brother, trans. Donald Attwater, *The Practice of the Presence of God* (London: Burns & Oates, 1931).*

Neri, St Philip, *If God be with us: The Maxims of St Philip Neri* (Leominster: Gracewing, 1994).

Newman, Blessed John Henry, *Parochial and Plain Sermons* in *John Henry Newman: Six Works Collection* (Amazon Digital Services, Kindle Edition, 2013).

Mother Teresa of Calcutta, *A Gift for God* (London: Collins, 1975).

Scupoli, Lorenzo, *Spiritual Combat* (London: Burns and Oates, 1960).*

Thomas à Kempis, *The Imitation of Christ* (London: Oxford University Press, 1900).*

Thérèse of Lisieux, St, trans. T. N. Taylor, *Story of a Soul* (London: Burns & Oates, 1912).

Underhill, Evelyn, ed. *The Cloud of Unknowing* (New York: Dover, 2003).*

Ward, Benedicta, ed., *The Sayings of the Desert Fathers* (Oxford: Mowbrays, 1975).

Arts, Aesthetics, Psychology, Reflections

Buber, Martin, *I and Thou* (New York: Charles Scribner, 1958).

Elchaninov, Alexander, *The Diary of a Russian Priest* (New York: St Vladimir's Seminary, 1982).

Emerson, Ralph Waldo, *Works of Ralph Waldo Emerson* (London: Charles Kelly, undated).

Flam, Jack, ed., *Matisse on Art* (California: University of California Press, 1995).

Fromm, Erich, *The Art of Loving* (London: Unwin, 1957).

Hazlitt, William, *Table Talk: Essays on Men and Manners* (London: Grant Richards, 1901).

Lewis, C. S., *The Problem of Pain* (London: Fontana, 1957).

May, Rollo, *Man's Search for Himself* (New York: Delta, 1973).

Pascal, Blaise, trans. A. J. Krailsheimer, *Pensées* (Harmondsworth: Penguin, 1966).

Rilke, Rainer Maria, trans. M. D. Herter Norton, *Letters to a Young Poet* (London: W.W. Norton, 1934).

Shakespeare, William, *The Complete Works* (New York: Nelson Doubleday, 1974).

Thoreau, Henry David, *Walden and On the Duty of Civil Disobedience* (New York: Collier Books, 1962).

Tillich, Paul, *The Courage to Be* (London: Fontana, 1962).

Tillich, Paul, *The Eternal Now* (London: SCM, 1963).

Vann, Gerald, *The Divine Pity* (London: Sheed & Ward, 1945).

Woolf, Virginia, *The Common Reader*, Volumes I and II (London: Vintage, 2003).

Poetry

Arnold, Matthew, *The Portable Matthew Arnold* (Harmondsworth: Penguin, 1949).

Barrett Browning, Elizabeth, *Aurora Leigh and Other Poems* (Harmondsworth: Penguin, 1995).

Brooke, Rupert, *Letters from America* (London: Sidgwick & Jackson, 1931).

Brooke, Rupert, *The Complete Poems of Rupert Brooke* (London: Sidgwick & Jackson, 1932).

Chesterton, G. K. *Complete Works of G. K. Chesterton* (Delphi Classics, Kindle edition, 2012).

Donne, J., ed. John Hayward, *Donne: Poems* (Harmondsworth: Penguin, 1950).

Eliot, T. S., *Collected Poems and Plays of T. S. Eliot* (New York: Houghton Miflin Harcourt Publishing Company, 1936).

Herbert, George, ed. F. E. Hutchinson, *The Works of George Herbert* (Oxford: Clarendon Press, 1941).

Hopkins, Gerard Manley, edited by W. H. Gardner, *Poems and Prose* (Harmondsworth: Penguin, 1953).

Keats, John, *Selected Poems* (London: Penguin, 1996).

Lawrence, D. H., *Complete Poems* (Harmondsworth: Penguin, 1993).

Milton, ed. John Carey, *Complete Shorter Poems* (London: Longman, 1968).

Milton, *Paradise Lost & Paradise Regained* (New York: Signet Classics, 1968).

Pope, Alexander, *Collected Poems* (London: Dent & Sons, 1983).

Thompson, Francis, *Complete Poetical Works of Francis Thompson* (London: Brooks Press, 2007).

Wordsworth, William, *The Works of Wordsworth* (London: MacMillan & Co. 1900).

Yeats, W. B., *Selected Poetry* (London: MacMillan, 1962).

Subject index